Using C in
Software Design

Using C in Software Design

Ronald Leach

Academic Press Professional
Harcourt Brace & Company, Publishers
Boston   San Diego   New York
London   Sydney   Tokyo   Toronto

Copyright © 1993 by Academic Press, Inc.

ACADEMIC PRESS PROFESSIONAL
955 Massachusetts Avenue, Cambridge, MA 02139

An Imprint of ACADEMIC PRESS, INC.
A Division of HARCOURT BRACE & COMPANY

United Kingdom Edition published by
ACADEMIC PRESS LIMITED
24–28 Oval Road, London NW1 7DX

Library of Congress Cataloging–in–Publication Data

Leach, Ronald (Ronald J.)
        Using C in software design / Ronald Leach.
              p.   cm.
        Includes bibliographical references and index.
        ISBN 0-12-440210-0 (alk. paper)
        1. C (Computer program language)   2. Computer software-
    -Development.   I. Title.
    QA76.73.C15L42   1993
    005.13'3—dc20   93-11903
                                                             CIP

Printed in the United States of America
93 94 95 96 97 98 EB 9 8 7 6 5 4 3 2 1

Contents

Contents

Contents

Preface

The C language was developed in 1978 at AT&T Bell Laboratories by Brian Kernighan and Dennis Ritchie. The language was intended for systems programming and was meant to replace the heavy reliance on assembly languages. C is the basis of the UNIX operating system as well as many systems-level and applications programs.

C was designed to be a language for which compilers would generate code that executes quickly. As a result, few of the facilities of run-time checking of variable types and array bounds are present in C. Consequently, C programs can be quite difficult to debug. This is especially true of C code written by programmers new to the C language even if they have considerable experience programming in other languages. Thus good software design practice is especially important in C.

You should be aware of a problem with programming in C – there is no such thing as "the C language." Because the original description of C by Kernighan and Ritchie was not completely precise, a few variants on their original intentions became widely available. A standardization effort has been completed by the American National Standards Institute (ANSI). However, the ANSI standard must allow all the existing C code that was used in existing major software projects to be compilable under the new system. To emphasize modern programming practice, we use ANSI standard C. The programs in this book are written in this version of C and will work on most standard compilers including those usually available for UNIX systems and PCs. There are a few times that some of the code will need to be changed for use with some compilers available on personal computers; this is indicated where appropriate.

Software engineering is a recurring theme in this book. Most of the chapters include a discussion of a large software system and some of the trade-offs involved with design decisions and the software engineering methods used. This system includes enough features and complexity to provide a real test of your ability to write a complex software system. After following this example and understanding the reasons we used for making decisions about design and implementation, you will be able to understand how the principles of software engineering can be incorporated into programming in C and how the language supports these goals.

This book is organized into two parts. Part I (Chapters 0 – 6) describes the features of C that are easily understood and that are unlikely to cause any difficulty because of the language syntax or semantics. Many examples emphasize syntax that is specific to C, and many other examples specify what not to do when programming in C. Part I also assumes that the reader has a general understanding of programming a computer, hopefully using a structured high level language such as Pascal, Ada, Modula-2, or similar languages. There are many examples of relatively short C programs that illustrate correct programs. Some of the examples are used to demonstrate typical problems that beginning C programmers have. Since the topics of structured data types and pointers are postponed until Part II, all of Part I should be accessible to a person whose only high level computer language is FORTRAN or BASIC.

The text is organized somewhat differently from most books on C. The primary reasons for the organization chosen are the sound pedagogical principles that simple concepts should be introduced before complex ones and that people learn best by imitation. Accordingly, the topics of input and output in C are introduced in Chapter 1, while a discussion of reading input streams is delayed until Chapter 2. A more fundamental change from other books on C is that arrays are treated before pointers. This is not as elegant as a combined approach but it has the advantage of building on the students' knowledge of arrays which is likely to be better than their knowledge of pointers. Throughout the book there is an emphasis on the use of the computer as a learning tool. Most colleges and universities, as well as computer companies, have enough computers and compilers so that a student is not limited in the amount of computer access. Indeed, many people have powerful personal computers available to them so that they have essentially unlimited access. This book contains a large number of suggested experiments that can and should be carried out on the computer. These experiments generally consist of extremely short programs that the reader can enter on the computer and run, thereby testing the results and achieving a greater understanding of the language. This is especially important in the first part of the book, which stresses syntax. The exercises in Part I are fairly straightforward. Part II (Chapters 7–12) describes more advanced, subtle features of the language and emphasizes the features of C that are likely to be used in larger complex programs than those considered in the first part. It includes chapters on separately compiling C source code files into large C programs, pointers, structured data types, and bit operations. The exercises in Part II are somewhat less straightforward than those in Part I and may take more programming time. The exercises are important since they demonstrate how the important data structures in C are actually implemented and used.

The title of this book is *Using C in Software Design*. This book includes introduction to the C programming language as well as those features of software engineering that aid in the development of very large software systems. "Very large software systems" means programs that are developed by large teams of programmers and that contain hundreds of thousands of lines of code. Obviously, we will not write programs anywhere near that size. In order to incorporate these fundamental ideas, we will have a single, large example of a fairly complex piece of software developed throughout the text. It includes enough features and complexity to provide a real test of your ability to write a complex software system.

A comment needs to be made about the disk that is available with this book. The disk contains all of the source code for the examples in this text in ASCII format. It is organized so that example 11 in Chapter 1 is in the file named ex1_11.c. Filenames were chosen this way so that they can be run on PCs or uploaded to other computers. All of the C programs were tested on a SUN workstation running UNIX with the standard UNIX C compiler for this machine. The programs were also run on a PC using Turbo C, on an Alliant FX/2800 supercomputer, and on an AT&T computer running AT&T System V UNIX with the front-end of the standard UNIX C++ compiler used as an ANSI C compiler. Emphasis is on portable code and not on any special nonstandard features of the compilers used. Thus there are no programs that include specific calls to graphics functions or to the BIOS on PCs using Turbo C, or to "far pointers" on PCs. The code here will probably run on any computer with commonly used ANSI C compilers.

I would like to thank the following individuals who helped to make this a better book: the reviewers, the Academic Press "book team" (Jenifer Niles, Lynne Gagnon, and Elizabeth Tustian), the students at Howard University (especially Ullysses Evans, Jr., who made a fortune finding errors at 10 cents each), and my colleagues Richard Bayne, Robert Gault, Reza Hashemi, and Don M. Coleman at Howard University, who made incisive (and painful) comments on earlier versions of this book. Any errors found in the text should be reported to me using electronic mail at the address rjl@scsla.howard.edu

LIMITED WARRANTY AND DISCLAIMER OF LIABILITY

PART I

CHAPTER 0

Software Engineering Principles

The term "software engineering" refers to a generally accepted set of goals for the analysis, design, implementation, testing, and maintenance of software. These software engineering goals include: efficiency, reliability, usability, modifiability, portability, testability, reusability, maintainability, interoperability, and correctness. These terms refer both to systems and to their components. Many of the terms are self-explanatory; however, we include their definitions for completeness.

Efficiency. The software is produced in the expected time and within the limits of the available resources. The software produced runs within the time expected.

Reliability. The software performs as expected. In multi-user systems, the system performs its functions even with other load on the system.

Usability. The software can be used properly. This generally refers to the ease of use of the user interface but also concerns the applicability of the software to the computer environment.

Modifiability. The software can be easily changed if the requirements of the system change.

Portability. The software system can be ported to other computers or systems without major rewriting of the software. Software that needs only to be recompiled in order to have a properly working system on the new machine is considered to be very portable.

Testability. The software can be easily tested. This generally means that the software is written in a modular manner.

Reusability. Some or all of the software can be used again in other projects. This means that the software is modular, that each individual module has a well-defined interface, and that each individual module has a clearly defined outcome from its execution. This often means that there is a substantial level of abstraction and generality in the modules that will be reused most often.

Maintainability. The software can be easily understood and changed over time. This term is used to describe the lifetime of systems such as the air traffic control system that must operate for decades.

Interoperability. The software system can interact properly with other systems. This can apply to software on a single, stand-alone computer or to software that is used on a network.

Correctness. The program produces the correct output.

These goals, while noble, do not help with the design of software that meets such goals. The choice of proper software design methodologies is currently a matter of considerable debate in academia, government, and industry. Some commonly used methods are data-structured systems design, Jackson structured design, data-flow design, rapid prototyping, spiral designs, etc. All of these methods are useful in certain software projects. We are not going to follow a particular method to exclude all others. Instead we will show how systems can be designed in C using these software engineering principles.

Software engineering will be a recurring theme in this book. Most of the chapters will include a discussion of a large software system and discuss some of the tradeoffs involved with design decisions and methods used.

CHAPTER 1

Elementary Programming in C

"Elementary" means different things to different people; in this book it refers to those concepts that have exact analogs in the computer language Pascal. This is not to say that programming in Pascal is a simple task – far from it. However, Pascal was originally intended to be a teaching language and therefore avoids certain complicated features of C. Topics taught in a college or university are frequently considered as being more elementary than typical industrial or government applications; this is the appropriate meaning of "elementary" in Part I, especially in Chapter 1. In this chapter we consider the simplest kinds of C programs. We will learn about simple program structure, typing of variables, coding conventions, documentation, and about several of C's input and output statements.

1.1 History of the C Programming Language

The C language was developed at AT&T Bell Laboratories by Brian Kernighan and Dennis Ritchie. The language was intended for systems programming and was meant to replace the heavy reliance on assembly languages. It was an outgrowth of other languages developed at Bell Laboratories. The UNIX operating system was the first major software project written using C. Approximately 90% of the more than 100,000 lines of code in the original version of the UNIX operating system was written in C with the rest being written in assembly language. The system has grown much larger recently, but most of the system is still written in C.

   Given its origins, it is not surprising that C has become one of the most popular languages for systems-level programming for a variety of computers, ranging from microcomputers to large mainframes and advanced high-performance workstations. In addition, C is a general-purpose programming language that can and has been used for a variety of software projects. For example, the University of Waterloo Symbolic Computation Group has developed a symbolic computation program called Maple, which performs all the typical operations of algebra, such as solving equations, factoring polynomials, simplifying, and adding fractions, as well as the typical operations of differential and integral calculus. All of this software has been written in C. The Maple software is similar in function to a much older software system called MACSYMA which is written in LISP and has grown increasingly complex since the original idea of such a program was developed in the 1960's. (The acronym MACSYMA includes abbreviations of the terms "symbolic" and "algebra.") The reason for the redesign of the system is that the much older MACSYMA, while extremely powerful, was originally developed before the concepts of software engineering were developed. It was felt that a symbolic computation program would benefit by having a new design that supported the basic principles of software engineering and by being coded in a language that supported these principles. The C language was chosen for this project since it supports most of the modern principles of software engineering better than LISP and allows the creation of very efficient programs.

Other examples of large C software projects include graphics software, database systems, communications packages, and numerous applications programs. Equally important, C has become the language of choice for a large amount of systems programming and for software that should run on many different computers with few changes. For these reasons, C has become almost a "universal assembly language."

The goal of software engineering is to develop correct software that meets the specifications set for the software on schedule and within budget limits. The software produced must be easily understood, modifiable, and reliable, and should be written in a modular fashion so that portions of the software may be reused in other projects. The software should be able to be ported easily to other systems (hardware or software) and any errors should be easy both to detect and to correct.

C was designed to be a language for which C compilers would generate code that executes quickly. As a result, few of the facilities of run-time checking of variable types and array bounds are present in C although they are present in strongly typed languages such as Pascal or Ada. C is a typed language but is not strongly typed. This means that each variable must have a type associated with it but that the checking of types is the responsibility of the programmer and not of the compiler. Consequently, C programs can be quite difficult to debug because of the lack of compiler support for the checking of types. This is especially true of C code written by programmers new to the C language even if they have considerable experience programming in other languages.

1.2 What Is C?

Unfortunately, there is no such thing as "the C language." There are at least five dialects that either are important now or are likely to be important in the next few years. The ANSI standard for C has been available since the middle of 1989. Compilers for ANSI standard C code and related variants are likely to be available on most microcomputers. This book uses ANSI C exclusively.

The original dialect of C was the Kernighan & Ritchie version. UNIX and several other operating systems for larger computers are written in the Kernighan & Ritchie version of C.

Concurrent C and Exceptional C are being developed at AT&T Bell Laboratories, with the development headed by Nahrain Gehani. Concurrent C is used for writing programs that perform streams of computations that appear to an observer to be executing at the same time, even if the computations are being switched rapidly on a single processor. Exceptional C is designed to encourage writing programs that can recover smoothly from run-time errors such as division by 0, or overflow of a floating point variable.

C++ is an object-oriented language that was invented by Bjarne Stroustrup, again at AT&T Bell Laboratories, to provide a facility for object-oriented programming. It incorporates an additional level of data abstraction into C-like programs. A C++ program that does not use the special object-oriented features of C++ is essentially an ANSI C program, although there are some small differences in syntax and semantics. Often C++ is implemented as a preprocessor that generates C code.

1.3 Structure of a Single-Unit C Program

A C program consists of one or more functions together with any necessary data declarations. A C program may consist of several source code files. In this chapter, we consider the simplest possible format for C programs:

- A single function
- No external data information
- All the source code in a single file

This structure is analogous to a simple BASIC program or to a Pascal program that has no functions or procedures and simply consists of a main program.

Every C program must have a function called main( ) that is the place where the program begins execution. The first example of a complete C program is given in example 1.1.

Example 1.1

```
main(void)
{
  int i;

  i = 1;
}
```

This program is quite simple, yet it has several features common to C programs. It has a function called main in which the program execution begins. The use of the reserved word "void" inside the pair of parentheses ( ) after main indicates that the function main has no parameters passed to it. In C, the body of the function is always enclosed in a pair of braces '{' and '}'. The semicolon ';' is used as a statement terminator, at least for most of the lines. It uses a variable called i and declares i to be a special type, called int (for integer). This is a requirement of C: every variable used in a C program must have a type associated with it. Finally, the program has an assignment statement that uses the symbol '=' to place the value 1 in the memory location where the variable i is stored.

Note that the program is written in lowercase letters. This is common practice in C. The generally accepted style of C programming has all variables, function names, and reserved words in lower case with only a few global constants given in upper case. This convention makes it easier for C programmers to read one another's code. C is case-sensitive, so that two variables named i and I represent different memory locations and therefore can refer to different quantities.

C programs do not require the special formatting that FORTRAN programs do. The program can be written using blank spaces, carriage returns, or tabs in any manner, as long as the individual tokens such as int and main, are not broken up. The term "token" is used in a technical sense to mean the information about names of variables; reserved words such as int; reserved punctuation symbols such as commas, semicolons, and braces; operators such as the = sign; character strings representing important portions of the program such as the word main in example 1.1; and any other distinct pieces of information used by the compiler to represent the syntax and semantics of the program. Blanks, tabs, and carriage returns are generally used to separate tokens during the compiler's lexical analysis phase. For more information on tokens and lexical analysis, see any good text on compiler construction.

A major goal of software engineering, maintainability, requires that programs be written so as to make them readable. This requires the use of a consistent programming style. Most companies have style guidelines that must be followed by programmers. We will follow a few simple rules that we will present gradually as we learn more of the programming constructions in C. For now, just notice that each line of the main program between the beginning and ending braces is indented two spaces; this allows the beginning and the end of the body of main( ) to be seen easily. Also notice that we have used a blank line to separate the declaration of type of the variable i from the rest of the code.

The program is not very interesting. To remedy this partially, we will add some output. The C language is unlike certain other languages in that input and output are not considered as being a part of the language but are instead available in a library. To use this library we must include some information about it in our program. The modified example to show some output is given in example 1.2. It uses the function printf( ), which is the most commonly used C output function.

Example 1.2

```
#include <stdio.h>

main(void)
{
  int i;
```

```
    i = 1;
    printf("%d\n",i);
}
```

The output of the program in example 1.2 is what is expected, namely a printing of the number 1.

The output statement is a call to a function named printf( ) that takes arguments of different types. In this example, the control statement "%d\n" says that the variable to be printed is a base 10 integer (which is said to be of type decimal integer) and that the cursor is returned to the next line by the request to print a '\n'. The '\' is called the backslash and is used to tell the C compiler that the next symbol is to have a special meaning. In this case, the combination '\n' means new line. Sequences of characters beginning with the '\' are called escape sequences and are treated as a single character with a special meaning. Thus the sequence '\n', which appears to a human reader to have two characters between the delimiting single quotes, is interpreted by the C compiler as a single character.

The program in example 1.2 uses the C preprocessor which understands that the file stdio.h, which is found in a special place by the compiler and linker, is to be included so that input and output can be done. The first statement of the program is called an "include" or "#include" statement and has a particular syntax that is unique to instructions to the C preprocessor – the # sign must be the first character on a line and cannot be preceded by blanks or tabs, at least for many compilers. The preprocessor is at the start of the compilation process, as shown in Figure 1.1.

Textual information can also be included in print statements, as shown in examples 1.3 and 1.4.

Example 1.3

```
#include <stdio.h>

main(void)
{
    int i;
    i=1;
    printf("The first positive integer is :%d\n",i);
}
```

Example 1.4

```
#include <stdio.h>

main(void)
{
    int i;
```

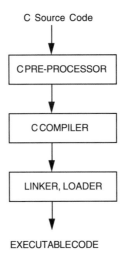

C Source Code

CPRE-PROCESSOR

CCOMPILER

LINKER, LOADER

EXECUTABLECODE

Figure 1.1 The C compilation process.

```
    i=1;
    printf("%d is the first positive integer\n", i);
}
```

Example 1.3 illustrates printing the variable i (whose value was 1) at the end of a string of characters. Its output is

```
    The first positive integer is : 1
```

The second program (example 1.4) illustrates that the variable can be embedded anywhere within a print statement; its output is

```
    1 is the first positive integer
```

1.4 Elementary Data Types in C

C is a language in which every variable must have a specific type. Previous programs have shown the method of declaration used for variables of type int, which is C's terminology for integer. Similar constructions are used for variables of other types in C.

The elementary data types in C are

int (for variables that consist of a single integer)

char (for variables that consist of a single character)

float (for floating point numbers)

double (for double precision floating point numbers)

Example 1.5 shows how these declarations of the type of a variable might be used in a C program.

Example 1.5

```
#include <stdio.h>

main(void)
{
  int i;

  char c;
  float f,g;
  float h, aardvark, chicken_hawk;
  double d, mint;
}
```

As you can see from this example, variables can be declared in any order inside the program and declarations of different variables of the same type can be given together on the same line or on separate lines. Variables of the same type may be declared on the same line by separating the variable names by commas. The variables can also be initialized by the programmer, as shown in example 1.6.

Example 1.6

```
#include <stdio.h>

main(void)
{
  int i= 10;
  char c = 'Y';
  float f,g;
  float h, aardvark, chicken_hawk;
  double d, mint;

  h = 3.14559;
  aardvark = 6.02E23;
}
```

Initialization of variables is not required. An uninitialized variable may contain any leftover data from previous memory use. **Never use a variable in C unless you know what its value is!** Garbage can result from using uninitialized variables before setting their values.

The variables i and c are initialized in example 1.6, but not in example 1.5. The variables f, g, h, aardvark, chicken_hawk, d, and mint are not initialized and using their values will give unpredictable, meaningless results. Since we have assigned the value 3.14159 to the floating point variable h in the program, the value of h may be used without problems from the point of giving it a value to the end of main( ). A similar statement holds for the value of the variable aardvark.

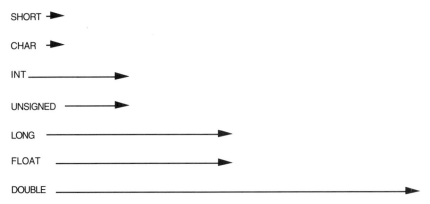

Figure 1.2 Relative sizes of some data types on one 32-bit computer

Note the use of the constants 10, 'Y', 3.14159, and 6.02E23 in example 1.6. The constant 6.02E23 is in exponential notation.

Many C compilers do not check for agreement between the actual values of a variable and its type. Thus if we had included statements such as h = 'a', mint = 5, etc., in example 1.6, the compiler might not complain but the program might have unexpected results. Recall that every variable in C must have a type declared for it.

This lack of checking between variables and their types is called "weak typing"; therefore C is called a weakly typed language. C's weak typing could be an advantage if we wish to transfer data without knowing its type; however, weak typing is also the source of many programming errors that are difficult to locate. In C, it is the programmer's responsibility to know the type of each expression at each step of the program's execution. The prudent C programmer does not depend on the compiler's type checking.

Each of the qualifiers short, long, and unsigned may be associated with the int data type; they indicate that the variable may be stored in a particular way. For example, if the variable j is declared in the statement

```
short int j;
```

then j will be stored in a space in computer memory no larger than the space available for an integer; this may save space in some cases, especially if the computer has both 16-bit and 32-bit integers available. More commonly, the qualifier long is used to specify that a larger space may be given for storage. It is important to note that the qualifiers short and long do not necessarily change the actual amount of storage allocated on any particular machine. The amounts of space actually needed for the storage of an integer, float, or double are machine dependent. All that you know is that the space used for a short integer will be no larger than the space used for an ordinary variable of type int. The qualifier long may also be used with the type double, and the same statements about actual storage allocation apply. The qualifier unsigned means that the value of the variable is non-negative.

Figure 1.2 shows a typical relationship between the sizes of various data types on one 32-bit computer.

The data type char also allows the qualifiers signed and unsigned to be applied to character data. This is useful in a situation where the computer stores 8 bits for each character and unsigned chars have values between 0 and 255 when the character is stored and interpreted as an int. (More detail about this point will be given later when we discuss reading variables from an input stream in Chapter 2.)

One data type that is **not** present in C is the boolean type. Hence evaluation of statements as being true or false cannot be done directly. The usual solution to this problem is to consider an expression to be false if it has the value 0 and to be true otherwise. This is reasonable if the expression takes on only integer values, but it appears quite strange for expressions of data types other than integer.

1.5 Output with printf and putchar

We have seen how to print simple statements that include textual information as well as the values contained in certain variables. These are special cases of a general concept in C: the *expression*. An expression is any quantity that has a value. Examples of expressions are constants, variables, arithmetic expressions, and values returned by functions. Any expression in C can be printed. The general printf statement consists of two parts: a control part describing how the expressions are to be printed and a list of variables to be printed. The two parts are separated by a comma, as are the various portions of the list of expressions. The control part contains instructions about the number and types of the expressions to be printed using printf( ). The syntax of the control statement is given in Table 1.1.

Table 1.1   Specification of a printf statement

Printing control statements must be enclosed in double quotes.

Any reference to the printing of an expression must have a description of how it is to be printed.

The percent sign (%) signifies the format of the expression to be printed in a conversion specification; everything between the quotes except conversion specifications or escape sequences will be printed as written.

A %d means that the expression is to be printed as a base 10 integer.

A %c means that the expression is to be printed as a single character.

A %f means that the expression is to be printed as a floating point number.

A %o means that the expression is to be printed as a base 8 (octal) integer.

A %x means that the expression is to be printed as a base 16 (hexadecimal) integer.

A %lf means that the expression is to be printed as a double-precision floating point number.

A %Lf means that the expression is to be printed as a "long" double-precision floating point number.

A %s means that the expression is to be printed as a string of characters.

There are optional specifications that describe the width of the various fields so that output can be nicely formatted. For example, the statement

```
printf("%5.2f\n",123456.789);
```

causes the following output:

```
123456.79
```

The specification %5.2f means that the floating point number

```
123456.789
```

is to be displayed in a field of at least five spaces, with two spaces after the decimal point. In this case, the fractional part of the number is converted to the appropriate size of two decimal places and the integer part of the number is displayed in the number of places necessary. Similar field restrictions are available for other types of variables – you should experiment to see how these work.

The complete specification of the formatting capability of the printf( ) statement requires nearly 10 pages of text in at least one current reference manual. It is probably more important to get programs to work and to experiment with formatting as you need it. The essential format specifications are

- Characters with special meaning must be preceded by either the backslash or the percent sign. For example, a double quote " must be preceded by a \ to form the escape sequence \", which is printed as a single character. (If we didn't use the escape sequence, the quote symbol " would be interpreted as the end of a string of characters and the remaining part of the character string would cause a syntax error to be generated by the compiler.)

- A tab can be included in the output by placing a \t in the control statement, a new line or carriage return can be included by using a \n, and the printing cursor can be backed up (perhaps for underlining or overstriking a character) by using the \b.

- A percent sign may be printed by preceding it by another percent sign. However, a single quote can be printed with or without using the preceding backslash.

Many other control specifications are available for use with the printf( ) function. Any disagreement between the control specification and the type of the expression to be printed will usually result in output that is both strange-looking and incorrect; however, it will generally not produce an error at either compile time or run time. If an error does occur, it is usually a run-time error caused by incorrectly using character strings.

Examples 1.7 and 1.8 demonstrate the use of the printf( ) statement for several different control specifications; the last printf( ) uses two lines in each example. The program in example 1.7 does it right. Example 1.8 produces strange and garbled output because we misused the control specifications and had a deliberate mismatch between the control specification and the type of the expression to be printed.

Example 1.7 Correct use of control specifications

```c
#include <stdio.h>

main(void)
{
   int i= 10;
   char c = 'Y';
   float f;
   float h = 3.14159;
   double d, mint = 6.023E3;

printf("%d\n",i);
printf("\t\t%c\n",c);
printf("\t\t%c\n",'Y');
printf("\t\t\t\t%7.2f\n",f);
printf("\t\t\t\t%7.5f\n",h);
printf("\t\t\t\t%7.4f\n",3.14159);
printf("\t\t\t\t%7.2f\n",d);
printf("\t\t\t\t%7.2f\n",mint, "\t\t\t\t%7.2f\n",6.023E3);
}
```

Example 1.7 gives the correct output

```
10
                        Y
                        Y
                                             0.00
                                    3.14159
                                    3.1416
                    0.00
                    6023.00
                                    6023.00
```

The output has been separated into columns in order to make it easy for you to see which variables are of type char, which are of type int, and which are of type float. Notice the alignment of the decimal points in the third column and the rounding of the value of 3.14159 to four decimal places.

Compare the correct use of control specifications of example 1.7 with an incorrect use in example 1.8. Note the way that we have split up the long printf( ) statement in the last line of the program and avoided having a carriage return within the quotes.

Example 1.8 Incorrect Control Specifications

```
/* incorrect output */
#include <stdio.h>

main(void)
{
   int i= 10;
   char c = 'Y';
   float f, h = 3.14159;
   double d, mint=6.023E3;

   printf("%d\t\t%c\t\t%7.2f\n",i);
   printf("%d\t\t%c\t\t%7.2f\n",c);
   printf("%d\t\t%c\t\t%7.2f\n",'Y');
   printf("%d\t\t%c\t\t%7.2f\n",f);
   printf("%d\t\t%c\t\t%7.2f\n",h);
   printf("%d\t\t%c\t\t%7.2f\n",d);
   printf("%d\t\t%c\t\t%7.2f\n",mint,
       "%d\t\t%c\t\t%7.2f\n",6.023E3);

}
```

On my computer, the program had the strange output given below. (Your computer might have different, but still incorrect, output.)

```
10                                        0.00
89                                        0.00
89                                        0.00
0                                      6023.00
1074342605                                       6023.00
0                                      6023.00
1085769472                                       6023.00
1085769472                                           ^L
```

Very little of this output is correct because we did not follow the rules for using the control specification; the quantities to be printed must agree with the control specification in their number and type. Notice that we have two tabs between every pair of output results on the same line. Most of the output in the character format %c is missing. We also have integers such as 1074342605 that clearly make no sense at all; this is a strong indicator that we are using an incorrect format in the control specification of the printf( ) statement. Note also that 3.14159 is never printed.

It ought to be clear that C is somewhat loose in the attempt to print variables in whatever format is indicated, even if the result is nonsense.

There are some situations in which a numeric value in either base 8 or base 16 is important, especially in systems programming. These values can be printed using the %o and %x print specifications. See the exercises for more information.

C has another method that can be used for the output of characters. This method uses the putchar( ) function, which is used as in the two statements

```
c='L';

putchar(c);
```

or the single statement

```
putchar('H');
```

Of course this can also be done using the function printf( ) with the %c specification; putchar( ) is just implemented to execute faster in most C compilers. Use of the function putchar( ) is restricted to characters only.

There is a useful variant on putchar( ) that can be used for the output of character strings: puts( ). This can be used as in

```
puts("This message was printed using puts");
```

This is somewhat simpler than using the equivalent printf( ) statement

```
printf("This message was printed using printf\n");
```

Note that puts( ) always returns the cursor to the beginning of a new line, so the \n is not needed in the argument to puts( ). Note also that it is not necessary to have a \n in each printf( ) statement; it is not always necessary to have the cursor return to the beginning of a line.

1.6 Input with scanf and getchar

It is time to learn about input in C. The C language has very rich input facilities. It allows input as a stream of bytes and also permits the programmer to make use of complicated formatting of the input data. We discuss the simpler input facilities of C in this section. Reading a stream of input will be discussed in Chapter 2.

The function scanf( ), which is used for input, is somewhat similar to the printf( ) function used for output. Use of the function scanf( ) for input requires a control statement as well as the names of the variables that the input is read into. Here is an example of a program to read a single integer from input and print the square of the integer.

Example 1.9

```
#include <stdio.h>

main(void)
{
    int i;
```

```
printf("Please enter a positive integer\n");
scanf("%d",&i);
printf("%d",i*i);
}
```

The program has two new features: evaluation of expressions and a new syntax for input. The argument to printf( ) contains an expression i*i that is evaluated before the number is printed. This is a general principle in C: use any expression in any context where its equivalent can be used. This is shorter than having additional variables such as

```
int j;
```

and doing something like

```
j = i* i;
printf("%d",j);
```

More strangely, the call of the function scanf( ) has an ampersand (&) before the variable i as well as a type control specification (%d); this is necessary for the scanf( ) function to place the correct value in the correct variable i. The & is necessary whenever reading integer, character, or float variables with the scanf( ) function. The ampersand is used because the scanf( ) function uses the address of the variable read in. We will discuss addresses when we study pointers later in this book. For now, simply use the ampersand with the function scanf( ) as shown in the examples.

(A note for readers with some familiarity with C: the ampersand & in the scanf( ) function has nothing to do with the "and" operator.)

It is easy to write C programs that read several variables from input. An example of such a program is

Example 1.10

```
#include <stdio.h>
main(void)
{
  int n,m,p,q;

  printf("Enter 4 integers, separated by blanks,\n");
  printf("tabs, returns, or any combination of these\n");
  scanf("%d %d %d %d",&n,&m,&p,&q);
  printf("%d %d %d %d",n,m,p,q);
}
```

This program illustrates the use of a single scanf( ) function to read all four of the integers from input. The four variables are all read using the & notation, as before. The input message was split into two printf( ) statements since a carriage return cannot be embedded into a string of characters to be printed by printf( ); the new line is forced by using \n within the string. Notice that the message promises that the numbers can be read in using any combination of tabs, blank spaces, and carriage returns. Don't take this statement at face value – type in the program and **experiment** until you are convinced that it works!

It is possible to enter other types of variables such as floats, characters, and character strings. To read in floating point numbers, you can simply use the scanf( ) function with the control format %f. For example, to read in a floating point number x and an integer i, you can simply use the statement

```
scanf("%f %d", &x, &i);
```

in your program. You should experiment with this statement using both regular floating point representation such as 123.456 and exponential notation such as 123.45 E10.

We can use the %c control specification to read in characters; a simple example of this is

```
scanf("%c",&ch);
```

There is another function in C that can be used for the input of characters: getchar( ). An example of its use is

```
ch = getchar();
```

The function getchar( ) reads its input from the standard input device (the keyboard) one character at a time. The function has no arguments and returns as a value the character read in. This character may be assigned to a variable for further use in the program.

Thus we have two functions in C that can be used for the reading of a single character. This is similar to the relationship between printf( ) and putchar( ) for the output of a single character. Clearly putchar( ) is a simpler function to use than printf( ) for writing a single character. Similarly, getchar( ) is simpler to use than scanf( ) for reading a single character.

Note that the syntax of the function getchar( ) is different from the usual syntax of putchar( ):

```
putchar(ch);
```

Example 1.11 is a simple echo program that reads in a single character and prints as its output the character that was read in.

Example 1.11

```
#include <stdio.h>

main(void)
{
  char ch;

  ch = getchar();
  getchar();
  putchar(ch);
}
```

The program has quite simple specifications – read a character and display the character read. It seems a little awkward at first glance to have two calls of the function getchar( ). The reason for this is that when input is read from the keyboard, the input has not been sent to the executing program until the return key is pressed.

The problem does not occur and the second getchar( ) is not necessary when reading input from a file or using input redirection either on a PC with Turbo C or on a UNIX-based system. On each system (PC or UNIX) we used a text editor such as edlin or vi to create an input file consisting of one character. Suppose that this input file was named "toy." Since the name of the C source code file was ex1_11.c, the name of the executable file was ex1_11.exe on the PC using Turbo C; on the UNIX system it was the default executable file a.out. Redirection of input using

```
ex1_11 < toy
```

on the PC and

```
a.out < toy
```

on the UNIX system avoided the need for the extra getchar( ).

Notice that we could have used several variations on this code. For example, we could have used the function printf( ) with the %c control specification in order to produce the same output.

We could have followed the general C language principle of substituting an equivalent expression whenever possible. Thus we could have avoided the use of the extra variable ch and used a smaller amount of memory by rewriting the program as in example 1.12.

Example 1.12

```
#include <stdio.h>
main(void)
{
    putchar(getchar());
}
```

The same type of construction avoiding the temporary variable ch could have been used with the function printf( ) instead of putchar( ).

Note that these programs would have had a nicer appearance if they had had some instruction to a user with code such as

```
printf("Please enter a character\n");
```

The function getchar( ) is only used for reading in unformatted data. You may know that an input of

```
123E10
```

represents a floating point value, but getchar( ) sees it as six bytes (ignoring the initial tab and the new line character). In order for the program to be able to use this value as a floating point expression, we must use getchar( ) six times, save the intermediate characters, convert them to decimal, accumulate the results with the proper interpretation of decimal places, interpret the E properly, and save the accumulated results in a floating point number.

You should be especially careful about one thing when using the function getchar( ) in an interactive program. Every character entered can be read by getchar( ). For example, suppose that you are writing a program to allow the user to enter data into a database and you ask the user if there is any change in his or her address. You expect to read the character 'Y' or 'N' (or perhaps 'y' or 'n'). If the answer is 'Y', then you wish to prompt for input and read in the new address. Most people who use such a program will type their answer ('Y' or 'N') followed by hitting the return or enter key. This is interpreted by getchar( ) as two characters, messing up the reading of the next data.

What can you do about this? Just be extremely careful in your programming to allow for unexpected input data in interactive programs.

We thus have two functions, scanf( ) and getchar( ), that can be used for reading input. This is somewhat analogous to having the two functions printf( ) and putchar( ) for printing output. There is a fundamental difference between the two situations, however.

Using printf( ) for output is safe if you are careful to ensure that the type of the variable being printed agrees with the control specification of the printf( ) statement. This is under the control of the programmer and good programming style requires that you know the type of any expression in your program.

The programmer can exercise no such control over the entering of input. Input to a program can come from two external sources: a human user or a data file. Humans can make errors, thus any programs that get input from a human user must check the format of any input and must allow for the smooth correction of any errors in input. This applies to errors in both the values being input and their data types.

Consider what happens if the program requests the user to enter a number and the user enters the characters

1 / 2

This is a perfectly good construction in mathematics. However, it causes great difficulty if the program tries to read input using the scanf( ) function. Try this input with various scanf( ) control specifications and you will understand the difficulty. There is only one way to read in such input – use the getchar( ) function to read in the data one character at a time and store the three characters 1, / , and 2 in some type of data structure (probably an array) and then let the program interpret the input. This causes an obvious complication in the coding but lets the program be more robust so that bad input doesn't cause the program to crash.

A program that reads data from a data file doesn't have quite as much of a problem as one that interacts with a human user. However, data files often have some data that is in the wrong format. A programmer needs to be careful in this case also.

Let's summarize the advantages and disadvantages of the functions getchar( ) and scanf( ).

```
getchar():
```

> reads in data one character at a time
>
> always succeeds in getting the input data
>
> is very fast (no type conversions)

```
scanf():
```

> reads in data in any specified format
>
> often fails if format is unexpected
>
> requires difficult error checking
>
> executes slower than getchar() (type conversions)

Both of these functions are essential to programming in C. You should use getchar( ) whenever you are processing data that is considered to be pure text and has no special format other than as a stream of characters. You should use scanf( ) whenever you want the input data to be in some special form.

The full range of input facilities of C is more complex than can be described in detail at this point. Reading streams of characters will be described in the next chapter, and the entry of character strings will be postponed until the discussion of arrays and pointers.

1.7 Constants in C Programs

You may have noticed that most of the variables in our sample programs were not changed after they were initialized. Imagine that we were writing a small portion of a large software system and that we wished to have the value represented by a symbol unchanged during the execution of the program. We cannot leave this to chance, thus we need some mechanism for making sure that the value of the symbol is unchanged. In C, this is done using constants.

Example 1.13 shows a typical use of constants in C programs. It has a single constant and is a slight modification of the code that we presented in example 1.6.

Example 1.13

```
#include <stdio.h>
main(void)
{
   int i= 10;
   char c = 'Y';
   float f,g;
   float h, chicken_hawk;
   double d, mint;
   const float aardvark = 3.14159;
}
```

The value of the symbol "aardvark" cannot be changed in this program, but all of the other variables can have their values changed by later statements. Any attempt to change the value of a symbol described as constant will cause an error when the program is compiled.

Note the syntax of the constant declaration of "aardvark." The reserved word "const" is used, followed by the type of the variable, the name of the variable, and the value to which it is initialized. The constant here is a floating point number in exponential form.

The ability to designate symbols as constants is a feature of ANSI C that was not always present in the earlier dialects of the C language. This is helpful in building maintainable software systems in C since the effect of changes can be determined with more certainty. Since most modern programming languages have the ability to declare constants, this facility removes a deficiency of earlier dialects of C.

Another feature available in ANSI C but not in all earlier dialects of C is the enumeration data type in which a variable of type int can be restricted to take on one of a fixed number of pre-defined constants of type int. An example of this is the days of the week:

```
enum days {MON, TUES, WED, THUR, FRI, SAT, SUN} ;
```

The C reserved word enum must be used with an enumerated data type. In this example, the enumerated type is called days. The enumerated constants need not be upper-case.

1.8 Documentation and Commenting of C Programs

C programs can include comments that provide information to a person reading the program. Comments in C are preceded by the two characters / and * and are followed by the same characters * and / in reversed order. A common feature of most programs written by professional programmers is that there is a program heading that includes the name of the programmer, date of program, name of programmer who modified code, date of any succeeding modifications, purpose of program, computer system used, as well as any information about the particular compiler. This will be especially important in the future since there are several different C compilers that cause slightly different versions of the language to be used.

Here is a simple example.

Example 1.14

```
/*********************************************
   PROGRAMMER NAME:  A. B. See
   DATE:    January 17, 1993
   PURPOSE OF PROGRAM: To print "Hello"
   COMPUTER:  HAL 9000
   COMPILER: Fred's  C compiler, version 1.23
   OPERATING SYSTEM: Elvira's OS version 2.3
 *********************************************/
```

```
#include <stdio.h>
main(void)
{
printf("Hello\n");
}
```

In addition to providing a program heading, programmers include comments in the program to make it easier to understand. Important variables and constants are generally commented. Comments are usually placed at the beginning of each function and at the beginning and the end of each complicated block of code. They are often placed at the beginning of the branches of an if-else statement if the conditions describing the alternatives are complicated. They are also frequently placed after braces that signify the end of a loop. (We study the if-else and loop statements in Chapter 2). Examples of one suggested approach to commenting are provided throughout the rest of this book. To save space we frequently omit the program header from sample programs.

There is one final note on commenting of programs. There are many possible ways that the same amount of information can be presented as commenting within a program. The objective of commenting software is to provide an adequate amount of information for use by yourself and others, either at the time that the software is being written or at some later date when it is maintained or modified. The most important thing is to be consistent with the visual style of indentation and the amount and type of information provided.

You will often have a standard commenting format provided to you, either by your instructor in a classroom, by a rigorous company guide to programming style, or by an informal company discipline. In the absence of such guidance, just be consistent. In any event, be careful to comment your programs, and recognize that large, complex systems need more documentation than do small, simple ones.

Summary of Chapter 1

We have seen our first examples of C programs. Programs in C must include a function called main at which execution begins. The body of main must be enclosed in braces.

Each variable in C must have a type. The elementary data types in C are int, float, double, and char. There is no boolean data type in C.

C is a case-sensitive language. This means that symbols named i and I represent different variables. The custom in C is to have nearly all of the program written in lowercase letters.

C is a weakly typed language. While each variable in C must have a definite type, type checking is usually not done by the C compiler. Type changes and conversions are common and often lead to unexpected results.

Variables in C can be initialized using an assignment statement. Uninitialized variables can have garbage values. The value of a variable can be kept fixed throughout a C program if we declare it to be a constant at the time of its initial definition.

Output in C can be done using the printf( ) function. Each value to be printed must have a control specification. Possible specifications include int (%d), char (%c), float (%f), double (%f or %e), octal (%o), hexadecimal (%x), and string (%s – to be discussed later). Field size can be controlled by including a field specification such as

```
printf("%5.2f",x)
```

with printf( ). Characters can also be printed using the putchar( ) function so as to run faster Putchar( ) can be used for character output only, while printf( ) is much more versatile in the sense that it can be used to print any type of expression. A useful function for printing a string of characters is puts( ).

Input in C is similar to output. We can use scanf( ) for formatted input using control specifications. Character data can be read either using scanf( ) with the %c control specification or by using the function getchar( ). The function scanf( ) uses the address of variables by means of the & symbol.

Comments in C programs can be enclosed within the delimiters /* and */. They may be placed anywhere in a program.

A variable of type int may be given as an enumerated type if its set of allowable values is a fixed set of values, each of which is of type int.

Exercises

1. Write a C program to produce the following two lines of output:

This is a good book.
Please buy 5 copies.

2. Write a C program that prints the output of exercise 1 with four blank lines between the two lines in that exercise. Use several of the newline characters \n within a single printf( ) statement.

3. Write a C program that shows what happens when you use a backslash (\) in front of other characters besides t and n in a printf( ) statement. Be sure to test the case of \b.

4. Find out the length of the largest string of characters that can be included within the quotation marks in a printf( ) statement. You will probably have to run many versions of your program to find the answer.

5. Write a C program to print your initials in large size type using the letters of your initials as components of the output. An example of the type of output expected for my initials is:

```
RRRRR
R    R
R    R
R    R
R    R
RRRRR
R    R
R    R
R     R

     J
     J
     J
     J
J    J
J    J
 JJJJ

L
L
L
L
L
LLLLLLL
```

6. Write a C program that explores other controls for printing output. Try to print the single value 7 in different formats. How many of the controls other than %d, %f, %g, %c, %o, %x, or %O are accepted by the compiler? Explain your answers in terms of your computer's character set, size of computer word, or base (10, 2, 8, 16). What happens if you try the format control %s?

7. Write a C program that explores other controls for the reading of input. Try to enter the single value 7 in different formats. Print the output using the %d control specification. How many of the controls other than %d, %f, %g, %c, %o, %x, or %O are accepted by the compiler? Explain your answers in terms of your computer's character set, size of computer word, or base (10, 2, 8, 16). What happens if you try the format control %s?

8. Repeat exercise 7 using the input of 7.0 and using the %f printf( ) control specification.

9. Write a program header that provides documentation for a C program that is a compiler; that is, the C program that you are providing documentation for will read in other C program files as input and will produce as output a program that can be run.

What kinds of information would you have to include in the documentation?

10. Experiment with the position of the #include statement in example 1.7. What happens if it is placed after the closing braces? What if it is placed within the delimiting braces in main( )?

II. List the basic data types in C. Which can be used with the qualifiers unsigned, short, or long?

12.

(a) What are the values stored in the variables c1 and c2 if the seven characters

```
Hello\n
```

are typed (the first character is the escape sequence for the tab character, \t and the last character is the escape sequence for the newline character, \n) after the statement

```
scanf("%c%c%c%c",&c1,&c1,&c2,&c2);
```

is executed?

(b) Does your answer to part a depend on the types of the variables c1 and c2?

13. Write a program to demonstrate the information lost in repeated changes from int to long to float to double to float to long to int. Run your program on many different inputs including 1 and 100000. Try to test this program on several different types of computers and compilers. Is the output different in different programming environments?

14. Write a program to demonstrate the information lost in repeated changes from unsigned int to int to long to long to int to unsigned int. Run your program on many different inputs including the four values −1, −10,000, 1 and 100,000. Try to test this program on several different types of computers and compilers. Is the output different in different programming environments?

CHAPTER 2

Control of C Programs

Like every other programming language, C has provisions for executing statements in the order in which they occur, for repeating statements or groups of statements, and for making decisions that affect the flow of control of the program.

In this chapter, we describe the C constructions for doing these common programming operations. We also consider some of the operations that are available in C for comparison of expressions. As a fundamental example of an application of loops, we show how to read in an input stream of characters.

2.1 Iteration in C: The for-loop

In this section, we discuss the for-loop. The simplest case of the for-loop is similar to the DO loop in FORTRAN and the for statement in Pascal.

The syntax of the loop is quite simple:

```
for (expression1 ; expression2 ; expression3)
    zero_or_more_statements_to_be_repeated
```

We have used the terminology "zero_or_more_statements_to_be_repeated" to indicate the body of the loop; that is, the set of statements executed at each iteration of the loop. In nearly all programs, there are some statements in the body of the loop other than the null statement (an empty statement terminated by a semicolon), and thus we will use the term "one_or_more_statements_to_be_repeated" instead of using the slightly more precise term "zero_or_more_statements_to_be_repeated." The body of a loop is always indented the same amount for clarity. A complete description of the precise syntax of for-loops is given in appendix 3, where the syntactic description of the C language is given.

the other two identical expressions are extremely unusual). Another method of obtaining an infinite loop (which might be useful in a program that must run forever such as an air traffic control program) is

```
for ( ; ; )
    one_or_more_statements_to_be_repeated
```

Do not run a program with an infinite loop unless you know how to stop the program on your computer system!

Any looping construction can be done with a for-loop although the code might be much simpler if another looping mechanism is used. In general, for-loops are most useful when the number of repetitions of the body of the loop is known in advance.

How would you test a program containing a for-loop? You would check that the loop is entered and that the body of the loop is executed the appropriate number of times. You would also check that each iteration of the loop left the program in a correct state. These three steps should be used whenever a for-loop is being tested.

In many computer programs, iterations of a computation need to be done for each of several variables. It is often convenient to nest several for-loops by having the body of the second loop contained inside the first. For example, to print the contents of 5 lines, each of which has the digits 0 through 9 separated by spaces, we could write the nested loops

```
for (i = 1; i <=5 ; i = i + 1)
    {
    for (j = 0; j <= 9; j = j + 1)
       printf("%d",j);
    printf("%d\n");
    }
```

We will see several examples of this construction later in programs. For now, just keep in mind that any set of iteration constructions can be nested. The number of loops that can be nested is limited only by the compiler's storage and this is usually much more nesting than is used in any real C program.

Up to this point all the loops that we have studied use relatively simple expressions for control of the number of iterations. There are more complicated expressions that can be used to control loops. We will meet some of them later in this chapter when we study the comma operator.

2.2 Iteration in C: The while-loop

While-loops can be used to repeat one or more statements based on the value of some controlling expression. The controlling expression can be quite general. As with the for-loop, the body of the while-loop is always indented the same amount.

The while-loop in C has the following syntax:

```
while (expression1)
    zero_or_more_statements_to_be_repeated
```

The execution of the while-loop consists of two steps. The first step is the evaluation of expression1 and the determination if it is true (nonzero) or false (zero). If the value of expression1 is non-zero, then the one_or_more_statements_to_be_repeated that form the body of the loop will be executed. On the other hand, if the value of expression1 is zero, then the body of the loop will not be executed. The testing of the control expression1 is done before the body of the loop is entered; therefore the body of the loop need not be executed at all if the value of expression1 is initially 0.

We will follow the coding convention of indenting the body of each loop. As we did with the sample programs in Chapter 1, we will place the beginning and ending curly braces { and } on separate lines. This makes programs somewhat easier to read. Other coding conventions will be given later in the book.

Any for-loop can be coded as a while-loop by using the transformation that changes the for-loop

```
for (expression1 ; expression2 ; expression3)
    one_or_more_statements_to_be_repeated
```

to the equivalent while-loop construction

```
expression1;
while (expression2)
    {
    one_or_more_statements_to_be_repeated;
    expression3;
    }
```

The equivalent while-loop has the loop controller expression2 and has the same statements in the body as the for-loop except that the statement expression3 is included in the while-loop body to allow the same changes to the controlling variable.

As an example of the method of transformation from for-loops to while-loops, consider the for-loop of example 2.1. which is changed to a corresponding while-loop in example 2.3.

Example 2.3

```
#include <stdio.h>
main(void)
{
  int i;

  i=0 ;
  while (i <=5 )
```

```
        {
        printf("Please buy this book.\n");
        i = i + 1;
        }
    }
```

Using the same transformation method, the for-loop of example 2.2 is transformed into the equivalent while-loop shown in example 2.4.

Example 2.4

```
#include <stdio.h>

main(void)
{
   float x;

   x=0.0;
   while (x < 3.0)
      {
      printf("The value of x is %4.2f\n",x);
      x = x + 0.5;
      }
}
```

In these examples, we have placed the statement that changes the value of the loop control variable at the end of the while-loop. This is done for the sake of clarity since it makes it obvious precisely which changes are made to the variable controlling the loop.

It is almost as easy to change from a while-loop to a for-loop. The only difficulty occurs when the statement that changes the loop controlling variable is not part of the loop. This can happen if the changes are caused by using some function that changes the loop controller but the changes are not obvious without reading all of the code. In any event, you should recognize that the most appropriate loop control mechanism for any loop is the one that makes the program easiest to understand and that you shouldn't arbitrarily choose one particular mechanism for all of your programs.

The while-loop of the form

```
        while (expression1)
           one_or_more_statements_to_be_repeated
```

is equivalent to the for-loop

```
        for ( ; expression1; )
           one_or_more_statements_to_be_repeated
```

Note that the body of this loop is executed as long as expression1 has a nonzero value. In particular, the body of the loop is executed indefinitely if it has no statements that change the value of expression1.

The while-loop is especially useful when the number of repetitions of the loop is not known in advance. Testing of while-loops should include a test of the program's state if the body of code in the while-loop is never executed because the loop control condition is never satisfied. Testing should also include the case where some random number of repetitions of the body of the while-loop is performed. Of course, the final test is whether or not the loop is ever exited.

Note that the controlling expression can be quite complex. It can be a simple inequality such as

```
x < 3.5 ;
y > 0 ;
```

a general arithmetic expression such as

```
3 * x + 7 ;
```

a constant such as

```
1
```

or

```
0
```

as well as combinations of expressions like these using logical operators.

Recall that the relational operators in C are <, <=, >, >=, ==, !=, and !.

The logical negation operator is used in the form !expr. It returns the value 0 if the value of expr is nonzero and returns the value 1 if the value of expr is 0. In C, we could do this to test for the value of an expression being equal to 0 with something like

```
while (expr != 0)
    do_something;
```

but C allows a simpler form using the logical negation operator

```
while ( !expr)
    do_something;
```

This tests if the value of expression expr is 0; if it is not zero, then the code indicated in do_something is executed.

Compound logical expressions are accomplished in C by means of the two operators

```
logical AND operator && (two ampersands)
```

and

```
logical OR operator || (two vertical bars)
```

Rather than remember a large number of precedence rules, you should use parentheses to separate portions of compound logical expressions as in the three sample statements below.

```
while ( (x < 0) && (y == 3) )
while (!done)
while ( ((x <= 3) && (!clear) ) || (!fullmoon) )
```

We will study the precedence rules in Chapter 3. If you wish to use the precedence rules before then, consult Appendix 5.

Warning: Be sure to type two ampersands (&&) and two vertical bars (||) when you want the logical AND or logical OR, respectively, as we generally do. There are other operators & and | that perform the bit operations of bitwise AND and bitwise OR and that provide unexpected results when applied to expressions that are not bits. We will meet these operators when we discuss bit manipulation in Part II.

As before, while-loops can be nested. Any combination of for-loops and while-loops can be nested up to the nesting depth allowed by the compiler.

2.3 Iteration in C: The do-while-loop

The last loop structure in C is the do-while-loop. This mechanism is like the while loop in that it is appropriate when the number of iterations is not known in advance. The syntax is

```
do
   one_or_more_statements_to_be_repeated
while (expression1);
```

The difference between the while-loop and the do-while-loop is that the do-while construction makes the test of expression1 being 0 after the execution of the body of the loop. Thus the body of the loop is always executed at least once. Every do-while-loop can be transformed into a while-loop by following the pattern

```
one_or_more_statements_to_be_repeated
while (expression1)
   one_or_more_statements_to_be_repeated
```

This construction guarantees that the statement or statements to be repeated will be executed at least once (before the while-loop) and thus the number of times that the statements will be executed will be the same in the while-loop and the do-while-loop.

It is not so simple to reverse the transformation from an arbitrary while-loop to a do-while-loop, because the body of the do-while-loop is guaranteed to be executed at least once and the body of the while-loop may not be executed at all. The easiest way to rewrite a while loop as a do-while-loop is to add a guard so that the while-loop

```
while (expression1)
      one_or_more_statements_to_be_repeated
```

can be transformed into the much more difficult to understand

```
do
   if (expression1)
      one_or_more_statements_to_be_repeated
while (expression1)
```

As before, any combination of loops can be nested. Note also the level of indentation.

Many people think that use of the do-while-loop makes C code hard to understand because the test is written after the body of the loop. An informal count of loops in a collection of many C programs from a variety of sources suggests that the do-while-loop is used less than 3% of the time that loops are used. You can provide additional help for the reader of the program (other than the common indentation of loops) by using blank lines to surround the entire do-while-loop in order to make its construction stand out from the rest of the program.

2.4 Reading an Input Stream with a while-loop

An important example of the use of a while-loop is a program that will read all characters from the terminal as input to the program and will print out each character in the format of one character per line. The step performed is to read each character and to print it together with a new line \n as the character is read. The problem is that there is no obvious way for the program to tell when no more data is to be read since a carriage return \n in the input is simply printed to the output together with an additional \n. Thus the two lines of input, each of which ends in a carriage return, of

```
begin
end.
```

will give as output the 11 lines

```
b
e
g
i
n

e
n
d
.
```

(the 11 lines consist of everything between the b and the period including the carriage return at the end of the first line and the carriage return at the end of the second line).

What is needed here is a marker to indicate the end of the input. In C, this is done using the constant EOF that is defined in the file stdio.h that should be included in the program. The problem is the test of the value of the character c being equal to the value of EOF that is defined in the file stdio.h. We expect that when we see the indicator EOF that signals no more input, the statement c != EOF will become false and the while loop will terminate. However, the function scanf( ) actually does two things: it reads the value ch from the input **and** it returns the value of EOF when we reach EOF.

A program to read in an input stream of characters is given in example 2.5.

Example 2.5 Correct reading in of character data

```
#include <stdio.h>
/* program to read in a stream of characters using scanf */
main(void)
{
  char ch;

  while( scanf("%c",&ch) != EOF)
    printf("%c\n",ch);
}
```

This is typical of many C programs in that it combines several operations in a single statement. The condition being tested in the while statement is that the value that is returned by the function scanf( ) is EOF; the actual reading of the value of ch, which is the important action, is performed as an effect of the function scanf.

What is printed here is the carriage return \n in the printf( ) statement; the value returned by the function scanf is meaningless unless it reads EOF.

There are many other ways of trying to do this program. Two of them are based on a function that we have seen before: getchar( ). The purpose of getchar( ) is to read in any character in the input without skipping over any intervening blanks, tabs, or carriage returns. It has an unusual feature that will become apparent when you run the next program.

Example 2.6 Works on some computer systems, but not all

```
#include <stdio.h>
/* incorrect attempt to read a stream of characters */
/* uses getchar() - but has a subtle problem */
main(void)
{
  char ch;

  while( (ch = getchar()) != EOF)
    printf("%c\n",ch);
}
```

This program uses a correct algorithm. The same program was run using exactly the same input on two different computers – an AT&T 3B2/310 and a SUN Microsystems model 2/120. Each of these computers was running under a version of the UNIX operating system and in each case, the C compiler was the standard C compiler provided with the original system software. On one of the computers, the program worked correctly, while on the other computer the program went into an infinite loop filling the screen with blank lines. Obviously, there was a problem with the reading of the end of input (EOF).

The error is caused by the manner in which the computer internally stores characters. On one of the computers, characters are stored using a numerical representation that is between 0 and 255; the other uses numbers between –127 and 128. The end of input marker EOF is defined on each system as having the value –1, which is not in the range of values allowed for characters on the computer for which the program failed. The solution, **which works for all computers**, is to use a different DATA TYPE for the values read in. In example 2.7, which works properly, the variable read in is considered to be of type int so that EOF can be matched successfully. Note that the printf( ) statement uses the %c control specification for the output.

Example 2.7 Successful reading in and echoing of character data

```
#include <stdio.h>
/*.Finally a correct program - uses getchar() and int type
for the input */

main(void)
{
   int c;

   while( (c=getchar() ) != EOF)
       printf("%c\n",c);
}
```

This program works correctly on each system and is the only one that is guaranteed to do so on all computers, including the UNIX-based ones and on a personal computer using Turbo C.

You should remember the important features of this program to read an input stream of unformatted data.

To read a stream of unformatted data using getchar:

(1) Use the function getchar( ) to read in the input one symbol at a time.
(2) The value returned by getchar( ) is to be of type int to agree with the range of values used for storage of the character set.
(3) The test for EOF is made before we print anything so that there will be no output if there is no input.
(4) Parentheses are used to force the assignment of the value returned by getchar( ) to the variable c before comparing the value to EOF. They were necessary because of the precedence rules of C, which in the absence of parentheses determine which of the operations = or != is performed first.

There is one other observation that needs to be made about the input into these programs. Recall that both UNIX and MS-DOS allow the use of input and output redirection to replace the submission of input from a keyboard with input from a file by using the less than character '<'. Suppose that the input file is named "infile." On UNIX-based systems, in which the default name for an executable file is "a.out", we could use the UNIX shell command

```
        a.out < infile
```

On MS-DOS systems, we can use the DOS command

```
    2_7 < infile
```

(assuming that we are running the executable file created from a program called 2_7.c).

The difference between reading from a file and reading from the standard keyboard input is the way that the input data is terminated. The character that indicates the end of transmission of data in the UNIX-based systems is a CTRL-d, which is created by pressing the control and 'd' keys simultaneously. The DOS-based systems used a variety of symbols to indicate the termination of keyboard input, including the DOS standard CTRL-z for file termination, CTRL-c, and CTRL-y, but not including CTRL-d. You need to read your compiler manual for more information.

You might wonder about the use of scanf( ) within a loop to read in a stream of character data. This can certainly be done. However, it is a less efficient way of getting a large amount of data because of the overhead of scanf( ). However, scanf( ) is more efficient (in terms of run-time speed) for formatted input data than reading it in character by character and then attempting to interpret the data after it is read in.

It is easy to read in a stream of formatted data using scanf( ). Example 2.8 shows how to do this for a stream of floating point numbers. (**Warning** – on DOS-based systems, the end-of-input character should be separated from the valid input by a space, tab, or new line character.)

Example 2.8 Reading and echoing a stream of floats

```c
#include <stdio.h>
main(void)
{
   float fl;

   while (scanf("%f",&fl) != EOF)
     printf("%f",fl);
}
```

2.5 Branching in C: The if and if-else Statements

The if statement is similar in semantics (if not syntax) to most other programming languages. The simple if statement has the form

```
    if (expression1)
        zero_or_more_statements
```

The term "zero_or_more_statements" means either 0 or 1 statements followed by a semicolon or else it means a compound statement enclosed in braces. As before, the value of expression1 is considered false if it is equal to 0 and is considered true otherwise. If the value of expression1 is nonzero, then the set of C code statements denoted by zero_or_more_statements is executed. If not, then the next statement after the if statement (if any) is executed.

C also has the if-else statement. The syntax is

```
if (expression1)
    zero_or_more_statements
else
    zero_or_more_statements
```

An example of an if-else statement in a program is

```
if (i == 5)
    printf("The value of i is 5");
else
    printf("The value of i is not equal to 5");
```

This program segment has two new syntax features in addition to the if and else reserved words. The expression i==5 represents the comparison of the value of the variable i and the constant 5. This is equivalent to the .EQ. in FORTRAN and the = in Pascal. We have already seen that the assignment operator in C is =, which is the same as in FORTRAN. This is easier to write than the := which is used for assignment in Pascal.

Warning: Misuse of the == and = symbols is a common error in C. Consider example 2.9.

Example 2.9

```
#include <stdio.h>
main(void)
{
    int i = 0;

    if (i == 0)
        printf("i = 0\n");
    else
        printf("i is not = 0\n");
    if (i = 0)
        printf("i = 0\n");
    else
        printf("i is not = 0\n");
}
```

It has the surprising output

```
i = 0
i is not = 0
```

The first line of output is correct and is a result of the correct use of == in comparing the value of i to 0. The second line of output, which is incorrect, is a result of testing the value of the expression i = 0. This expression is an assignment statement whose value is the value that was actually assigned to the variable on the left-hand side of the assignment symbol =. This value is clearly 0 and hence the second if statement is interpreted as 0. Hence the program of example 2.9 is actually the same as

```
if (0)
   printf("i = 0\n");
else
   printf("i is not = 0\n");
```

which gives the incorrect result seen in the output of example 2.9.

When you test your programs, you should try to test any possible path that execution of the program might take. This means that, as a minimum, you should check each possible branch of an if-else statement. This type of testing will often find errors such as the misuse of == and = that we indicated.

The syntax of C's if-else statement is different from that of the if-then-else of Pascal in that the "then" is not used and the statement before the else is terminated by a semicolon if the statement before the else is not a compound statement enclosed in braces.

A slightly more complex if-else statement is

```
if (i == 5)
     {
     printf("The value of i is 5");
     }
else
     {
     printf("The value of i is not equal to 5");
     printf("The value of i is not equal to 5");
     }
```

In this if-else statement, no semicolon is inserted before the else since the braces signify the end of a compound statement. Note however that the statements before the right braces are always terminated by a semicolon.

The use of semicolons and braces in C is somewhat confusing, especially to those who are proficient in the Pascal language, which uses semicolons differently. A semicolon in C is used as a statement terminator. Thus the only time that a semicolon is **not** used is when the statement is already terminated. Each of the statements inside braces must be terminated by a semicolon. A compound statement in C consists of the statements inside plus the delimiters { and }; thus no semicolon is used after the closing right brace.

The expression evaluated in the if (expression) statement is not restricted to simple tests for equality using the logical operator ==. It can use the other logical operators that we have seen. It can also use compound logical expressions such as:

```
if ( (x < 0) && (y == 3) )

if (!done)

if ( ((x <= 3) && (!clear) ) || (!fullmoon) )
```

The logical AND operator && and the logical OR operator ‖ have *short-circuit evaluation* – evaluation of a compound logical expression stops as soon as its value is determined. Thus a C statement involving a logical "or" will stop execution as soon as the statement is known to be 0 or nonzero. This means that the second of the two alternatives need not be evaluated and indeed will not be evaluated in such a C statement. Here is an example of a program that produces no output even though there is a division by 0 in the statement 3==1/i.

Example 2.10

```
#include <stdio.h>
main(void)
{
  int i=0;

  if( (1==0) && (3==1/i))
    printf("In main, value returned is %d\n", i);
}
```

Warning: Be sure to type two ampersands (&&) and two vertical bars (‖) when you want the logical AND or logical OR. There are other operators & and ‖ for bit manipulation that behave oddly on expressions that are not guaranteed to be one of the bits 0 or 1. We will meet these operators when we discuss bit manipulation in Part II.

Again, you should use parentheses for clarity rather than use the precedence rules.

The if and else reserved words can be used for the selection of one option from among many by using what is frequently called the else-if construction. The syntax of this construction is

```
if (expression1)
  zero_or_more_statements_1
else if (expression2)
  zero_or_more_statements_2
else if (expression3)
  zero_or_more_statements_3
  .
  .
  .
else if (expression n)
  zero_or_more_statements_n
else
  zero_or_more_statements_otherwise;
```

This construction has the following meaning. If expression1 is nonzero (true) then the set of statements indicated by zero_or_more_statements_1 is executed and we then continue execution of the program with more_statements. If the value of expression1 is zero, then execution of the program ignores the zero_or_more_statements_1 and the next statement executed is the next if statement. If expression2 is nonzero, then zero_or_more_statements_2 is executed and we then continue execution of the program with more_statements. This continues until we get to expression n. If expression n is nonzero, then we execute zero_or_more_statements_n. If none of these expressions is nonzero, then we execute the statement zero_or_more_statements_otherwise.

In other words, if any of the expressions in the if portions is nonzero, then we execute the associated statements, break out of the else-if portion of the code, and continue execution after the last else. The statements are executed in order so that once an expression becomes non-zero, we exit this portion. The final else statement is optional.

Be careful with the if-else construction. For example, the C statements

```
if (expression1)
if (expression2)
  statement_1 ;
else
  statement_2 ;
else
  statement_3 ;
```

mean that the second "if" (and the corresponding "else" are executed only if the first "if" is executed because the value of expression1 is nonzero. This code should be written as

```
if (expression1)
  if (expression2)
    statement_1;
  else
    statement_2 ;
else
  statement_3 ;
```

where the indentation indicates which "else clause" is subordinate to which "if."

There are some things to watch out for. Many of them are caused by the fact that expressions in C have a value. For example, the statements

```
printf("%d\n", 1 < 2 < 3);
printf("%d\n", 1 > 2 > 3);
if (x<0)
  printf("x < 0");
```

have quite different output from what you might expect. The double inequality is evaluated from left to right.

It is generally a good idea to test all possible branches in a program. This may become impractical if you are at the innermost branch point of a program segment with many earlier branches since the maximum number of possible branches is multiplied by a factor of 2 at each level of branching. In this case, you should see if the program is overly complex. If you are forced to use a huge number of nested branches, then you should choose the most important test cases of the program and test them as well as a reasonable number of other, less important branches of program execution.

We close this section with a mention of a C operator called the conditional operator. It uses the symbols ? and : to shorten an if-else statement. For example, the C code

```
if (i)
      j=3;
else
      j=x;
```

can be written more compactly as

```
i ? j=3 : j=x;
```

The two forms are completely equivalent. Many people find this construction very hard to read; others use it frequently. It will not be used very much in this book. However, it is available in the language and you should at least be able to understand it if you see the ?: used in other people's programs.

2.6 Branching in C: The switch Statement

There is another mechanism in C for choosing among alternatives when a selection is to be made from a fixed number of constant values of type integer: the switch statement. The syntax of the switch statement is

```
switch (expression1)
  {
  case constant_integer_1: zero_or_more_statements_1
  case constant_integer_2: zero_or_more_statements_2
      .
      .
      .
  case constant_integer_n: zero_or_more_statements_n
  default: zero_or_more_statements_default
  }
more_statements;
```

A statement using the switch construction is often clearer than the corresponding collection of else-if statements. There are several points to keep in mind however. The individual choices must be expressions that evaluate to integers, and the values of these choices must be constant. There is no method in C of specifying a range of values in a switch statement; an else-if statement must be used instead.

Unlike the else-if construction, after a match of the value of the constant_integer, control of execution does not go to the statement indicated by more_statements after the enclosing brace. Execution simply continues to attempt to match some other constant within the body of the switch. This can be prevented by putting the break statement after each case where you want to exit the switch statement. The purpose of the break statement is to shift control of the program's execution to the smallest enclosing block of code containing the break statement. The smallest enclosing block is the innermost switch statement in which the break statement appears.

Consider a switch statement in which either there were no matches or there was a match not followed by a break statement. We would then fall through to the last block of code within the switch statement.

The default option forces the last block of code to be executed. It is used to match automatically any constant integer value of the expression controlling the switch. The default option is optional. If no default option appears within the switch, then control of the program resumes at the next line after the switch.

Example 2.11 shows a simple block of code using a switch statement. It also uses the break and default constructions. We have not bothered to initialize the loop control variable digit since it will be given a value upon execution of the body of the do-while-loop. The body of the do-while-loop will always be executed at least once. Note the two space indentation of the body of the do-while loop and the style and indentation used for the various cases in the switch statement.

Example 2.11

```c
#include <stdio.h>
main(void)
{
  int digit;

  do
    {
    puts("Enter a digit in the range 0 .. 9");
    puts("A 0 quits the program");
    scanf("%d",&digit);
    switch (digit)
      {
      case 1:
        digit=2;
        break;
      case 2:
        digit=3;
        break;
      case 3:
        digit=4;
        break;
      case 4:
        digit=5;
        break;
      case 5:
        digit=6;
        break;
      case 6:
        digit=7;
        break;
```

```
        case 7:
          digit=8;
          break;
        case 8:
          digit =9;
          break;
        case 9:
          digit =1;
          break;
        }
      printf("The new value of digit is %d\n",digit);
      }
  while (digit);
}
```

The use of the break statement allows the control of execution of the program to resume at the beginning of the smallest enclosing loop or switch statement enclosing the break. A break statement often speeds up the program's execution slightly since there is no need to check the value of the variable digit against the later values since only one of the possible cases can be matched. The program would still execute. However, note that the value of digit is changed by the statements executed in the possible options in the switch statement. This could affect the control of the program's results if there were no break statements. For example, if we remove all the break statements from example 2.11, the program would have two possible outputs from each iteration of the loop: 1 or 0.

The break statement can eliminate many program errors that are difficult to find. In order to write programs that are easy to understand and easy to debug. **Always use the break statement inside a switch statement to separate options**.

A switch statement should be tested in exactly the same manner as a collection of if-else statements. This means that each possible branch should be tested and that the default statement should be tested also.

In example 2.12, we show a portion of a program that uses the switch statement in conjunction with some of the other statements that we have discussed in this chapter. Note the use of the default option to guarantee a match. Note also the commenting of the ends of the switch statement, the for-loop, and the main program. This is very helpful in writing readable programs.

Example 2.12

```
#include <stdio.h>
main(void)
{
  int i, number_of_students;
  int number_of_A = 0, number_of_B = 0, number_of_C = 0;
  int  number_of_D = 0, number_of_other = 0;
  float average;
  char grade;
```

```
      puts("Enter the number of students in the class");
      scanf("%d", &number_of_students);
      if (number_of_students > 100)
        puts("Remember to ask for raise");
      for (i = 1; i < number_of_students; i = i + 1)
        {
        /* code to compute the average and grade goes here */
        switch (grade)
          {
          case 'A' :
            printf("Grade is A\n");
            if (average >= 95.0)
             printf("Outstanding job!!!\n");
            number_of_A = number_of_A + 1;
            break;
          case 'B' :
            printf("Grade is B\n");
            number_of_B = number_of_B + 1;
            break;
          case 'C' :
            printf("Grade is C\n");
            number_of_C = number_of_C + 1;
            break;
          case 'D' :
            printf("Grade is D\n");
            number_of_D = number_of_D + 1;
            break;
          case 'W' :
            printf("Grade is W\n");
            number_of_other = number_of_other + 1;
            break;
          case 'I' :
            printf("Grade is I\n");
            number_of_other = number_of_other + 1;
            break;
          default:
            printf("Sorry\n");
            number_of_other = number_of_other + 1;
          } /* end of switch */
      } /* end of  for loop */
} /* end of main */
```

We can also use enumeration types as labels within a switch statement. An example of this is a code fragment to count the number of occurrences of the weekdays and weekend days of a particular period. We can use this code fragment if the constants would have to have been declared previously using an enum statement.

```
switch (day)
  {
  case MON:
      Monday_total = Monday_total + 1;
      break;
  case TUES:
      Tuesday_total = Tuesday_total + 1;
      break;
  case WED:
      Wednesday_total = Wednesday_total + 1;
      break;
  case THURS:
      Thursday_total = Thursday_total + 1;
      break;
  case FRI:
      Friday_total = Friday_total + 1;
      break;
  default:
      Weekend_total = Weekend_total + 1;
      break;
  }   /* end switch */
```

In the exercises you will be asked to change the grading program to use an enumerated data type to act as the labels within the program.

2.7 The Comma Operator

It is possible to have extremely complicated expressions as the control expression in loops or branches in C. This is usually done using the comma operator. The comma operator uses the symbol ',' to allow the performance of more than one operation within a set of delimiters.

Commands embedded within a statement that uses the comma operator are executed from left to right. Thus a statement such as

```
i = 1;
j = 2;
i = j , j = 3;
```

gives i the value 2 and gives j the value 3, in that order.

A more interesting example of the use of the comma operator is the for-loop that we present in example 2.13. This loop uses the comma operator to perform two computations in the space that we have usually described as being "expression3."

The C code in "expression3" is translated by the compiler as follows. The expression

```
j = j + 1
```

on the right-hand side of the comma operator is performed first. Its value is then given to the expression on the left-hand side of the comma and this expression is now evaluated. This means that in this example, the first time through the loop, the value of i printed is 0, since the value of i makes expressions 1 and 2 both nonzero. The value of expression3 is computed according to the above rules, and thus both i and j are changed as part of the evaluation of expression3. This means that the value of i is incremented by 2. The second time through the loop, the value of i is again incremented by 2 as a result of the two component expressions making up the portions of expression3 and thus the loop terminates. The value of the variable i after exiting the loop is 3.

Example 2.13

```
#include <stdio.h>

main(void)
{
   int i, j = 1 ;
   float f;

   for (i = 0; i < 3; i = j + 1, j = j + 1)
     printf("%d",i);
   printf("After loop, i is %d\n",i);
}
```

Expressions separated by a comma are evaluated from left to right. The values, if any, of expressions on the left-hand side of the comma operator are ignored after the execution of the statements that involve the expression. The value of the complete statement using the comma operator is the value of the rightmost expression that is comma-free, and the type of the comma expression is the type of this rightmost expression.

The comma operator can lead to compact code that executes quickly. On the other hand, it can make programs hard to read. Be careful if you use this construction.

2.8 Processing of an Input stream: An Example

We can use the control structures in this chapter together with some readily available C facilities to process streams of text. We show how to do this by a simple example to compute the number of upper and lowercase letters, digits, spaces, punctuation marks, and other characters in an input stream. The program makes use of the predefined facilities included in the file ctype.h which have been incorporated in this program by use of an include file directive to the C preprocessor. (The contents of a typical ctype.h file are included in Appendix 4.) The facilities provided in this file are very useful in programs that process streams of character data. Note the use of meaningful names for variables.

Example 2.14

```c
#include <stdio.h>
#include <ctype.h>
main(void)
{
  int ch;
  int character_count = 0, punct_count = 0;
  int letter_count = 0, digit_count = 0;
  int space_count = 0, other_count = 0;

  while (( ch = getchar() ) != EOF)
    {
    character_count = character_count + 1;
    if isalpha(ch)
      letter_count = letter_count + 1;
    else if isdigit(ch)
      digit_count = digit_count + 1;
    else if ispunct(ch)
      punct_count = punct_count + 1;
    else if isspace(ch)
      space_count = space_count + 1;
    else
      other_count = other_count + 1;
    }

  printf("There are %d characters in the input.\n",
          character_count);
  printf("There are %d letters, %d digits,", letter_count,
          digit_count);
  printf("and %d punctuation marks.\n", punct_count);
  printf("There are %d spaces, tabs, or new lines\n",
          space_count);
  printf("and %d other characters.\n", other_count);
}
```

The while-loop of example 2.14 can be changed to use the comma operator as in:

```c
    while (character_count = character_count+1,
        (ch= getchar()) != EOF)
      {
      if isaplha(ch)
        letter_count = character_count + 1;
```

```
    else if isdigit(ch)
      digit_count = letter_count + 1;
    else if ispunct(ch)
      punct_count = punct_count + 1;
    else if isspace(ch)
      space_count = space_count + 1;
    else
      other_count  = other_count + 1;
  }
```

This use of the comma operator simplifies the body of the loop at the expense of complicating the loop control expression. The coding practice shown in example 2.14 is much more commonly used.

There are many other possibilities for processing input streams using the facilities available in the include file <ctype.h>. These facilities include detecting uppercase and lowercase letters, alphanumeric characters, and ASCII characters, and facilities for changing to either uppercase or lowercase letters. Use these facilities as needed in your programs.

Summary of Chapter 2

C has several facilities for iteration and for branching of programs. All of these statements are controlled by evaluation of one or more expressions.

Iteration can be done using the for-loop, the while-loop, or the do-while-loop. Each of these is convenient for certain applications. Any type of expression can be used to control the number of iterations of a loop. A for-loop is most commonly used when the number of iterations of the loop is essentially controlled by a numeric variable. The primary difference between a while-loop and a do-while-loop is that the testing of the controlling expression is done at the start of a while-loop (before execution of the statements in the body of the loop) and at the end of a do-while-loop (after execution of the statements in the body of the loop).

The expressions controlling any kind of loop can be arithmetic expressions such as $3 * x + 1$ or logical ones such as $x < 7$. Logical operators that can be used are <, <=, >, >= , ==, !=, and !. Expressions can be combined using the logical operators && (logical AND), || (logical OR), or ! (logical NEGATION).

Iterations can be nested. We can have for-loops that are inside of for-loops that are inside of while-loops, and so on.

All loops should have the body of their code indented. A do-while loop should be further marked by using blank lines to set off the loop from the surrounding code.

An important use of loops is to process a stream of information. The while loop is especially useful for reading from an input stream. The function scanf( ) can be used to read formatted data and getchar( ) can be used to read in data without requiring any assumption about the format. The file stdio.h should be included in order to access the system constant EOF, which is used to indicate the end of the input stream.

C uses the == symbol to denote comparison; it is important to distinguish its use from that of the = symbol, which is used to indicate an assignment.

Branching can be done using the if, if-else, or switch statements. The if and if-else statements are used for determining which of two branches can be followed in the control of a program.

The switch statement is used when there are many possible branches in a program's control flow. It can use numerical constants as the choices; the constants can also be given using an enumerated type. The only requirement for the choices in a switch statement is that they must be integer constants.

Many combinations of conditional and branching statements can be made within a program. Switch statements can be combined with if and if-else statements in any order. They can be combined with any reasonable number of loop control statements.

There are many facilities for the processing of character data such as isspace( ), isalpha( ), and isalphanum( ). These can all be found in the file ctype.h, which can be included in C programs using the C preprocessor.

Exercises

1. Write a C program that assigns grades. The program will have the control structure that will indicate a grade of 'A' if the value of average is greater than or equal to 90.0, 'B' if the value of average is greater than or equal to 80.0 but less than 90.0 and so on down to 'F' if the the value of average is less than 60.0. This program should use the if statement but should not use the C reserved words else or switch. Test your program logic by running it several times.

2. Repeat the previous exercise using the if-else construction. You may also use the else-if construction if you wish.

3. Describe an algorithm that will change an arbitrary switch_statement with all its options into a collection of if-else or else-if statements. Do not attempt to implement this algorithm at this time.

4. In this exercise and the next, we consider two incorrect attempts to read in a stream of characters from input using scanf( ). In each case, test the program to see if it works on your system and explain what the error is. The first attempt at writing a program to do this has two errors, one of which is subtle.

```
#include <stdio.h>
/* first attempt - doesn't work quite right */
main(void)
{
   char ch;
```

13. Rewrite the grading program of example 2.12 using the enumeration data construction for the possible letter grades. Compare the two programs. Which is easier to read?

14. We have seen a fairly large number of simple C language statements and a few C programs, probably enough to be able to distinguish most of the simple notations that are used in C programs. Describe an algorithm that will take as input a file that contains a C language program and that produces as output a listing of the separate tokens that make up the program. Assume that tokens are anything other than blanks, tabs, or new lines. Be sure that your algorithm can handle such things as the comment delimiters /* and */. Do not attempt to implement this algorithm at this time.

CHAPTER 3

Arithmetic and Other Operations in C

This chapter provides a description of some fundamental operations that are available in the C language. It describes a more general notion that is central to C: expressions. The term "expression" includes any simple variables or constants and any combinations of these using allowable sequences of operations in C. It introduces the notion of precedence of operators and indicates the precedence of some of the more common C operators. The chapter also provides an introduction to a design project that we will study throughout the remainder of this book.

3.1 Integer Arithmetic

In this section we will learn how to perform arithmetic operations on numbers that are of type int. Floating point arithmetic will be discussed later in this chapter. The arithmetic operations that are readily available in C for variables of type int are addition, subtraction, multiplication, division, and the modulus operation. They are denoted by +, −, *, /, and %, respectively. The operations +, −, and * behave in the expected manner: the values of the result are what you would normally expect, and if two expressions that are both of type int are added, subtracted, or multiplied, then the result is also of type int. Division of int expressions always produces a result of type int, so that 7/2 has the value 3, which is of course of type int also. Division fails if the divisor is 0.

The modulus operator works in the following way. If the numbers n and m are positive, then the modulus of n modulo m is the remainder when n is divided by m. The modulus operator fails if the divisor is 0. For example, the value of 7 % 2 is 1 since 1 is the remainder when 7 is divided by 2. Note that for any two positive ints n and m, n is equal to $n/m + n \% m$; this equation need not be true if either n or m were negative.

All the operations listed above are binary operations; that is, they take two operands. The – symbol is overloaded in the sense that it can stand for either the binary operator for subtraction or the unary operator for negation. There is no ambiguity in the evaluation of any arithmetic expression by C compilers, and this overloading causes very few problems in practice.

The previous paragraphs in this section could apply with minimal changes to most programming languages. Since C was originally designed for systems programming with the associated need for rapidly executing code, its syntax permits providing direct information to the compiler about certain operations that are to be done fast. By far the most common arithmetic operations that can be done fast are those of the form

```
variable = variable + 1;
```

as well as similar statements for subtraction. C has the incrementation operator ++, which is used for adding 1 to an expression, and the decrementation operator ––which is used for subtracting 1 from an expression.

The incrementation and decrementation operators can be used as in the following C statements:

```
i++;
++i;
i--;
--i;
```

The first two statements add 1 to the variable i while the last two subtract 1 from i. The statements i++ and ++i are equivalent in their effect on the variable i. The difference in the action of the two statements occurs when they are used as part of more complicated expressions such as

```
x = ++i
```

and

```
x = i++
```

In the first statement, the assignment takes place after i is incremented, and in the second, the assignment takes place before the incrementation. Thus if i were equal to 4 initially, x could be either 5 or 4, depending on which statement you use for the assignment. This difference is due to the different precedence of the operators = and ++. Example 3.1 indicates the results of the operations.

Example 3.1

```
#include <stdio.h>
main(void )
{
    int i=4, x;
```

```
    x = ++i;
    printf("Increment before the assignment: %d\n",x);
    i=4;
    x = i++;
    printf("Assignment before the increment: %d\n",x);
}
```

The output is what is expected, namely

```
    Increment before the assignment:  5
    Assignment before the increment:  4
```

Needless to say, the relative precedence of the -- and = operators is the same as the relative precedence of ++ and =.

We have defined the term "expression" as anything that can be formed by variables, constants, and any sequence of allowable operations in C. An expression can be substituted for any other expression in C. Thus it is perfectly legitimate to have the code of example 3.2 in which we print the value of the expressions x = ++i and x = i++. The values of these expressions are 5 and 4, respectively, assuming that the value of x had been set to 4 before the evaluation of each of these two statements. This happens because a side effect of the assignment statement is to provide a value for the expression and not just for the variable on the left-hand side of the assignment statement. Example 3.1 and example 3.2 produce the same output.

Example 3.2

```
#include <stdio.h>
main(void)
{
    int i=4, x;

    printf("Increment before the assignment: %d\n", x=++i);
    i=4;
    printf("Assignment before the increment: %d\n", x=i++);
}
```

See the precedence table later in this chapter or in Appendix 5 for more details about the relative precedence of operators. As a beginning C programmer, it is probably better for you to use the i++ and i-- forms together with parentheses. Use parentheses to avoid complicated arithmetic expressions by breaking them up into expressions that are easier to understand.

Notice how much cleaner the code from example 2.12 looks when we use the incrementation operator ++ in example 3.3. This is a much better programming style.

Example 3.3

```c
#include <stdio.h>
/* Same as example 2.12 except for using the ++ operator */

main(void)
{
  int i, number_of_students;
  int number_of_A = 0, number_of_B = 0, number_of_C = 0;
  int  number_of_D = 0, number_of_others = 0;
  float average;
  char grade;

  puts("Enter the number of students in the class");
  scanf("%d", &number_of_students);
  if (number_of_students > 100)
    puts("Remember to ask for raise");
  for (i = 1; i < number_of_students; i ++)
    {
    /* code to compute the average and grade goes here */
    switch (grade)
      {
      case 'A' :
        printf("Grade is A\n");
        if (average >= 95.0)
          printf("Outstanding job!!!\n");
        number_of_A ++;
        break;
      case 'B' :
        printf("Grade is B\n");
        number_of_B ++;
        break;
      case 'C' :
        printf("Grade is C\n");
        number_of_C ++;
        break;
      case 'D' :
        printf("Grade is D\n");
        number_of_D ++;
        break;
      case 'W' :
        printf("Grade is W\n");
        number_of_other ++;
        break;
```

```
          case 'I' :
            printf("Grade is I\n");
            number_of_other ++;
            break;
          default:
            printf("Sorry\n");
            number_of_other ++;
        } /* end of switch */
      } /* end of  for loop */
    } /* end of main */
```

(The code of example 2.14 will also be much shorter and more readable using the ++ operator.)

The next type of statement is also extremely common:

```
    variable = variable + increment;
```

There are similar needs for statements that use the subtraction, multiplication, and division operators. These can be annoying to type frequently and can be hard to read, especially if the variable names are long and the statement has been indented a large amount. C allows the shorthand operators +=, -=, *=, and /= to replace these forms so that we can simply write

```
    variable += increment;
    variable -= increment;
    variable *= increment;
    variable /= increment;
```

to make the C source code easier to read. This is especially useful in improving readability when one of the variables has a long name. The changed program probably doesn't run any faster; the C compiler uses the two forms interchangeably.

Note that the operators ++, --, +=, -=, *=, and /= cannot be used with an expression that has been defined as being a constant using something like

```
    const int x = 4;
    x += 3;        /* illegal - will not compile */
```

Each of the operations in this section produces a result that is of type int when all its operands are of type int. The result of an operation in which all operands are of type long int, short, unsigned int, or unsigned long int are also of that type.

The situation is slightly more complicated when the operands of an operator have different types. We discuss the case of mixed types of integer operands in this section and consider floating point types and mixed floating and integer expressions in the next section.

The rules for conversion of mixed expressions are complicated. They all have the underlying principle of "convert each operand to a single common type, operate on that type, and produce a result that is of that type."

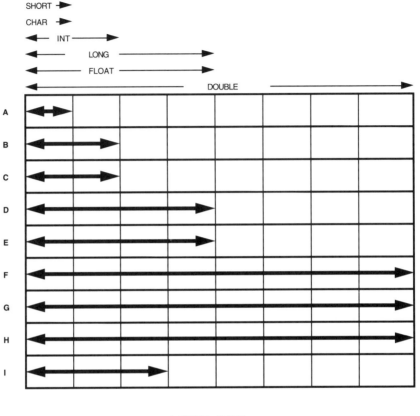

A: SHORT + SHORT
B: SHORT + INT
C: CHAR + INT
D: INT + FLOAT
E: FLOAT + FLOAT
F: FLOAT + DOUBLE
G: INT + DOUBLE
H: CHAR + DOUBLE
I : SHORT + LONG

Figure 3.1 Some typical sizes of types on a 32-bit computer

arithmetic on the right-hand side was carried out in double precision, but the assignment to the variable on the left-hand side only had the single-precision accuracy available to float variables. Thus some information was lost in the conversion.

It is clear from the conversion rules that floating point arithmetic in C is always done in double-precision format.

As before, the value of constants cannot be changed.

We can combine our knowledge of floating point arithmetic in C with our grade program to get a simple program to compute grades. This program is shown in example 3.4.

Example 3.4

```c
#include <stdio.h>
/* Grade computation program  */
main(void)
{
  int i, number_of_students;
  int number_of_A = 0, number_of_B = 0, number_of_C = 0;
  int  number_of_D = 0, number_of_other = 0;
  float project1, project2, project3, midterm1, midterm2,
  final;
  float average;
  char grade;

  puts("Enter the number of students in the class");
  scanf("%d", &number_of_students);
  if (number_of_students > 100)
    puts("Remember to ask for raise");

  /* code to compute both the average and grade goes here */
  /* There is no provision for incomplete grades.       */
  for (i = 1; i < number_of_students; i ++)
    {
    scanf("%f%f%f%f%f%f", &project1, &project2, &project3
          &midterm1, &midterm2, &final);
    average = (project1 + project2 + project3) *0.3 +
          midterm1 *0.2 + midterm2 *0.2 +final*0.3 ;

    if (average >= 90.0)
      grade = 'A';
    else if ((average >= 80.0) && (average < 90.0) )
      grade = 'B';
    else if ((average >= 70.0) && (average < 80.0) )
      grade = 'C';
    else if ((average >= 60.0) && (average < 70.0) )
      grade = 'D';
    else
      grade = 'F';
    switch (grade)
      {
      case 'A' :
        printf("Grade is A\n");
        if (average >= 95.0)
```

```
      printf("Outstanding job!!!\n");
    number_of_A ++;
    break;
  case 'B' :
    printf("Grade is B\n");
    number_of_B ++;
    break;
  case 'C' :
    printf("Grade is C\n");
    number_of_C ++;
    break;
  case 'D' :
    printf("Grade is D\n");
    number_of_D ++;
    break;
  case 'W' :
    printf("Grade is W\n");
    number_of_other ++;
    break;
  case 'I' :
    printf("Grade is I\n");
    number_of_other ++;
    break;
  default:
    printf("Sorry\n");
    number_of_other ++;
  } /* end of switch */
 } /* end of for-loop */
} /* end of main */
```

There is one additional point to keep in mind about the program in example 3.4. If actually used to compute student's grades, this program could affect people's lives. Thus it must be subjected to an extremely high level of analysis, design, and testing. An accuracy of 99 percent is adequate for many situations, but certainly not here. Some software has even more critical performance requirements. Consider the case of banking programs, software control of nuclear or chemical reactions, software control of airplanes, life-support systems in hospitals, etc. Programmers have a major responsibility to society to make sure that their systems work correctly.

3.3 Precedence of Operations

The usual rules for precedence of arithmetic operations also hold in C, so that $2 + 3 * 5$ is 17 and not 25; multiplication and division have a higher precedence than addition and subtraction. The operators ++, --, and – all have the same precedence, which is higher than that of multiplication and division. If you wish to change the order in which some expression is evaluated, then simply insert parentheses to force evaluation in the desired order.

Here is an example to show the results of some arithmetic operations and to show the action of the precedence rules.

Example 3.5

```
#include <stdio.h>
main(void)
{
  int i = 0;
  float x = 0.0;

  printf("%d\n",2 + 3 * 5 );
  printf("%d\n",i += 3);
  printf("%d\n",i += 3 * 5);
  printf("%d\n",i *= 3 * 5);
  printf("%f\n",2.0 + 3.0 * 5.0);
  printf("%f\n",x += 3.0);
  printf("%f\n",x += 3.0 * 5.0);
  printf("%f\n",x *= 3.0 * 5.0);
}
```

It has the output

```
17
3
18
270
17.000000
3.000000
18.000000
270.000000
```

One of the most difficult features to understand in C is the role of operator precedence. Every expression in C is made up of operators and operands, and the order in which these operators are evaluated depends on the place of the operator in a table called the precedence table and on the associativity of the operators. This table includes all operators, including several that we have not yet seen.

The portion of the precedence table that is relevant to the operators we have seen so far is given in Table 3.3; for easy reference, it is repeated in Appendix 5, where the complete table is given.

The table is used as follows. Suppose that we have an expression to be evaluated. The expression is read left to right. Operands such as 5, 3.1415, and "Hello" are evaluated as you might expect, and their values are placed on a stack for later combinations, if necessary. The operations indicated by the operators are either performed immediately or

Table 3.3 Portion of precedence table. Operators within groups have same precedence.

Operator	Comments on Use
( )	grouping
!	negation, right-associative
++	increment, right-associative
– –	decrement, right-associative
–	unary minus, right-associative
*	multiplication
/	division
%	modulus
+	addition
–	subtraction
<	less than
<=	less than or equal to
>	greater than
>=	greater than or equal to
==	equal to (comparison)
!=	not equal to
&&	logical AND
||	logical OR
? :	if-else, right-associative
=	assignment, right associative
+=	assignment (with addition), right-associative
–=	assignment (with subtraction), right-associative
*=	assignment (with multiplication), right-associative
/=	assignment (with division), right-associative

placed on the stack for later execution. The decision to perform an operation or to delay its execution is determined entirely by the position of the operator in the precedence table relative to the previously seen operators that have already been stored in the stack. Stacks are discussed in detail later in this book. For now, just interpret a stack as a place where intermediate computations are stored.

Consider the two expressions

```
5 * 3 + 7
```

and

```
5 + 3 * 7
```

The normal rules of arithmetic provide us with values of 22 and 26, respectively. The way that you would evaluate the expressions is to determine if the + and * are to be performed immediately or which one, if any, is to be deferred. The portion of the precedence table is read in the same way. Multiplication has a higher precedence than addition and thus must be performed first.

(If you compared the portion of the precedence table given here with the complete one given in the appendix, you may have already noticed that the * symbol appears in several places in the table. This is because * has two meanings in C. We are only interested in the arithmetic meaning in this example and will discuss the other meaning when we discuss pointers.)

Consider a more complex statement such as

```
x = 5 + 3 * 7
```

There are three operators here: =, +, and *. We have already discussed the precedence of the last two operators. The assignment operator = has a precedence lower than the arithmetic operations and thus is performed after the complete evaluation of the arithmetic expression, which is how it should be.

The precedence table also describes how operators with the same precedence are to be evaluated. This is needed for evaluation of expressions such as

```
5 - 3 - 7
```

Here is an unusual type of combination. It is presented here to show how the table works. It uses the fact that assignment statements in C have both lvalues, for the variable to which a value is being assigned, and rvalues, for the value being assigned to the variable. The example is intended to show precedence and assignment statements rather than to exemplify good coding practice.

```
x = 5 > 3 + ( x = 7 )
```

This combination seems impossible. However, it has a perfectly good meaning based on the concept that expressions in C have values. How do we evaluate it? By the precedence table and by observing that expressions have both an lvalue and an rvalue.

Reading the precedence table shows that the left and right parentheses have equal precedence and that this precedence is higher than that of the other operators. Thus after reading this expression from left to right, we see that we must evaluate the expression

```
x = 7
```

inside the parentheses. The intent of the assignment is clear. We are to give the value 7 to the variable x. What is the value of this expression? It is the lvalue, namely 7.

In general, the lvalue of an assignment statement is the value assigned to the variable on the left-hand side of the assignment operator.

Following this principle, we reduce the evaluation of the expression to the evaluation of

```
x = 5 > 3 + 7
```

after evaluating the effect of the parentheses. How do we complete the rest of the evaluation of the expression? Use the precedence table.

We use the table again to see that the > operator has lower precedence than does the + operator; hence we perform the addition first. The expression simplifies to

```
x = 5 > 10
```

Some of the special operators available in the C language but not generally available in other languages are the incrementation operator ++ and the decrementation operator --. C also allows several compound operators such as +=, −=, *=, /=, and %=. All of these operators can be applied to expressions of type int, and the results will be of type int. Addition, subtraction, multiplication, and division can be applied to float or double types. Mixed-mode arithmetic is possible in C, and the results will always be of type double.

C allows a large number of operations to be performed on expressions. Precedence and associativity of operations are critical to a good understanding of how these operations are performed in C. An extensive precedence table is used to determine the order in which operations are performed. Default precedence can be overridden by the use of parentheses.

Expressions in C can have lvalues, which may have values assigned to them, and rvalues, which may not have values assigned to them. Expressions declared as constants cannot have their values changed and therefore are rvalues only. In general, expressions can be used in placed of variables with the same value in any situation in which the expression is used as an rvalue.

Exercises

1. Write a C program to print the number of times that the single character 'T' occurs in its input.

2. Write a program to read its input and print out the number of words of length 1, the number of words of length 2, ..., the number of words of length 10. The output is to be a horizontal bar chart of *'s. For example, the input of

```
Hello. How are you today my little chickadee?
```

should give the output

```
words of length 1
words of length 2     *
words of length 3     ***
words of length 4
words of length 5     **
words of length 6     *
words of length 7
words of length 8
words of length 9     *
words of length 10
```

3. Write a C program to print all the prime numbers less than 1,000. Use the following test for divisibility of an integer p by an integer q: an integer p is evenly divisible by an integer q if

```
p = q * (p/q)
```

4. Write a C program to compute and print the factorials of all integers that are greater than or equal to 1 but less than or equal to 12.

5. Write a C program to test each of the integers between 1 and 1,000 for being triangular. An integer p is defined to be triangular if there is an integer q such that

```
p = q(q + 1)/2.
```

6. Write a program to remove all comments from its input. Assume that the input is a C program with correct syntax. Remember that C comments cannot be nested; that is, no syntactically correct C program can have a comment enclosed within a comment.

7. Write a C program that changes some of the features of simple C programs to look like simple Pascal programs. Perform each of the following steps in order. The idea is to have a set of transformations of the input that provide closer and closer approximations to what happens if the code were written in Pascal instead of in C. The steps of the exercise are to be applied in turn to the same input.

(a) Remove the line

```
#include <stdio.h>
```

(b) Replace the phrase

```
main()
```

by the phrase

```
PROGRAM MAIN(INPUT,OUTPUT);
```

This will make the first line look like a Pascal program instead of a C program.

(c) Replace "/*" by "(*" and "*/" by "*)". This will replace C comments by Pascal comments.
(d) Replace the symbol '{' by "BEGIN" and '}' by "END ;". This is necessary for the determination of the beginning and the end of Pascal compound statements.
(e) Replace '=' by ":=" (for assignment statements) and replace "==" by '=' (for comparison statements).
(f) The next step is much harder – replace C declarations such as

```
int c;
```

```
float x;
```

by Pascal declarations such as

```
c: INTEGER;
```

```
x: REAL;
```

It is probably easier to keep the variables such as 'c' and 'x' in lower case.

(g) The final step is somewhat harder still. The goal is to replace some of the control or branching statements by equivalent Pascal statements. In C, there are three types of control statements (the for, while, and do-while statements) and we might attempt to replace each of them. There are several types of branching statements involving use of either if or switch. The general replacement might be a very difficult problem, so it is wise to attempt at most one of these. Probably the easiest is the simple if statement.

As we saw in Chapter 2, simple if statements in C have the form

```
if (expression1)
    zero_or_more_statements
```

In Pascal, the equivalent statement is

```
IF (expression1) THEN
    zero_or_more_statements
```

Thus the primary difficulty is deciding where to put the "THEN."

(h) The final change is an easy one – add the last line

```
END.
```

to the Pascal program that you have created.

After you have completed this problem, try to run your output as a Pascal program.

8. This problem is the reverse of number 7 – change simple Pascal programs to C programs. This is somewhat easier than problem 7 in that it is easy to find the location of the word "THEN" in a Pascal program.

9. This problem tests the recognition of words as being reserved words in C. The input should consist of a single word and should be read in to the program using the getchar( ) function. The word should be tested character by character against each of the reserved words that are included in Appendix 1. As each letter of the input word is read in, the partially read-in input word should be tested against the list of reserved words. That is, if the first letter is an 'x', then we know that the word is not a reserved word because no reserved words start with 'x'. If the first letter is 'i', then there are two possibilities (if and int) and the decision cannot be made until more information is available. Note that even if the first few letters match, the word might not be a reserved word. For example, the word "ift" is not a reserved word. To make the program more manageable at this time, assume that the input consists entirely of lowercase letters.

10. Write a C program that will read in an integer, interpret this integer as a Fahrenheit temperature, and print a table of these temperatures in Fahrenheit and Centigrade. The output in the first column should include all of the temperatures that are multiples of 10 in the interval between 0 and the number read into the program. The second column should include the Centigrade equivalents of the Fahrenheit numbers in the first column. The entries in both columns should increase as you go down the columns. Be sure that your program handles both positive and negative numbers read in. Thus the input of 37 should produce an output of

```
FAHRENHEIT       CENTIGRADE
     0              -18
    10              -12
    20              -7
    30              -1
```

Note that 0 is a multiple of 10 but that 37 is not. An input of –25 should produce an output of

```
FAHRENHEIT       CENTIGRADE
   -20              -29
   -10              -23
     0              -18
```

This is an easy problem to get almost correct. Be very careful to test the extreme cases to make sure that your program works correctly. Use the suggestions about testing loops and branching statements that we discussed in Chapter 2.

11. In Chapter 2, we described the if, if-else, else-if, and other statements in a formal manner. One of the most common formal ways of specifying such formal language statements is the Backus-Naur form, which is called BNF for short. For example, the if-else statement that we described in Chapter 2 as

```
if (expression1)
      zero_or_more_statements

else
      zero_or_more_statements
```

can be described in BNF as

```
IF_ELSE_STATEMENT ::= if ( EXPRESSION1 )
              ZERO_OR_MORE_STATEMENTS
          else
              ZERO_OR_MORE_STATEMENTS
```

Here we have followed the BNF notational convention that any statements such as ZERO_OR_MORE_STATEMENTS that can be reduced to further actual computer language statements are written in upper case while actual symbols that represent actual language statements are written in lower case. Write a C program that changes the form of text data from a grammar statement written in the notation that we had given in Chapter 2 to BNF.

12. Another common type of formal language specification notation is used for the UNIX utility program yacc and is often called "yacc format". It differs from BNF in the following ways. (These rules are not all necessary for the UNIX yacc utility to work; however, they are helpful in writing yacc input files.)

- The symbol ::= is replaced by a single colon ':'.
- All grammar symbols that are punctuation marks are enclosed by '.
- The end of a grammar rule is denoted by a semicolon.
- The last semicolon is not enclosed by ''.
- The last semicolon is directly below the first colon.

Thus the grammar rule in BNF form in exercise 10 will be written in yacc format as

```
IF_ELSE_STATEMENT :if '(' EXPRESSION1 ')'
                  ZERO_OR_MORE_STATEMENTS
                      else
                  ZERO_OR_MORE_STATEMENTS
                  ;
```

Write a C program that changes the form of text data from a grammar statement in the notation that we have given in Chapter 2 to the yacc format described above. Note: the syntax description of C in Appendix 3 is written in yacc format.

13. Which of the following C programs correctly print the output shown below?

```
100 is 100 % of 100
```

Be careful about the space after the % sign. (The output is indented by a tab for clarity, but no tabs are included in the actual output.)

(a)

```
#include <stdio.h>
main(void)
{
printf("100 is 100 %% of 100\n");
}
```

(b)

```
#include <stdio.h>
main(void)
{
printf("100 is 100 '%' of 100\n");
}
```

(c)

```
#include <stdio.h>
main(void)
{
printf("100 is 100 \% of 100\n");
}
```

(d)

```
#include <stdio.h>
main(void)
{
printf("100 is 100");
printf("%c",'%');
printf("of 100\n");
}
```

(e)

```
#include <stdio.h>
main(void)
{
printf("100 is 100");
printf("\%");
printf("of 100\n");
}
```

(f)

```
#include <stdio.h>
main(void)
{
printf("100 is 100 %c of 100\n",'%');
}
```

14. Explain the program given here. How does it compare with example 3.1 in the text?

```
#include <stdio.h>
main(void)
{
const int i = 4;
const int x;
```

4.1 Functions

We will illustrate the way that functions work in C by giving a set of examples of increasing complexity.

We have already seen the use of the functions scanf( ), printf( ), and getchar( ) which perform I/O operations. Here is a simple example of a C program that uses a different function that is not provided by a standard library but instead is user-defined. We have used a long name for this function which describes the actions that the function performs. The user-defined function here has no parameters and returns no value.

Note: The terms "parameter" and "argument" are often used in the computer science literature to mean the same thing; we will use the two terms interchangeably throughout this book.

Example 4.1 A function with no parameters and no return value

```
#include <stdio.h>

void print_message(void);

main(void)
{
   int i;

   for (i = 0; i < 5; i++)
     print_message();
   printf("\nI agree!\n");
}

void print_message(void)
{
   printf("Buy many copies\n");
}
```

The program in example 4.1 has a simple syntax. It has three important features – a function prototype, a function call, and a function definition.

In this example, the function prototype

```
        void print_message(void);
```

is the first nonblank line after the C preprocessor directive to include the file stdio.h in the program. It says to the C compiler that there is a function whose name is print_message( ) and that this function has no arguments (because of the presence of the C reserved word "void" inside the parentheses) and returns no value (because of the first occurrence of the reserved word "void"). The function prototype allows the C compiler to determine the number and type of parameters to be used when linking the code generated for this function to the rest of the program. This is a great advantage for providing interoperability of software subsystems since the details of the interface between functions can be checked by the compiler.

Note the use of the semicolon ';' after the function prototype. It indicates that the definition of the function will be given elsewhere in the program. The compiler will test the definition of the function to see if the number and type of arguments and the return type of the function agree with the function prototype. A compile-time error occurs when the two do not agree.

If the compiler encounters the definition of the function before it sees a prototype, then the compiler must rely on default values for the function's arguments and return types. The default value for the return type of a function is int. This reliance on default values for return types of functions was common in older versions of C; it is now frequently considered to be poor C programming practice and we generally avoid it in this text.

The function call is the line

```
print_message();
```

that is within the curly braces enclosing the body of the function main( ). The function call tells the C compiler to move control from the current function, which in this case is main( ), to start executing the first statement in the function print_message( ). After exiting the function print_message( ), control will resume at the next statement in the calling function. The two parentheses in the function call are essential as we will see later.

The function definition of print_message( ) occurs in the last four lines of the program. The purpose of this function is to perform an action. It has no parameters and returns no values. The use of the reserved word "void" before the definition of the function print_message( ) shows the compiler that there is no value to be returned by this function.

The function in example 4.2 has a single parameter and returns no value. Compare the program in example 4.1 to the program in example 4.2. As before, we have a function prototype, a function call, and a function definition.

Example 4.2 A function with a parameter and no return value

```
#include <stdio.h>

void print_message(int i);

main(void)
{
   int i;

   for (i = 0; i < 5; i++)
      print_message(i);
   printf("\nI agree!\n");
}
```

```
void print_message(int i)
{
  int j;

  for(j=0; j < i; j++)
    printf("Buy many copies\n");
}
```

The function prototype

```
void print_message(int i);
```

in this program now indicates that the function print_message( ) has a single argument of type int and that the function returns no value. The compiler checks this against the later definition of the function. If they don't agree, then the compiler generates an error and the program does not compile.

You should be aware that we have included redundant information in our function prototype. Since the compiler only needs to know the types of any arguments and that this function returns no value, the name of the argument is redundant and the program could have worked equally well with the function prototype

```
void print_message(int);
```

which omits the name of the argument. Of course, the argument must be used in the function call and the formal argument to the function must also be present in the function definition. You might prefer to use the name of the variable in a function prototype since it often provides additional information about the purpose of arguments to a function to the reader of a program. In any event, we will use the name of the variable in the function prototype whenever it adds to the understandability of the program.

The program uses a parameter in the function print_message( ). It prints many more lines than the first program because of the loop in the body of that function.

The program works in the following manner. After the C source code is translated to binary code that is executable by the computer, the program counter is set to the first instruction. It then changes as the program is being executed until it gets to the function call. When the function call is reached, the current value of the program counter is stored, and the program counter is now set to the first instruction of the function print_message( ). By the term "program counter" we mean the variable used by the operating system to keep track of the instruction being executed. A copy of the value of the parameter i is made and is available to the function; this is why the value of i is available to print_message. After completion of the function print_message( ), the copy of the parameter is destroyed and program control is restored to the next instruction after the stored value of the program counter. The program counter now continues with the loop in main, and execution of the loop continues until the expression (i < 5) is false; that is, it takes the value 0, after which the last line is printed and the program stops execution.

Note that the program of example 4.1 prints the message to buy this book 5 times but the program of example 4.2 prints it 10 times, with an additional line of output for the printf( ) statement in main( ).

Many languages allow two types of subprograms: those that return a value, and those that do not. These subprograms are called functions and procedures in Pascal, Ada, and Modula-2; in FORTRAN they are called functions and subroutines. In C, only the function type of subprogram is available. C allows the flexibility of other languages in that functions are not required to return a value and even if a value is returned, it may be ignored. This allows a common syntax for function definitions and function calls.

In the first two programming examples in this chapter, the function print_message( ) had no value returned by it because its purpose was to perform an action. Consider examples 4.3 and 4.4. In each case, the function calculate( ) returns a single value.

Example 4.3 A function with a parameter: the function return value is never used

```
#include <stdio.h>

int calculate(int);

main(void)
{
    int i;
    for (i = 0; i < 5; i++)
        calculate(i);
}

int calculate(int i)
{
    printf("The original number was %d\n",i);
    return (i+2);
}
```

In example 4.3, the function calculate( ) takes a parameter i and returns the value of the parameter plus 2. This value returned by the function calculate( ) is never used in the calling function, because the value of calculate( ) is never used by assigning it to a variable; only the action of calculate( ) in printing the parameter was performed. In example 4.4, we actually use the value returned by calculate( ).

Example 4.4 A function with a single parameter: the program uses the returned value

```
#include <stdio.h>

int calculate(int);

main(void)
{
    int i;
```

```
    for (i = 0; i < 5; i++)
      printf("In main, value returned is %d\n", calculate(i));
}

int calculate(int i)
{
  printf("The original number was %d\n",i);
  return (i+2);
}
```

The output of the program in example 4.4 is

```
The original number was 0
In main, value returned is 2
The original number was 1
In main, value returned is 3
The original number was 2
In main, value returned is 4
The original number was 3
In main, value returned is 5
The original number was 4
In main, value returned is 6
```

As you can see, the value returned by the function calculate( ) is used in example 4.4 as an actual parameter to the function printf( ). In general, your functions will either return a value or not return one. If the function is to return a value, then you should use the return statement to indicate the value to be returned. A function can have several return statements such as those shown in example 4.5.

Example 4.5 A function with several return statements

```
f(int x)
{
  if ((0 < x) && ( x <= 10))
    return 7;
  else if (10 < x)
    return (x + 3);
  else
    return -1;
}
```

As soon as a return statement is encountered as the program runs, the function is exited and execution of the calling routine continues. Thus only one of the three return statements in the function f( ) can be executed in any single execution of the function.

In Part II, we will see how C programs can be spread out over several C source code files and how this affects the scope of variables and the part of the program in which the type returned by the function is visible. For now, simply use whatever organization you wish but only use functions that either return no value or return only values of type int. We will show how to use functions that return values other than of type int in section 4.6.

4.2 Passing of Parameters

Functions are the natural mechanism for creating modular programs in C. Data can be accessed by a function in several ways. The data can be made available to a specific function by using the data as parameters to the function. The function receives a copy of each parameter's value, so that only the function receiving the parameters can access the data. If we use global variables for data, then all functions in a program can access the data stored in these global variables.

The way that C uses global variables is easy to understand. The value stored in the variable is made available to all functions.

Parameters in C are somewhat trickier. When a function is called with a set of parameters, the compiler begins the execution of the machine code for the function by making a copy of the values of the parameters. The function is free to use its copy of the parameters in any way that it wishes. After the function finishes execution, it destroys the copy of the parameters, and the original set of values of the parameters is the same as the set of values of the parameters after the call to the function. This is called passing parameters by value and is the only way that parameters can be passed in C.

Parameters are passed to a function in a list. The list can be empty, in which case the reserved word "void" is used, as we have already seen. If the list consists of only one element, then the argument list is just the type of the single argument, followed by its name. If the list contains more than one element, then each of the formal parameters is given with its type followed by its name; the formal arguments are separated by commas.

Let's look at an example of a program that calls a function with two parameters. Notice the function prototype for mystery( ). There are two parameters of type int and so we indicate each of them (separated by a comma) in the function prototype as in

```
void mystery(int i, int j) ;
```

Since there are no values returned by mystery( ), we indicate a void return type in its function prototype. We have placed the names of the arguments in the function prototype because the names are important conceptually in this example as you will see.

Example 4.6

```
#include <stdio.h>
/* doesn't do what we want  */

void mystery(int i, int j) ;

main(void)
{
   int i,j;

   i=10;
   j=20;
   printf("Before mystery, i = %d and j = %d\n",i,j);
   mystery(i,j);
   printf("After mystery, i = %d and j = %d\n", i,j);
}
```

```
void mystery(int i,int j)
{
   int temp;

   temp = i;
   i = j ;
   j = temp ;
}
```

The intention of the function mystery is clear –we want to swap the values of the two variables. However, the output is rather surprising at first glance.

```
Before mystery, i = 10 and j = 20
After mystery, i = 10 and j = 20
```

Perhaps the problem was getting the parameters into the function mystery. We will add a new line to mystery so that we echo the parameters and add a line to echo the values after the swap. The function mystery now looks like

```
void mystery(int i , int j)
{
   int temp;

   printf("In mystery, i and j are %d and %d\n",i,j);
   temp = i;
   i = j ;
   j = temp ;
   printf("Leaving mystery, i and j are %d and %d\n",i,j);
}
```

but the output is still wrong:

```
Before mystery, i =10 and j =20
In mystery, i and j are 10 and 20
Leaving mystery, i and j are 20 and 10
After mystery, i =10 and j =20
```

In this program, parameters are passed to the function mystery, and the swap occurs in mystery as it should. The difficulty is that the values that were given to the function mystery( ) were copies of i and j. Mystery did what it was supposed to do by interchanging these copied values. After leaving mystery( ), these copies were destroyed so that the line after the call of the function mystery( ) by the function main( ) has the original unchanged values of i and j. This difficulty is a direct result of the design of the C programming language to permit passing only of copies of parameters. Recall that this is called passing parameters by value and it is the only way that parameters can be passed to functions in C. C encourages the writing of modular programs by this mechanism since passing values by value means that functions can only change the values of copies and not affect other parts of the program.

Use of the single method of passing parameters by value is aesthetically satisfying. However, it is not obvious how to solve the problem that mystery( ) was supposed to solve – swapping the values of its two parameters. We could always use the simple algorithm of mystery( ) to add three lines to the code of the main program. However, we want a general method for doing this since most functions will be too long to keep inserting in place. We want a solution of the problem that uses the function mystery( ). For simplicity, we have removed the printf( ) statements from mystery( ) and the first one from main( ).

We can use the technique of letting the variables i and j be global variables. That is, i and j no longer belong to any special function (not even main) but are visible to all functions in the source code file. We declare them outside of every function and for clarity write them before any function. The complete code is given in example 4.7.

Example 4.7 Swapping global variables

```
/* solution using global variables */
#include <stdio.h>

int i, j;

void mystery(void);

main(void)
{
   i=10;
   j=20;
   mystery();
   printf("After mystery, i = %d and j = %d\n",i,j);
}

/* mystery has no parameters */
void mystery(void)
{
   int temp;

   temp = i;
   i = j ;
   j = temp ;
}
```

This solution allows the variables i and j to be visible to all functions in the file and removes any need to declare i and j as parameters to mystery( ). The declaration of mystery is much simpler since we don't have to declare the types of the parameters (there aren't any). For this simple programming exercise, this is the shortest way to do this. You don't have to declare anything and all the variables are available to all functions. What's the disadvantage? Each of the variables is available in each function. This is especially bad for variables with common names such as i and j that are frequently used as counters in different functions. Try to imagine writing and understanding a 1,000 line program with many functions and only global variables; remember that 1,000 lines requires 17 pages of output if we have the usual 66 lines of print per page. Programs of 10,000 or more lines can have even more problems in program understanding. **Try to avoid the use of global variables**. Here is a reason for this suggestion.

There is an interesting study of student programmers by Dunsmore and Gannon [1980] in which they considered efficiency of writing programs by using either global variables only or parameters only. For the extremely short programs (about 80 lines of Pascal) that were part of the exercise, using global variables allowed the programs to be written faster. However, using only parameters and not permitting global variables to be used allowed the incorrect programs to be debugged faster, and this carried over into shorter time to understand programs. This pattern will not carry over into much larger programs of the sort that you will be able to write later; overuse of global variables will delay program development and debugging. The use of global variables causes immense difficulties if overused. You should avoid global variables whenever possible. We use them infrequently in this text.

Many languages allow another method of passing parameters based on the idea of passing as parameters the address of the variables to be passed. This is called passing parameters by reference and allows the contents of the address to be changed. In Pascal, we could accomplish this by using a function header such as

```
function f(var x :integer ):integer;
```

Because the C language only allows copies of parameters sent to functions, we cannot change the address; however, we can change the contents located at the address. This technique allows us to simulate passing parameters by reference, since we can change the contents of an address. Our complete solution using this simulation of passing values by reference will be postponed until we discuss pointers in Chapter 8.

4.3 Storage Classes: Automatic, Static, Extern, Register, and Void

We have already seen two types of variables in C: variables inside a function (main or otherwise) and those that were external to all functions (the global variable example). In this section, we discuss how the ways that variables are stored can affect C programs.

There are five qualifiers that describe the storage class associated with an expression in C: automatic, static, extern, register, and void. We have already met the use of the reserved word "void" to describe the argument list of functions with no formal parameters and also to describe the case of a function with no value returned. The storage class void means that there is no memory allocated to the object.

There are two storage classes that can be given to any type of variables that are inside functions: automatic and static.

Automatic variables are the easiest to understand – they are what you have been using already and require no special designation to be of this storage class. Indeed, there is no reserved word "automatic" in C; this is the default storage class. Every variable that is declared inside a function is considered to be automatic unless otherwise specified. A variable being automatic means that its value is not visible outside the function. It also means that the variable must be assigned a value before it is used, since the lack of initialization implies that there is no guarantee that there will not be garbage values in the memory location assigned to the variable. Because of the possibility of an automatic variable containing garbage values, successive calls to a function require new initializations of automatic variables. In particular, the value of an automatic variable is not retained between successive calls to a function.

Static variables inside functions behave differently from automatic variables. A variable that is intended to be retained between successive function calls must be declared using the static qualifier. This can be useful in situations such as generating pseudo-random numbers when the results of a multiplication obtained from one call of a function need to be available to successive function calls.

Consider the program of example 4.8 in which the two functions mystery( ) and not_a_mystery( ) are each called twice. Note that the variable i in mystery( ) is an automatic variable since it is internal to the function mystery( ) and no qualifier has been attached to it. The variable temp in the function not_a_mystery( ) is of storage class static because of the qualifier static being present in the declaration. The variable temp cannot be external since it belongs to a function. Of course we need a function prototype for each function in the program.

Example 4.8

```
/* produces garbage sometimes */
#include <stdio.h>

void mystery(void);
void not_a_mystery(void);

main(void)
{
  mystery();
  not_a_mystery();
  mystery();
  not_a_mystery();
}


/* use of uninitialized automatic variable - can cause
unpredictable results */
void mystery(void)
{
  int i;

  i = i + 1;
  printf("in mystery, i is %d\n",i);
}
```

```
/* correct use of local static variable */
void not_a_mystery(void)
{
  static int temp;

  temp++;
  printf("in not_a_mystery, temp is %d\n",temp);
}
```

The output on two different computers is

```
in mystery, i is 1
in not_a_mystery, temp is 1
in mystery, i is -2138569498
in not_a_mystery, temp is 2
```

and

```
in mystery, i is 1
in not_a_mystery, temp is 1
in mystery, i is 2
in not_a_mystery, temp is 2
```

The two outputs show that the use of values of automatic variables can lead to serious trouble if we are not careful. In the first example, the program worked as expected when the first calls were made to the functions, but the second calls gave a serious error. In the first call to mystery( ), we were fortunate enough to have the desired value of 0 stored in memory location i; in the second call we were not quite as fortunate. The calls to not_a_mystery( ) always worked because the variable temp was a static variable; therefore its value was retained between successive function calls. Static variables are always guaranteed to be initialized to 0 while automatic variables can have any values. (The name temp is probably a poor one for a static variable. The variable is not temporary since it keeps its value after successive function calls.)

The second example is more troubling since it appears to give the correct answer even though it does not follow the requirements of the C language. I ran this program eight times before I got an incorrect result. This is the type of error that is extremely difficult to detect. You should be careful in your use of the automatic and static classes of variables if you expect to reuse the values of these variables in successive function calls.

Variables that are not defined within any function are called external variables. We saw an example of their use when we wrote the swapping program using the variables to be swapped as global variables. If these external variables are given at the beginning of a C source code file, then they can be used by any functions in the file in which they are defined. As with static variables, they are guaranteed to be given the initial value of 0 if they are not explicitly initialized by the programmer.

We now discuss the "register" storage class for variables in C. The declaration of a variable preceded by the C reserved word register indicates that the variable is likely to be used frequently during the execution of the program and that it should be placed in a register if one is available. The restriction on register variables is that they should have a type that can be placed in a register. Usually the allowable types are int, float, double, or the address of variables. (Addresses of variables will be discussed in Part II when we consider pointers.)

In general, the only importance of register variables is to speed up certain programs. We will not use register variables in the remainder of this book. Some compilers spend a considerable amount of effort in attempting to optimize the executable code for speed. Often the use of register variables disturbs the optimization effort of the compiler.

The final storage class used in C is void. This storage class means that no memory is to be set aside for the expression. An example of this is the use of "void" to indicate that no value is to be returned by a function.

4.4 Scope Rules for Functions in a Single Source File

The term "scope" in a computer program means the portion of a program in which the value of some quantity can be used by other program statements. It refers to visibility of the quantity inside the various functions and files that make up the program. A large scope means that the quantity is visible to most of the program, and a small scope means that the quantity is visible to only a small portion of the program. The first situation describes a global variable that is easy to access by any function whatsoever. The second describes a highly modular program in which information is easily hidden.

Example 4.9 shows some of the pitfalls that can occur with an overuse of global variables. We start out by using two global variables i and j that are intended as counters. The program has a function called f( ) in addition to main. Without running the program, can you determine the value of i after the assignment in the fourth line of f( )?

Example 4.9 A confusing mess with global variables

```
void f(int) ;

int i , j;

main(void)
{
   int i, j;
   i = 4 ;
   j = 2;
   f(j);
}
```

```
f(int x)
{
   int i , j;
   i = 3;
   j = 1;
   i = j;
}
```

The answer is that the value of the variable i is 1. The variables i and j that are relevant inside the function f( ) are the local variables i and j, using the most local scope. These values are 3 and 1, respectively, after the assignment statements and thus i gets assigned the value 1.

This program is a bit silly. However, it is somewhat typical of the problems that you can get into with an overuse of global variables. It is hard to tell which i and j are indicated in the function f( ). The reason is that the scope of the variables is not clear to us as human beings reading the source code.

There are several rules for determining the scope of variables in C; these rules are different for programs that are contained in a single C source file and those that extend over several files. We give the rules for those programs that are in a single source file in this section and discuss the more complex topic of multiple source code files in Part II.

Recall that external variables are those that appear outside any function. Their scope is, at a minimum, the entire file from the point of declaration to the end of the file. Therefore if you wish a variable to be available to every function in a file, then you should declare it at the beginning of the file. External variables so declared are then available to any functions in the file without the programmer taking any additional action.

We can also make external variables available to functions in a file by defining them external to all functions and by explicitly declaring them inside any function where they are to be used. Here is an example of the syntax. Notice that the variable i is defined as having type int and that the declaration of i inside mystery( ) as being extern links the two together. The definition of i is given in the last line of the program; it could appear anywhere in the file as long as it is external to every function.

The difference between a declaration and a definition is that the compiler reserves space for a defined variable; it merely marks the type of a declared variable so that it can be interpreted later.

Example 4.10

```
#include <stdio.h>
void mystery(void);

main(void)
{
   mystery();
}
```

```
mystery(void)
{
   extern int i;

   i = i + 100;
   printf("in mystery, i is %d\n",i);
}

int i;
```

The output of the function is what is expected, namely

```
in mystery, i is 100
```

To summarize our discussion of scope, we list some of the possibilities for the scope of variables if the program is contained in a single C source file.

(1) If the variable is defined inside a function, then its scope is that function. Static variables retain their values on successive function calls while automatic variables do not. Neither is available outside the defining function.
(2) If the variable is defined outside every function, then it will be available to any function defined from that point to the end of the file.
(3) If the variable is defined outside every function, then it can be made available to any function in the file by declaring the variable to be extern in the function that wishes to use it. In this case the variable is global.
(4) The C language does not permit a function to be defined inside another function.

It is possible for variables to have a nested scope in C. A code fragment such as

```
f()
{int i = 1 ;
      {
      int i;
      i = 2;
      . . .
      }
   . . .
}
```

is possible. In this code fragment, the innermost definition of the variable i hides the outermost definition of the variable i, and thus the innermost block uses the initial value of 2 for i.

The advantage of nesting the scope of variables is that we can use the same name for such things as an internal index for arrays and not have to worry about influencing another index of the same name. Theoretically, we can use nested variables to have modular software building blocks comprising functions. The reality is that the values of the innermost variables are often difficult for the programmer to understand. In addition, several popular compilers do not implement the hiding of the values of nested variables properly. Therefore we will not use nested scope anywhere in this book.

4.5 The Type of a Function: Default Types and External Declarations

In many languages, the order in which the various subprograms are placed in the program is an essential part of the syntax of the language. In most implementations of Pascal, all subprograms must be in the same file as the main program and must precede the main body of the program. In addition, if declarations of constants, data types, or variables are present, then they must appear in this order, and any subprograms must appear after these declarations (but before the main program). In most implementations of FOR-TRAN, the main program must precede any subroutines or functions.

C has no such restrictions. In a C program, the function main( ) may appear anywhere in a file, and other functions and declarations may be placed anywhere in that file and in any order. The only changes that need to be made to a C source code file when functions or declarations are moved are those changes that are necessary because of the rules for determining the scope of variables and the types of functions. We discussed scope rules in section 4.4. Types of values that are returned by functions are the topic of this section.

We have used functions many times in this book. Most of the time we have not cared about the value returned by the function. Example 4.11 shows how dangerous a practice this can be.

Example 4.11

```
/* wrong output */
#include <stdio.h>

main(void)
{
  float x,y;

  x = 10.0;
  y = 30.0;
  printf("The average is %f\n",average(x,y));
}

average(float first, float second)
{
  return (first + second)/2.0;
}
```

The output of the program is surprising!

```
The average is 0.000000
```

What went wrong? The first possibility is that the parameters x and y were never sent to the function average( ). It is easy to check if they were passed correctly by writing an appropriate printf statement – if you do this you will see that the parameters were passed correctly. The logic of the function average( ) is obviously correct. The incorrect answer doesn't change if we move the definition of the function average( ) to be ahead of the declaration of the function main( ) – you should try this. The answer is found in the definition of the function average( ), not in its placement in the program. Change the definition of average( ) as in example 4.12 and things get worse.

Example 4.12

```
/* doesn't even compile */
#include <stdio.h>

main(void)
{
  float x,y;

  x = 10.0;
  y = 30.0;
  printf("The average is %f\n",average(x,y));
}

float average(float first, float second)
{
  return (first + second)/2.0;
}
```

It is even worse than before – the program of example 4.12 will not even compile, and we get the error message

```
"ex4_12.c", line 12: redeclaration of average
```

The problem is that the function always returns a value of a specific type. The default return type of a function in C is a value of type int. The function average( ) is intended to return a value of type float. We can communicate this to the compiler in two ways: by defining all functions before main( ) or by including a declaration before main( ) that the function average( ) is of type float. Experience shows that the second way is better since it does not depend on defaults but instead requires the programmer to take an action.

Example 4.13 Functions defined before main( )

```c
/* works -  all functions defined before main() */
#include <stdio.h>

float average(float first, float second)
{
  return (first + second)/2.0;
}


main(void)
{
  float x,y;

  x = 10.0;
  y = 30.0;
  printf("The average is %f\n",average(x,y));
}
```

and

Example 4.14 Functions declared in main( ), defined elsewhere

```c
/* This one is preferable - it uses function prototypes */
#include <stdio.h>

float average(float, float);

main(void)
{
  float x,y;

  x = 10.0;
  y = 30.0;
  printf("The average is %f\n",average(x,y));
}


float average(float first, float second)
{
  return (first + second)/2.0;
}
```

The second choice (example 4.14) is better since we can place the function main( ) first and see the program structure more clearly. This issue will also be critical when we consider C programs that are composed of several C source files.

If the function is not intended to return a value such as the print_message( ) function of example 4.1, then no return statement should be included in the body of the function. In addition, the definition of the function should be preceded by the word void to indicate to the compiler that there is no value returned and that any attempt to use such a value should be flagged as an error. EXPERIMENT. See what message your compiler gives if you insert the word void before the word calculate in the definition of calculate( ). The reason for the error message generated is that you should be warned about the possibility of using an uninitialized value for the returned value of calculate( ). A better way of writing the function print_message( ) of example 4.1 is given in example 4.15.

Example 4.15

```
#include <stdio.h>
void print_message(void)
{
   printf("Buy many copies of this book\n");
}


main(void)
{
   int i;

   for (i = 0; i < 5; i++)
     print_message();
   printf("\nI agree!\n");
}
```

The use of the void return type causes a small change to be made to the way that code is organized for C programs. This is the same sort of change that is necessary for functions returning something other than the default return type of int.

The function print_message( ) of example 4.15, which now has a void return type, could also be placed in the program of example 4.1 with a declaration before main( ) and a definition after main( ) and might look something like example 4.16.

Example 4.16 A new version of examples 4.1 and 4.15

```
#include <stdio.h>
void  print_message(void);

main(void)
{
   int i;

   for (i = 0; i < 5; i++)
     print_message();
   printf("\nI agree!\n");
}
```

information that is not available through function prototypes; this additional information would not otherwise be available to the programmer.

Many PC compilers provide a higher degree of type checking than is available on the standard UNIX compilers. You should always use the compiler with the largest amount of type checking for software development, even if your development compiler and computer are not the ones on which you will eventually run the code. The goal is to avoid problems in type differences that might be ignored by a compiler.

4.7 The C Preprocessor

The role of a preprocessor is to set values that are to be used in a C program. A pre-processor also transforms certain code into assembly language instructions that are included in the code as needed. Finally, the preprocessor arranges for appropriate files to be included in the program. Example 4.18 shows the operation of the C preprocessor. The numbers at the left are line numbers and are not part of the program. All the statements begin in the left-most column.

Example 4.18 A simple C program using the preprocessor. (Line numbers shown are not part of program.)

```
1    #include <stdio.h>
2    #define MAX 10
3    #define MSG "Hello"
4    #define min(x,y) ((x) > (y) ? (y): (x) )
5    main(void)
6    { int i;
7      printf(MSG);
8      for(i=0; i <= MAX ; i++)
9        printf("%d\n",min(i, 5));
10     printf(MSG);
11   }
```

Example 4.18 has the output

```
Hello
0
1
2
3
4
5
5
5
5
5
5
Hello
```

The C preprocessor works in the following manner. Line 1 is expanded to include the file stdio.h in the C source code program. Line 2 is interpreted to mean that every occurrence of the expression MAX, except for the three letters M, A, and X being embedded in a character string, is replaced by the integer 10. Line 3 means that every occurrence of the expression MSG, except for the three letters M, S, and G being embedded in a character string, is replaced by the string "Hello." The expression min(x,y) in line 4 is replaced by the right-hand side of line 4 whenever it occurs. After the preprocessor has completed its pass through the program, the C source code file is in the form of example 4.19, and this form is passed to the rest of the C compiler.

Example 4.19 Action of the C preprocessor on a C program. (Line numbers are not part of program.)

```
1      all of the information in the file
2            stdio.h
3      goes here
4      int MAX = 10
5      char *MSG = "Hello"
6      /* code for min goes here */
7      main(void)
8      {  int i;
9        printf("Hello");
10       for(i=0; i <= 10 ; i++)
11          printf("%d\n",( (x)>(y) ? (y): (x) ) );
12       printf("Hello");
13     }
```

The two examples 4.18 and 4.19 show that the effect of the C preprocessor is actually to replace quantities throughout a C program. You can convince yourself that the actual replacement is happening by leaving out a quotation mark on line 3 or a parenthesis on line 4 and noting that a compiler error indicates that the error is on the line where the replacement occurs instead of being on line 3 or 4 where the actual error is created. The C compiler now performs syntactic and semantic analysis on the transformed source code and generates object code for the output if no errors are found.

Since the two forms in examples 4.18 and 4.19 are equivalent in terms of the object code generated, you might wonder about the need for the C preprocessor to do anything but include files in programs. The most common application of the C pre-processor is for programs with constants. It is clear that MAX is a constant because it follows the C convention of having uppercase letters reserved for constants. Using constants avoids having numerical values in the program whose meaning is unclear and which make programs difficult to debug, maintain, or modify.

The use of #define statements such as on line 4 of example 4.18 is somewhat controversial. Having the value of min(x,y) defined on line 4 is certainly clearer than the complex printf( ) statement on line 11 of example 4.19. We could have defined min(x,y) as a function in the form

```
min(int x, int y)
{
  if ( x > y )
    return y;
  else
    return x;
}
```

Because of the overhead of function calls, this is somewhat slower running code than that of examples 4.18 and 4.19, which use the #define statement. However, it has the advantage of providing information about the types of the parameters x and y as well as the type of the value being returned by the function. The #define definition of min in example 4.19 provides no facility for type checking either of its arguments or of its return type. In general, you should avoid the use of the #define statement for compound C expressions unless you have excessive need for fast-running code or for an interface with the underlying operating system to use previously determined expressions.

You may run across another use of the C preprocessor: determination of the previous declaration of constants. It allows us to set a value for some (usually constant) expression if one is not yet given. This technique uses the #ifndef command and is used as follows:

```
#ifndef INT_MAX
#define INT_MAX 32767
```

If the constant INT_MAX was not already defined (in some other include file), then the constant would be defined as 32,767 (which is the largest 16-bit integer). Giving a definition to INT_MAX only if there is no previous one insures that a consistent value of INT_MAX exists across the entire system and that a #define statement for this file does not overwrite a previous one. (This constant is found in the file limits.h.)

4.8 Recursion

We have seen that C functions can easily call other C functions. When a function is called, a copy is made of each of the parameters to the function and execution now begins in the function which is called. The called function continues execution until either a return statement is reached or the function is exited because no more statements are to be executed. The copies of parameters are placed on a stack and they are popped off the stack when they are used. The manipulation of the stack of parameters is one of the most important actions of a compiler. (A stack is a data structure in which information is entered and retrieved in a last-in–first-out manner.) This is precisely the organization that is available for functions that are recursive in the sense that they call themselves. A simple example of recursion is given in example 4.20.

Example 4.20

```
#include <stdio.h>

int fact(int);

main(void)
{
   int i;

   printf("Please enter a positive integer\n");
   scanf("%d",&i);
   printf("The factorial of %d is %d\n",i,fact(i)) ;
   }

int fact(int i)
{
   if (i <=1)
     return 1;
   else
     return (i*fact(i-1));
}
```

The function fact( ) calls itself with a different argument each time. Each function call uses a new value of the parameter that is 1 less than the value of the previous one. The way to understand the behavior of a recursively defined function is to note the following:

(1) The values of the parameters to the function change. Each new function call means that copies of the new parameters are placed by the C compiler on a special place called the system stack.
(2) There is always some exit condition that provides an escape from the process of making an infinite number of calls. In this example, the exit condition is that if the parameter i is equal to 1, then we return the value 1 in step 2.

Here is some sample output. Notice that the computed results are incorrect if the parameter i is large; this is caused by the limitation on the accuracy of arithmetic on the computer because the amount of space allotted for storage of an int is exceeded.

```
Please enter a positive integer
1
The factorial of 1 is 1
```

```
Please enter a positive integer
5
The factorial of 5 is 120

Please enter a positive integer
7
The factorial of 7 is 5040

Please enter a positive integer
10
The factorial of 10 is 3628800

Please enter a positive integer
20
The factorial of 20 is -2102132736

Please enter a positive integer
50
The factorial of 50 is 0
```

If we rewrite the function fact( ) to show the parameters changing as we call this function recursively with a printf( ) statement such as in example 4.21, the behavior is clear. We present the output from the program when a value of 4! is being computed.

Example 4.21 Factorial with printing of recursive parameters.

```
int fact(int i)
{
  printf("The parameter is %d\n",i);
  if (i ==1)
    return 1;
  else
    return (i*fact(i-1));
}
```

The output from a program using this function is

```
Please enter a positive integer
4
The parameter is 4
The parameter is 3
The parameter is 2
The parameter is 1
The factorial of 4 is 24
```

The factorial function of example 4.21 shows the behavior of the recursive calls to fact with regard to the parameters. To see the values of fact( ) being created, look at example 4.22 in which the values returned by fact at each level are printed. We have also added a global variable named count to the program. That is, count has been defined at the beginning of the program file and external to every function. The initial value of count is 0, and each call of fact( ) increments count by 1.

Example 4.22 Factorial with printing of returned values

```
int fact(i)
{
  count++;
  printf("in fact, count is %d\n",count);
  if (i == 1)
    {
    printf("Value of fact(%d) at lowest level is 1\n",i);
    return 1;
    }
  else
    {
    printf("The value of fact(%d) is %d\n",i,i* fact(i-1));
    return (i*fact(i-1));
    }
}
```

With an input of 4, the output from the fact( ) function of example 4.22 is

```
Please enter a positive integer
4
in fact, count is 1
in fact, count is 2
in fact, count is 3
in fact, count is 4
Value of fact(1) at lowest level is 1
Value of fact(2) is 2
in fact, count is 5
Value of fact(1) at lowest level is 1
Value of fact(3) is 6
in fact, count is 6
in fact, count is 7
Value of fact(1) at lowest level is 1
Value of fact(2) is 2
in fact, count is 8
Value of fact(1) at lowest level is 1
Value of fact(4) is 24
in fact, count is 9
in fact, count is 10
in fact, count is 11
```

```
Value of fact(1) at lowest level is 1
Value of fact(2) is 2
in fact, count is 12
Value of fact(1) at lowest level is 1
Value of fact(3) is 6
in fact, count is 13
in fact, count is 14
Value of fact(1) at lowest level is 1
Value of fact(2) is 2
in fact, count is 15
Value of fact(1) at lowest level is 1
The factorial of 4 is 24
```

Note that there were a total of 15 separate calls to the function fact( ). The first four calls had no value printed since we were calling fact() recursively and no values of fact( ) were obtained. The first value of fact( ) returned was 1 and this value was returned only after four calls to fact( ), each one with a smaller argument until the argument was finally 1, in which case the lowest level value of 1 was returned. After fact(1) was obtained, other values of fact( ) for larger arguments were obtained and the final value of fact(4) was finally reached. You should note that the function fact( ) of example 4.23 has exactly the same output as the program of example 4.22. The two functions differ in the placement of the recursive function calls.

Example 4.23 Reversed order of the recursion in fact( )

```
int fact(int i)
{
  count++;
  printf("in fact, count is %d\n",count);
  if (i !=1)
    {
    printf("The value of fact(%d) is %d\n",i, i* fact(i-1));
    return (i* fact(i-1));
    }
  else
    {
    printf("The value of fact(%d)at lowest level is 1\n",i);
    return 1;
    }
}
```

You should experiment with the use of recursion in the exercises to see the effect of the placement of the recursive function calls on the output of recursive programs.

Obviously the program of examples 4.20 through 4.23 could have been written using iteration instead of recursion. In the next chapter we will see an example of how this program could be written in another way by manipulating the stack explicitly and thus removing the recursion.

4.9 Library Functions

It would be extremely unpleasant if all functions used in a C program had to be written by the programmer. Many functions are commonly used by a large variety of programs; typical examples are the input and output functions such as scanf( ) and printf( ) and the functions that are part of a mathematics library. These functions are commonly provided as external libraries by most C compilers. The ANSI C standard requires certain external functions to be provided and that these functions should be placed in specific libraries. To use such functions, we must have some way of accessing the libraries in which these functions are located. The methods for doing this are somewhat system-dependent. We will describe some general rules of thumb for doing this and show the method that is used for the standard AT&T UNIX C compiler.

Any functions that are in a system-supplied library must be made known to the compiler in a header file so that the compiler can recognize that the function is defined elsewhere. The functions stored in a library are stored in the form of object code and are linked to programs by a linker that uses the information contained in a header file to make the proper connection. This is the reason for the inclusion of the file stdio.h in every program that uses input or output.

In order to include the typical mathematics library functions it usually is necessary to have the statement

```
#include <math.h>
```

in every program in which the math functions are used. With the incorporation of this statement, the C compiler can use this header file to determine the names of the functions, the number and type of their arguments, and their return type. This step of including the appropriate header file is common to nearly all C compilers.

The next step in the generation of actual executable code depends on the links between the various functions used and the body of the program. This requires some form of communication to the linker that the necessary libraries are to be included when the final executable code is generated. The method of doing this is highly system-dependent. For example, compilation of the program shown in example 4.24 on the UNIX operating system requires the command

```
cc mathprog.c -lm
```

to be executed in order to generate code for this example. The last portion of this command says that the library denoted by 'm' , that is, the math library, is to be linked in. Other libraries have other designations. (The program of this example is in a file called mathprog.c.)

Example 4.24

```
#include <stdio.h>
#include <math.h>

main(void)
{
```

```
float x = 4.0;

printf("%f\n", sqrt(x));
}
```

If we simply enter the command

```
cc mathprog.c
```

the code compiles since it is syntactically and semantically correct, but we get the error message

```
Undefined:
_sqrt
```

because we have not set the links to the library functions properly.

An error message of this sort for a typical library function generally means that the library has not been linked correctly. If you see this message and are unable to resolve it, check the system manual for assistance.

This error does not occur with all compilers. Indeed, the code compiles and runs correctly on a PC using Turbo C.

The standard C library contains the object code for many functions. The standard library functions can be grouped logically into several sets of functions, each set used in different situations. You will need to use header files whenever your program uses some of the functions included in the standard or other libraries. The standard C library is very large and there is no need to link the entire library to many programs. Linking a library can greatly increase the size of the executable code needed for a program; why include unnecessary code?

The C library is grouped into 15 different sets that are accessed by using different header files. The header files are: assert.h, ctype.h, errno.h, float.h, limits.h, locale.h, math.h, setjmp.h, signal.h, stdarg.h, stddef.h, stdio.h, stdlib.h, string.h, and time.h.

The names of the header files and a brief description of the types of functions linked via these header files are given in Table 4.1. The contents and proper use of many of the library functions will be discussed later in the text and in the appendices. Note that we have included some functions and concepts in Table 4.1 that we have not discussed previously in this text. The constant LC_MONETARY in locale.h and the type definition wchar_t (for "wide character type") in stddef.h are indications of the movement of the C programming language from being a national language to being an international standard.

The header files for the standard C library may be included in any order within a C program.

In addition to the standard C library, there are additional library functions that are used on some other systems. Some typical libraries whose header files must be included in C programs on UNIX systems are curses.h (for controlling a cursor), usercore.h (for some graphics programs using a special library), and system.h (for special calls to the operating system). In some cases, the order in which header files for functions other than those in the standard C library are included and the order in which libraries are linked to the program are important. See a system manual for more information if you are using functions that are not included in the standard C library.

There are other special libraries that you may need, depending on your application. These are not generally portable across different environments. For example, a program called "node.c" running on an Intel iPSC/2 hypercube using the "node library" was compiled with the command

```
cc node.c -node
```

while the same code on an Intel iPSC/860 hypercube requires the compilation command

```
cc node.c -node -i860
```

Read your system's manual; nothing about linking of libraries is standard. Some systems automatically link in many libraries.

There is another problem that can occur when you are using libraries. A library function is separately compiled, and it is the responsibility of the programmer using the

Table 4.1 Header files for the standard C library

Header File	Purpose	Some Typical Functions
assert.h	used with preprocessor for debugging purposes	void assert(int expression)
ctype.h	character handling	int isalpha(int ch); int isdigit(int ch);
errno.h	error-handling macros	varies
float.h	floating point constants	FLT_MAX, FLT_MIN
limits.h	integer limits	CHAR_MAX, CHAR_MIN, INT_MAX
locale.h	local standards (countries)	LC_MONETARY
math.h	standard math functions	double sin(double expr)
setjmp.h	nonlocal jumps for nonlocal GOTOs	int setjmp(jmp_buf env) void longjmp(jmp_buf env, int val)
signal.h	signals, event detection	SIGKILL, SIGTERM, signal handlers
stdarg.h	writing functions with variable numbers of arguments	complex
stddef.h	commonly used constants	typedef char wchar_t
stdio.h	I/O functions	printf( ), scanf( )
stdlib.h	functions for general use	NULL, malloc( ), bsearch( ), rand( )
string.h	string handling	strcmp( ), strlen( )
time.h	system clock access	typedef long clock_t

FUNCTIONAL REQUIREMENTS:

- Provide opening message to user.
- Move data into memory directly, from memory to disk, or from disk to memory in fixed-sized units called blocks. Any movement of data to or from the disk must access the block using the track and sector numbers that uniquely identify the block. A block in memory is specified by identifying the starting position.

These requirements are given at a high level. We can expand them and provide more detail as described next.

SLIGHTLY REFINED FUNCTIONAL REQUIREMENTS:

Obtain input commands interactively. The input is read in one line at a time. If the first input character is 'i', then the next input line is a variable of type int, which is the type that we are using for data. The function put_in_memory( ) is then called with the parameter data that was read in. After the function put_in_memory( ) is called, then control returns to the main program.

If the input is 'd', then the next three input lines will contain variables of type int. These three lines represent the values of the memory location mem_loc and the disk location specified by track and sector, respectively. The function mem_to_disk( ) is then called with the parameters mem_loc, track, and sector read in. After the function mem_to_disk( ) is called, then control returns to the main program.

If the input is 'm', then the next three input lines will contain variables of type int. These three lines represent the values of the memory location mem_loc and the disk location specified by track and sector, respectively. The function disk_to_mem( ) is then called with the parameters mem_loc, track, and sector read in. After the function disk_to_mem( ) is called, then control returns to the main program.

Input is read in without error checking.

4.11 Software Engineering Project: The Next Prototype

Some of the functions that we will need are

```
void print_disk()

void print_mem()

void mem_to_disk(int mem_loc, int track, int sector)

void disk_to_mem(int mem_loc, int track, sector)
```

The functions print_disk( ) and print_mem( ) are used to display the contents of the simulated memory and disk on the screen. The functions mem_to_disk( ) and disk_to_mem( ) are used actually to move blocks of data from memory to disk or from disk to memory. The three parameters mem_loc, track, and sector are each of type int and indicate the starting locations of the blocks of data in memory or on the simulated disk. We will discuss the nature of these functions in the next chapter when we study arrays in C. For now, we simply assume that our program will have these functions and that the bodies of the functions are to be expanded later.

The user will have to be able to tell the software if data is to be moved from memory to disk or from disk to memory. In our system, data needs to be placed in memory before it can be sent to the disk. Thus we need some additional functions:

```
opening_message()

get_data()

put_in_memory(data)
```

To make life as simple as possible, we will require that the input commands are entered one per line, with 'i' for input into memory, 'd' for writing to disk from memory, and 'm' for writing from disk to memory. A command of 'd' or 'm' means that three additional parameters are needed to specify the memory location mem_loc and the two parameters track and sector needed to specify a disk location. The command 'i' means that data is to be sent to memory from the keyboard and thus is to be followed by the data. For now, we will assume that the data is of type int and that only one such data item will follow the command 'i'.

FUNCTIONS:

```
opening_message(void)
```

Presents an opening message explaining the system and its purpose to a user. It has no parameters and returns no value.

```
get_data(void)
```

This function has no parameters. It reads its input one line at a time. It has no parameters and returns no value.

If the input is 'i', then the next input line contains a variable of type int, which is the type of data that we are using for the disk. The function put_in_memory( ) is then called with the parameter data that is read in. After the function put_in_memory( ) is called, control returns to the main program.

If the input is 'd', then the next three input lines will contain variables of type int. These three lines represent the values of the memory location called mem_loc that is used to mark the start of a block of memory as well as the track and sector that are used to mark the start of a disk block. The function mem_to_disk( ) is then called with the parameters mem_loc, track, and sector that were read in. After the function mem_to_disk( ) is called, control returns to the main program.

If the input is 'm', then the next three input lines will contain variables of type int. These three lines represent the values of the memory location called mem_loc that is used to mark the start of a block of memory as well as the track and sector that are used to mark the start of a disk block. The function disk_to_mem( ) is then called with the parameters mem_loc, track, and sector that were read in. After the function disk_to_mem( ) is called, control returns to the main program.

```
void put_in_memory(int data)
```

Parameter is of the type of data that we will enter into memory. For now, this type is char. Details are given later. It returns no value.

```
void disk_to_mem(int mem_loc, int track, int sector)
```

Parameters are of type int. Details are given later. It returns no value.

```
void mem_to_disk(int mem_loc, int track, int sector)
```

Parameters are of type int. Details are given later. It returns no value.

```
void print_disk(void)
```

Prints the contents of the array simulating the disk. Details are given later. It returns no value.

```
void print_mem(void)
```

Prints the contents of the array simulating memory. Details are given later. It returns no value.

Notice that the design has at least one major flaw – we have no way of stopping the program smoothly. Thus we will add another input symbol to be processed by get_data( ) in order to allow the user to stop the program smoothly. The obvious choice is to ask the user to select a 'q' to quit.

We need to have some method of conveying the major features of the design. It would be nice to have some formal way of describing this. However, formal design methods are not common and are often hard to use. In the absence of such methods, we will do the next best thing – incorporate the description of the design into the documentation of a prototype that will serve as the basis for the program itself.

We will write the design in two parts. The top-down design will indicate the major modules of the system and their relationship. The data-flow design will show some of the flow of data through the system.

These two representations of the design are clearly well suited to graphical methods. However, we will choose a somewhat less attractive representation of the design using text to simulate the boxes and lines that are part of the graphical model. The reason is that such a representation can be easily kept as part of the system documentation and as part of the source file containing the code for the system.

We now consider the design of the system. We will use a top-down approach to our design by choosing appropriate functions and by "stubbing in" their definitions. Stubbing in means that even if we do not know precisely how the function will perform its actions, we include a description of the function in the design. For example, we do not yet know the structure of the disk but we can still indicate the printing of its contents by using a function called print_disk( ). The process of stubbing in requires that all parameters to a function be described in the function header. It is good practice to include documentation of the name, type, and purpose of each parameter used inside a function.

The function print_disk( ) is then stubbed in to the system in a form something like

```
/****************************************************
This function prints the contents of the simulated disk.
PARAMETERS : none
VALUE RETURNED: none
****************************************************/
void print_disk(void )
{
  printf("In print_disk\n");
}
```

The function print_disk( ) has been set up with no parameters and no values to be returned. We may change this later but for now it seems sufficient.

We must decide about the passing of variables to the functions in our prototype either by parameters to the functions or by means of global variables. Dunsmore and Gannon [1980] suggest that global variables are better for the original design of very small programs but are a poor idea for larger programs and are especially poor for the design of a program that will need to be modified many times (as this one will). We will therefore avoid the use of global variables as much as possible.

We now show the initial design of the system. (Perhaps this should be phrased as the design of the first prototype.) It has three parts: documentation of the top-down design of the system, documentation of the flow of data through the system, and a stubbed-in set of functions.

```
/****************************************************
****************************************************/
/*
DESIGN  OF DISK/MEMORY MANAGEMENT SYSTEM  PROTOTYPE
DESIGN TEAM: A. B. See
             C. D. Eff
             G. H. Eye

DESIGN LEADER:
             A. B. See

DESIGN DATE: February 30, 1993

HOST COMPUTER: xxx

COMPILER: UNIX C Compiler v 3.2

****************************************************/
```

```
/* FUNCTION BLOCK DESIGN:

               |-----------|
               |   main()  |
               |_____|
                     |
                     |
                     |
          |----------------------|
          |   opening_message()  |
          |_____|
                     |
                     |
                     |
          |--------------|
          |   get_data() |
          |_____|
                     |
                     |
                     |
_____|_____
        |          |           |          |         |
        |          |           |          |         |
   ----------      |     -------------    |    -------------
   put_in_memory() |     disk_to_mem()    |     print_mem()
   ----------      |     -------------    |    -------------
                   |                      |
                   |                      |
            ------------             ------------
            mem_to_disk()            print_disk()
            ------------             ------------

*/


/****************************************************
****************************************************/
/*
                DATA FLOW DESIGN

input choice:

--- 'i',                data  -->    put_in_memory()

--- 'd', mem_loc, track, sector    -->    mem_to_disk()
```

```
--- 'm', mem_loc, track, sector    --> disk_to_mem()

--- 'p'     --> print_mem()

--- 'P'     -->  print_disk()

*/


/**********************************************************
 **********************************************************
             MAIN

 **********************************************************
 **********************************************************/
/* list of functions in program */

void  opening_message(void ) ;
void get_data(void ) ;
void put_in_memory(int data) ;
void mem_to_disk(int mem_loc, int track, int sector) ;
void disk_to_mem(int mem_loc, int track, int sector) ;
void print_mem(void ) ;
void print_disk(void ) ;

#include <stdio.h>
main(void)
{
  char ch;

  opening_message();
  get_data();
}


/**********************************************************/
/**********************************************************/
/**********************************************************/


/**********************************************************/
/***************** FUNCTION opening_message()**********/
/**********************************************************

This function prints an opening message
```

```
            printf("m.........move data from disk to mem\n");
            printf("p.........print memory\n");
            printf("P.........print disk\n");
            printf("q.........quit\n");
            printf("\n\n");
            ch = getchar() ;
              switch (ch)
              {
              case 'i':/* place data directly into memory block */
               scanf("%d", &data);
               put_in_memory(data);
               break;
              case 'd': /* need three parameters */
                scanf("%d %d %d", &mem_loc, & track, &sector);
                mem_to_disk(mem_loc, track, sector);
                break;
              case 'm': /* need three parameters */
                scanf("%d %d %d", &mem_loc, & track, &sector);
                disk_to_mem(mem_loc, track, sector);
                break;
              case 'p':
                print_mem();
                break;
              case 'P':
                print_disk();
                break;
              case 'q':              /* exit get_data() */
              case 'Q':
                return;
              }      /* end switch */
        }    /* end for */
}              /* end get_data */


/********************************************************/
/************** FUNCTION put_in_memory() ************/
/********************************************************/
/*
This function places data into memory initially.
It has a parameter that represents the data that is to be
placed into each of the memory locations forming the first
available block */
```

```
/* CALLED BY: get_data()                                   */
/*                                                         */
/* FUNCTIONS CALLED:none                                   */
/*                                                         */
/* PARAMETERS: data (type int)                             */
/*                                                         */
/* VALUE RETURNED: none                                    */
/*                                                         */
/***********************************************************/
void put_in_memory(int data)
{
   printf("In put_in_memory - parameter is %d\n", data);
}




/***********************************************************/
/************** FUNCTION  mem_to_disk()  **************/
/***********************************************************/
/*This function controls the movement of blocks of data
from the simulated memory to the simulated disk.  It has
three  parameters: mem_loc, track, and sector.  */
/*                                                         */
/* CALLED BY: get_data()                                   */
/*                                                         */
/* FUNCTIONS CALLED: none                                  */
/*                                                         */
/* PARAMETERS : mem_loc, track, sector                     */
/*                                                         */
/* VALUE RETURNED: none                                    */
/*                                                         */
/***********************************************************/
void mem_to_disk(int mem_loc, int track, int sector)
/* int mem_loc is the  starting point of memory block */
{
   printf("In mem_to_disk -");
   printf("parameters are %d %d %d \n",
           mem_loc, track, sector);
}
```

8. Rewrite the function of exercise 5 using recursion.

9. Here is a program to compute the greatest common divisor of two integers; the greatest common divisor is the largest positive integer that divides evenly into both the given integers. The program is nonrecursive.

```c
#include <stdio.h>

int min(int, int);

main(void)
int i, j,k, m;

printf("Enter two integers on a line\n");
scanf("%d %d",&i,&j);
k =0;
m=min(i,j);
while ( k< min(i,j))
   {
   if (((i% ( m -k)) ==0) && ((j %( m - k)) ==0))
     {
     printf("gcd is %d\n",m-k);
     break;
     }
   ++k;
   } /*end while */
} /* end main */

min(int i,int j)
{
   if (i <j)
     return i ;
   else
     return j ;
}
```

Write a recursive C program to use this algorithm to find the greatest common divisor of two integers.

10. Write a recursive program to print the first 10 Fibonacci numbers. The Fibonacci numbers are given by the formula

```
f(0) = 1
f(1) = 1
f(n) = f(n - 1) + f(n - 2) if  n > 1
```

Determine the largest Fibonacci number that can be determined correctly on your computer using your recursive program.

11. Write a recursive program to compute some of the values of Ackermann's function. This function is defined recursively in each of its arguments. It has integer arguments, returns integer values, and is defined by the set of rules

```
a(n, m) = 2n, if n = 0;
a(n, m) =  0, if m = 0 and n > 0;
a(n, m) =  2, if n > 1 and m = 1;
a(n, m) = a(n - 1, a(n, m - 1)), if n > 0 and m > 1;
```

The function a( ) grows extremely large as its arguments increase. This is probably the fastest growing function that anyone is likely to encounter. A computer magazine recently printed a challenge to its readers for anyone to compute the value of a(5,5) in standard integer notation using exponential notation, if necessary. **Your program to compute the value of a(n, m) should be tested for values of the parameters n and m no larger than 3**. The reason for this is that the function grows so rapidly.

12. Write three main programs, each of which is to use one of the three functions in examples 4.21, 4.22, and 4.23. Which of the programs was easiest to write? What feature of the functions and variable scope caused the most difficulties?

13. The next two exercises concern random number generation in C. The rand( ) function is included in the standard C library and produces random integers in the range 0 to RAND_MAX. (The value of RAND_MAX is the difference INT_MAX −1. Recall that the value of the constant INT_MAX was declared in the header file limits.h.) Use the modulus operator % and the function rand( ) to generate 100 random integers in the interval 1..20. (Be careful about the lower limit.) Run this program several times and save the output of each program's execution in a file. Compare the various output files.

14. In the previous exercise, you used the rand( ) function provided in the standard C library. This function suffers from the consistency of results. In a true random number generator, results of different program runs would be different. The use of the standard C library function srand( ) seeds the random number generator so that there is no exact replication of output. The function srand( ) uses a single argument, which is an unsigned int. For a true random number generation, use the time( ) function (with the header file time.h) to provide the argument time(NULL) to srand( ). Compare the results of several runs of generation of random integers in the range 1..20 with those of the previous exercise.

Software Engineering Exercises

15. Think about the way that a file system is organized, especially with regard to directories; information on the location, time of modification, and size of files; file access security; and the maximum file size. Determine a list of functions needed and write a set of requirements.

16. List a set of functions that you would use to control a database. The elements of the database consist of student records including personal information (such as name, address, telephone number) and academic information (grade point average, grades in major courses, course schedule, etc). For each function, indicate the return type and the types and meaning of each parameter.

17. The purpose of this exercise is to introduce you to some of the ideas involved in software estimation, which is the prediction of the number of people, computers, software tools, and time needed for delivery of a software project. Maintenance time and effort is also a subject of estimation. For each function in our prototype, list the total number of external files, interactions with users, or data objects needed. Multiply these numbers by 3, 5, and 5, respectively. The total is a rough approximation to the number of months needed for a first-class software project, including delivery, installation of the system, production of supporting documents, and the initial software maintenance. For more information, see [Boehm, 1981].

CHAPTER **5**

Arrays

Arrays are appropriate data structures for storing objects of the same type. Any object in the array can be accessed by knowledge of its index as an element of the array. Most of the common data organizations such as stacks and queues can be implemented in terms of an array. For example, if it is necessary to have access to the objects that are stored in the array in a last-in–first-out order, then we can use a stack that uses the elements of the array to hold the items on the stack, and we can access the item on the top of the stack by using as the array index the variable top. For a queue, we can use the array for storage and access the elements by using the variables front and rear for deletion and insertion.

In this chapter you will learn how to implement arrays in C. C permits and even encourages the use of arrays of both fixed size and variable size. It also permits the concept of multiple-dimensional arrays to be implemented as one-dimensional arrays whose elements are themselves arrays. Since arrays of fixed size are easier to understand, we consider them first.

5.1 One-Dimensional Arrays of Fixed Size

Arrays are used when a number of objects of the same type are to be considered together. The elements in the array can be accessed by simply indicating their position in the array; this is done using an index. Here is an example of a program that declares a variable named arr to be an array of 10 integers and assigns to each element of the array arr a value equal to the square of its index.

```
main(void)
{
  int i,  key;
  int arr[NUM_ELEMENTS];

  printf("Please enter the key to be searched for\n");
  scanf("%d",&key);
  for(i=0;i<NUM_ELEMENTS;i++)
    arr[i] = 300 + i;
  i=0;
  while (i < NUM_ELEMENTS )
    {
    if (arr[i] == key)
      {
      printf("The key is found in position %d.\n",i);
      break;
      }
    else
      i++;
    } /* end else */
  if (i == NUM_ELEMENTS)
    printf("The key %d is not in the array.\n",key);
}  /* end program */
```

The output is

```
Please enter the key to be searched for
324
The key is found in position 24.
```

The code of example 5.3 was easy to understand and quite efficient.

The next example of array use is binary search. In binary search, the array is already sorted and we use a divide-and-conquer approach to the problem by dividing the size of the array portion that we search in two every time we make a comparison between the array element and the key. Since the array is previously sorted, this method will eventually close down on the key to be searched for if it is present in the array. If the key is not present in the array, then the search will fail and a value of –1 will be returned. An example of a binary search program is given in example 5.4. Note the similarity to a root finding algorithm given in the exercises at the end of the previous chapter.

Example 5.4

```
/* nonmodular implementation of binary search for arrays */
#include <stdio.h>
#define NUM_ELEMENTS 100
```

```
main(void)
{
  int low, high, mid, key;
  int found = 0 , i;
  int arr[NUM_ELEMENTS];

  for(i=0; i < NUM_ELEMENTS; i++)
    arr[i] = 300 + i;
  printf("Please enter the key to be searched for\n");
  scanf("%d",&key);
  low=0;
  high = NUM_ELEMENTS - 1;
  while (low <= high)
    {
    mid = (low + high ) /2;
    if (key < arr[mid])
      high = mid - 1;
    else if (key > arr[mid])
      low =  mid + 1;
    else     /* key found */
      {
      low = high + 1;
      found = 1;
      }
    }
  if (!found)
    printf("The key %d is not in the array.\n",key);
  else
    printf("The key is in position %d. \n",mid);
}
```

The code works correctly. However, as presented, it has several flaws. The most serious flaw is that it requires the array size to be hard coded into the program. The second serious flaw is that the program is not modular. That is, it requires that the assignment of the array values, the reading in of the key to be searched for, the actual search, and the output of the result all be incorporated into the main program.

We can somewhat solve the modularity problem by declaring the array arr as an external variable that will be accessible to all functions. You will be asked to rewrite the program using this technique in one of the exercises. A solution that corrects both of these flaws will be presented in section 5.2.

The binary search technique is much faster than linear search for arrays of more than eight elements or so, at least in the average case. In the worst case, we have to keep dividing the array into two equal pieces until we get to an array portion that consists of only one element, arr[mid].

It is easy to see how to use arrays to store data and to allow the elements of the array to be accessed simply by knowing the index of the element. We can also use arrays to implement one of the most important data structures in computing – the *stack*. A stack is a method of organizing data so that only a single element can be seen by the rest of the program at any time – the so-called top of the stack. Think of a stack of trays in a cafeteria where the allowable operations are place a tray onto the top of the stack (the push operation), remove a tray from the top of the stack (the pop operation), and test the stack for being empty (no trays).

There are several ways to implement stacks. In this chapter, we will implement a stack whose elements are integers by using an array to store the integers and we will access the element on the top of the stack using a variable called top.

Example 5.5

```
#define MAXSTACK 20          /* maximum items in stack */
int top = -1;
int stack[MAXSTACK];         /* array of char         */

/*----------------------------------------------------*/
/* Pushes argument onto stack if stack is not full.   */
/* If the stack is full,  an error message is printed.*/
/*- no return value                                   */
/*  input parameters are of type int                  */
/*----------------------------------------------------*/
void push (int n)
{
  if (top < MAXSTACK - 1)
    {
    top++;
    stack[top] = n;
    }
  else
      printf("error — stack full.\n");
}


/*----------------------------------------------------*/
/* Pops the top value from stack and prints an error  */
/* message if stack is empty.                         */
/* Negative value for top means that stack is empty   */
/* no parameters are used in the call                 */
/* the value returned is int                          */
/*----------------------------------------------------*/
```

```
int pop(void)
{
int temp = top;

  if (top >= 0)
    {
    top--;
    return (stack[temp]);
    }
  else       /* stack empty */
    {
    printf("error -- stack empty.\n");
    return (-1);    /*  error */
    }
}
```

These routines can be used in any program to manipulate a stack of integers, assuming that we arrange the main program to accommodate them. We will show how to accommodate them into a program that emulates a simple desk calculator that uses reverse Polish notation such as most HP calculators. To add 2 and 3 and then multiply the result by 7 on such a calculator, you would enter the keystroke sequence

```
    7 2 3 + *.
```

The program we show here is very limited since it only does one operation at a time. That is, it expects input to be in the form

```
    integer integer operator
```

The calculator will then print the result and stop. It does not allow for larger input and does no error checking for things like too few integers to operate on. A program to do this is given in example 5.6. Note the declaration of push( ) as having return type void.

Example 5.6

```
#include <stdio.h>
#define MAXSTACK 20            /* maximum items in stack */

int top = -1 ;
int stack[MAXSTACK];           /* array of characters */

void push(int n);
int pop(void);
```

```
main(void)
{
  int n,m,second;
  char c;

  printf("Welcome to the cheap calculator program\n");
  printf("Please enter two integers followed by an
  operator\n\n");
  scanf("%d %d %c",&n,&m,&c);
  push(n);
  push(m);
  switch(c)
    {
    case '+':
      printf("The answer is %d\n", pop()+pop() );
      break;
    case '-':
      second = pop();
      printf("The answer is %d\n", pop()-second );
      break;
    case '*':
      printf("The answer is %d\n", pop()*pop() );
      break;
    case '/':
      second = pop();
      printf("The answer is %d\n", pop()/ second );
      break;
    default:
      printf("Not a valid operator - sorry\n");
    }
}


/*----------------------------------------------------*/
/* Pushes argument onto stack if stack is not full.   */
/* If the stack is full, then an error message.       */
/*- no return value                                   */
/*  input parameters are of type int                  */
/*----------------------------------------------------*/

void push (int n)
{
  if (top < MAXSTACK - 1)
    {
    top++;
```

```
          stack[top] = n;
          return(stack[top]);
          }
     else
        printf("error -- stack full.\n");
   }



   /*----------------------------------------------------*/
   /* Pops top value from the stack. It prints an error  */
   /* message if one tries to "pop" from an empty stack. */
   /* A negative value for top means that stack is empty */
   /* no parameters are used in the call                 */
   /* the value returned is int                          */
   /*----------------------------------------------------*/

   int pop(void)
   {
      int temp = top;

      if (top >= 0)
         {
         top--;
         return (stack[temp]);
         }
      else
         {
         printf("error -- stack empty.\n");
         return (-1);     /*  clear stack */
         }
   }
```

This program works (try it!) for the restricted input. How can we develop this program so that it works for an arbitrary input? We clearly cannot assume that the input occurs in any special order since any combination of operators and operands is possible in reverse Polish notation as long as the number of operands that we have seen at any point of the input is greater than the number of operators. Anything else will cause an error. Since we do not know the order, we must read in the input one character at a time and interpret the input as needed. This means that we must convert a sequence of the characters 0 through 9 into an integer. This function is generally available in the standard C library and is called atoi( ). The purpose of this function is what is suggested by its name since it transforms an input from ASCII (the most common encoding scheme of characters into binary form) into an output of the form integer. If your computer doesn't use ASCII, the built-in function atoi( ) will still work, changing character input into integer. We will not use this function since it is simpler to write our own as we do in the switch statement.

To make things easier, assume that the input is given with only one operand or operator per line. Also, in order to have the results make sense (in case we enter a string of characters whose integer equivalent is larger than the largest integer representable on the computer), we will assume that each integer read in has no more than eight places; this will be stored in an array of eight characters. The main program now looks like this; the functions push and pop are the same as before and will not be repeated.

Example 5.7

```c
#include <stdio.h>
#define MAXSTACK  20              /* maximum items in stack */
#define MAXSIZE 8                 /* size of int using char */

int top = -1 ;
int stack[MAXSTACK];              /* array of characters */

void push(int n);
int pop(void);

main(void)
{
  int i, n, second;
  int c,temp[MAXSIZE];

  printf("Welcome to the cheap calculator program\n");
  printf("Enter an expression in reverse Polish form\n");
  printf("one operator or operand per line\n");
  while ((c = getchar()) != EOF)
    switch(c)
      {
      case '0':
      case '1':
      case '2':
      case '3':
      case '4':
      case '5':
      case '6':
      case '7':
      case '8':
      case '9':    /* first digit of int */
        i=1;
        n = c - '0';
        while ((i <= MAXSIZE) &&
                ((temp[i] =getchar())!= '\n'))
```

```
        {
        n= 10 * n + temp[i] - '0';
        i++;
        }
    push(n);
    break;
case '+':
    push( pop()+pop());
    break;
case '-':
    second = pop();
    push( pop()-second);
    break;
case '*':
    push( pop()*pop());
    break;
case '/':
    second = pop();
    push( pop()/ second );
    break;
case '=':
    printf("%d\n",push(pop()) );
    break;
case '\n':
    break;
case 'c':          /* clear the stack */
    top = -1;
    break;
default:
    printf("Unknown command\n");
    }
}

/* code for push and pop would go here */
```

The program in example 5.7 assumes that input is in the form of one operator or operand per line. It does not allow for the input to be given on a single line, and it does not handle input characters other than 0 through 9, the arithmetic operators, 'c', and '='. In the exercises you will have an opportunity to improve this program.

So far, we have only implemented the stack data structure using arrays. All of the other standard data structures are as easy to implement in C as in any other modern, high-level language. You will have an opportunity to write a C program to use arrays for implementing queues in the exercises at the end of this chapter and will meet some of the other data structures in Part II.

One point needs to be mentioned about the initialization of arrays. We can always write a loop to place easily computed values into an array as we did in examples 5.1 and 5.3. However, it is sometimes easier to initialize the array; that is, to give values to the array elements when the array is first defined. This can be done by assigning values to the array using braces to delimit the array elements; the elements are separated from one another by commas. External arrays can always be initialized as can static arrays (whether internal or external) and automatic arrays (those arrays that are inside of functions but are not qualified by "static"). Thus the five programs

```c
#include <stdio.h>

void f(void);

main()
{
    f();
}

static int arr[10] = {1,2,3,5,7,11,13,17,19,23};

f()
{
    printf("%d\n",arr[5]);
}


,



#include <stdio.h>

void f(void);

main()
{
    f();
}

f()
{
    static int arr[10] = {1,2,3,5,7,11,13,17,19,23};

    printf("%d\n",arr[5]);
}


,
```

```
#include <stdio.h>

void f(void);

int arr[10] = {1,2,3,5,7,11,13,17,19,23};

main()
{
  f();
}

f()
{
  printf("%d\n",arr[5]);
}
```

,

```
#include <stdio.h>

void f(void);

main()
{
  f();
}

int arr[10] = {1,2,3,5,7,11,13,17,19,23};

f()
{
  printf("%d\n",arr[5]);
}
```

and

```
#include <stdio.h>

void f(void);

main()
{
f();
}
```

```
f()
{
int arr[10] = {1,2,3,5,7,11,13,17,19,23};

printf("%d\n",arr[5]);
}
```

all produce correct results because the array is either static, external, automatic, or some combination of these (The initialization of automatic arrays is a new feature of ANSI C that was not present in earlier dialects of the C programming language.)

5.2 One-Dimensional Arrays of Variable Size

Many computer languages do not allow arrays of variable size because of the extra information that must usually be kept with arrays if we do not specify the number of elements. In strongly typed languages such as Pascal, an array consisting of the four integers 1, 2, 3, and 4 cannot be the same type as an array of three integers 1, 2, and 3 since the arrays have different sizes and therefore cannot be the same type. C is not a strongly typed language and therefore has no such restriction. However, to work properly, we must either specify the size of an array before it is used or else have a special character to indicate the end of the array. Both methods are used in C, with the special termination character being used primarily for character arrays. (The two methods are sometimes called the length-byte and null-byte methods. We will not use this terminology in this book.) We will show the use of arrays of variable size by an example.

A typical use of arrays is in computer graphics when we wish to draw the graph of a polygon. In such programs, we must usually initialize a graphics mode, define the size of windows on the screen, and the color, thickness, and style of the lines (dotted, dashed, unbroken, etc.), and move the cursor appropriately. This is usually done by making calls to functions that are part of a graphics library that is linked to the code written by the programmer. In this discussion, we will consider only that portion of the code that sends information to a separate polygon-drawing function that would be linked using a graphics library. We will want something general that does not require the number of vertices of the polygon to be known in advance.

To be specific, suppose that we wish to draw the polygon in Figure 5.1 which is centered at the origin (0, 0) with the coordinates of the vertices given.

We could use the elementary move and draw commands for something like

Example 5.8

```
move_abs_2(50.0,0.0);
line_abs_2(0.0,100.0);
line_abs_2(-50.0,0.0);
line_abs_2(0.0,-100.0);
line_abs_2(50.0,0.0);
```

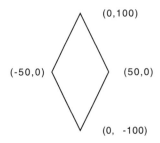

(0,100)

(-50,0)   (50,0)

(0, -100)

Figure 5.1   A simple polygon

This is simple enough for this polygon. The move_abs_2( ) function moves the cursor from its current position to the point whose coordinates are specified by its arguments. (There is a related function move_rel_2( )) that moves from the current position the relative amounts specified in its arguments.) The function line_abs_2( ) draws a line from the current position to the arguments specified in its arguments; both functions require floating point arguments in most standardized computer graphics libraries.

Note that we have no easy way of specifying the polygon as a complete object if we use this method. A better way is to use a function that is often called polyline and that uses three arguments: an array for the x and y coordinates and the number of points.

Example 5.9

```
float x[5], y[5];
x[0] = 50.0; y[0] = 0.0;
x[1] = 0.0;  y[1] = 100.0;
x[2] = -50.0; y[2] = 0.0;
x[3] = 0.0; y[3] = -100.0;
x[4] = x[0]; y[4] = y[0];
polyline_abs_2(x,y,5);
```

The call to the function polyline_abs_2( ) uses the three arguments x, y, and 5 differently. We have specified the arrays x and y to have five floating point elements each and have told polyline_abs_2( ) to consider only the first five of these; that is, elements with indices 0, 1, 2, 3, and 4. Note that the function polyline_abs_2( ) needed only the first five elements of the arrays x and y. C uses the construction of variable-size arrays to avoid constraining functions such as polyline_abs_2( ) as in example 5.10; the two code segments will work equally well.

Example 5.10

```
float x[], y[];
x[0] = 50.0; y[0] = 0.0;
x[1] = 0.0;  y[1] = 100.0;
x[2] = -50.0; y[2] = 0.0;
x[3] = 0.0; y[3] = -100.0;
x[4] = x[0]; y[4] = y[0];
polyline_abs_2(x,y,5);
```

Note that in example 5.10, we do not specify the size of the array at all. We assign values to the array elements as needed. The construction

```
float x[] ;
```

is interpreted by the C compiler to mean that there will be a contiguous set of memory locations that are to be set aside for floating point numbers at some point in the program; the actual setting aside of these memory locations in this program is done when the assignments to x[0], x[1], x[2], x[3], and x[4] are made. The technical language here is that the first mention of x[] is a "declaration" of its type and the type of its elements; the second use of x[] is in the assignment of values and the actual setting aside of memory storage, which constitutes a "definition" of the elements of x[].

We can use these ideas to write a better binary search program than what was presented in example 5.4. The code in example 5.11 shows the passing of the array arr[] as a parameter to the function search( ). Note that the array is "declared" as a parameter to the function search( ) but is "defined" in the main program so that space can be set aside for it. The binary search function is written in a form that can be used for any size array as long as the array is an array of integer elements only. To remind us of good documentation style, a typical minimal amount of documentation has been included in the code to describe briefly the functions needed and their interfaces.

Example 5.11

```
/*-------------------------------------------------*/
/* Program for binary search                       */
/* The main program calls the function search      */
/*    GLOBAL constants : NUM_ELEMENTS              */
/*    GLOBAL variables : none                      */
/*-------------------------------------------------*/
#include <stdio.h>
#define NUM_ELEMENTS 100

int search(int a[], int n, int k);

main(void)
{
   int i, arr[NUM_ELEMENTS];
   int key, found ;

   for(i=0;i<NUM_ELEMENTS;i++)
     arr[i] = 300 + i;
   printf("Please enter the key to be searched for\n");
   scanf("%d",&key);
   found = search(arr,NUM_ELEMENTS,key);
   if (found == -1)
     printf("The key %d is not in the array.\n",key);
   else
     printf("The key is in position %d\n",found);
}
```

```
/*-------------------------------------------------*/
/* Function search                                 */
/* INPUT:                                          */
/*   a[] an array of integers                      */
/*   n:   the size of the array                    */
/*   key: an integer representing the              */
/*        key to be searched for                   */
/* OUTPUT :    an integer that indicates the       */
/*        position of the key in the array         */
/*        if the key is found                      */
/*        -1 is returned if the key is             */
/*        not in the array                         */
/* METHOD :    binary search technique             */
/*-------------------------------------------------*/
int search(int a[], int n, int key)
{
   int low = 0, mid, high = n -1 ;

   while (low <= high)
     {
     mid = (low + high ) /2;
     if (key < a[mid])
       high = mid - 1;
     else if (key > a[mid])
       low =  mid + 1;
     else    /* key found */
       return mid ;
     }
     return -1;            /* we get here if low > high and key
                           is not in the array */
}
```

Unfortunately, there is a subtle difficulty with the distinction between the declaration and the definition of an array. If we do not explicitly allocate memory storage using a definition, then the compiler might use some available space and the program might give correct output for some small arrays. Replacing the definition in the program of example 5.11

```
int arr[NUM_ELEMENTS];
```

by the declaration

```
int arr[];
```

the program worked most of the time for up to 48 array elements on one computer, but not on the others. The results are highly dependent on the compiler used. This type of error is very difficult to find, so be careful.

You should be careful to check that the number of values initialized within the braces is the same as the dimension of the array. If there are two few values within the braces, the program will be hard to read; if there are too many, then the compiler will generate an error and the array initialization will fail.

5.3 Character Strings

Many languages do not have built-in facilities for handling character strings. Many versions of Pascal do not have this facility and use the notion of a packed array of characters as a substitute. FORTRAN is even worse. Many older versions of FORTRAN implement characters as portions of integers using a highly machine-dependent method. Other languages such as SNOBOL have excellent facilities for string manipulation. C allows the use of string constants and the passing of strings as parameters to functions but is somewhat unusual in that input and output are not part of the language but are part of the standard library.

There are two typical ways that character strings appear in programs: as constant strings and as variable strings. Typical uses of constant strings are shown in the next example.

Example 5.12

```
#include <stdio.h>
#define MESSAGE "I love the C language."

main(void)
{
  printf("%s\n",MESSAGE);
  printf("Hello\n");
}
```

which has the expected output

```
    I love the C language.
    Hello
```

The constant strings are brought into the programs by defining them using the #define statement or by simply presenting them as arguments to printf( ).

How does the C compiler know where the string ends? There are really only two ways to do this in any language: either count the number of characters in the string or use a marker to indicate the end of the string. Using a marker to indicate the end of the string is more flexible and is the method used in C. The end-of-string marker must be a character that cannot be mistaken for a normal printable character. In C, this is done using the "escape sequence" of a backslash followed by a 0. This is almost always enclosed in single quotes because it represents a single character. It represents a special byte that has all its bits set to the value 0.

As an example of this philosophy, consider the next two programs.

Example 5.13

```
#include <stdio.h>

main(void)
{
  int i;
  char arr[10];

  arr[0]='I';
  arr[1]=' ';        /* blank space */
  arr[2]='l';
  arr[3]='i';
  arr[4]='k';
  arr[5]='e';
  arr[6]=' ';
  arr[7]='C';
  arr[8]='!';
  arr[9]='!';
  for(i=0;i <= 9;i++)
    printf("%c",arr[i]);
  printf("\n");
}
```

The program of example 5.13 has the output

```
I like C!!
```

This is correct output but it depended on our printing the string character by character and knowing the length of the string (or at least of the portion that we wanted) in advance. There was no use of the string termination symbol at all.

To see what problems this can cause, consider the next example.

Example 5.14

```
#include <stdio.h>

main(void)
{
  int i;
  char arr[11];

  arr[0]='I';
  arr[1]=' ';        /* blank space */
  arr[2]='l';
  arr[3]='i';
  arr[4]='k';
```

```
arr[5]='e';
arr[6]=' ';
arr[7]='C';
arr[8]='!';
arr[9]='!';
i=0;
while (arr[i] != '\0')
  {
  printf("%c\n",arr[i]);
  i++ ;
  }
}
```

When you run this experiment, be prepared to stop the program. The infinite loop is caused by the escape sequence '\0' not being in the array since we have not placed it there. You might be bothered by the huge number of array elements printed since we only declared arr to be an array of 11 characters. The reason for this will become clear when we discuss pointers in Part II; for now consider the arbitrary access to all elements of an array as something to be avoided unless the array has a termination symbol. The termination symbol can be inserted manually as in adding a line of the form

```
arr[10] = '\0';
```

to example 5.14 or by forcing the termination symbol to be placed there automatically. A termination symbol is automatically placed at the end of a string that is created using a #define instruction; thus the array called MESSAGE in example 5.15 is exactly 6 characters long.

Example 5.15

```
#include <stdio.h>
#define MESSAGE "Hello"

main(void)
{
  printf("%s",MESSAGE);
}
```

It works correctly since the array of characters in MESSAGE has six entries: H, e, l, l, o, and \0. More information on this topic will be presented in the next section.

An examination of the header file string.h shows that there are many functions available for manipulation of character strings. Among them are

- strcmp() – to compare the contents of two strings
- strcpy() – to copy one string to another
- strlen() – to compute the length of a string
- atoi() – to change an ASCII string to integer

These functions expect a particular input format for the strings that are their arguments, namely the convention of ending the string of characters by a \0 in the appropriate array position. We will return to their use in Chapter 8. The exercises suggest how we can write similar functions now for our own use.

5.4 Printf Revisited

You have used the function printf( ) many times for output, using the %c, %d, or %f control specifications for character, integer, or floating point expressions, respectively. You have also printed character strings using code similar to

```
printf("Hello\n");
```

or the popular

```
printf("The %s is underpaid. Please send money \n",
          "author");
```

Consider the code of example 5.16, which at first glance seems to be correct.

Example 5.16

```
#include <stdio.h>
/* error in second printf statement */
main(void)
{
  printf("Happy February %d to you\n",28);
  printf("Happy February %s to you\n",30);
}
```

This code doesn't work and the result is terrible. The error is so severe that control of the program is taken over by the operating system to prevent damage to other programs resident in memory. The typical error message when this program executes (at least on one system) is

```
Segmentation fault (core dumped)
```

which tells us that we are using memory that we were forbidden by the operating system to have access to. What is causing the error? It is possible that the compiler knows that there are only 28 days in February (except for a leap year). I don't think so and neither do you. The real reason is that the C compiler expected a string argument in the second printf( ) statement in example 5.16. Since strings in C are stored as arrays of characters with a symbol '\0' used to indicate the end of the string, the program looks for a '\0' in the computer's memory to indicate the end of the string. Since no such entry is found in memory, the search continues until we address a memory location that is not available to us, and therefore the error occurs. Note also that treating the 30 as an address of a string causes a violation unless we have privileges that allow us to access memory address 30.

There is no easy way automatically to avoid this problem by using software tools. Most C compilers do not mention this type of error, and lint does not complain about it either. The programmer must be extremely careful to check that the type of the expression being printed and the control specification in the printf( ) statement agree; this is critical if character strings are to be printed.

Some C compilers are more robust than others with regard to differences between control specifications in printf( ) statements and the type of the expression being printed. In Turbo C, the output of the program of example 5.16 is

```
Happy February 28 to you
Happy February 88  Borland Intl. to you
```

which indicates that a memory location (where the trademark information is found) is being accessed incorrectly. I don't know if this is better than a core dump. A core dump gets your attention quickly, while the error in output might be missed when testing the program.

You should be especially careful to avoid functions that have different types of values returned. In example 5.17 we show a poorly written binary search function that causes a disaster if it is called by a simple printf( ) statement such as

```
printf("%s\n",search(arr,n,key) );
```

I agree that the code is silly, but it does illustrate the point. I hope that you write better code than this. Note that if this search function were commented carefully, then the mixed return type would have been easier to find.

Example 5.17

```
/* bad example, mixed return types            */
/*---------------------------------------------*/
/* Function search                             */
/* INPUT:                                      */
/*    a[] an array of integers                 */
/*    n:   the size of the array               */
/*    key: an integer representing the         */
/*         key to be searched for              */
/* OUTPUT :   an integer that indicates the    */
/*         position of the key in the array    */
/*         if the key is found                 */
/*         -1 is returned if the key is        */
/*         not in the array                    */
/* METHOD :   binary search technique          */
/*---------------------------------------------*/

int search(int a[],int n,int key)
{
   int low = 0, mid, high = n -1 ;
   while (low <= high)
```

```
        {
    mid = (low + high ) /2;
    if (key < a[mid])
        high = mid - 1;
    else if (key > a[mid])
        low =  mid + 1;
    else     /* key found */
        return mid ;
    }
    /* we get here if low > high and key is not in the array*/
    /* software design error - no return value          */
    printf("key not found\n");
}
```

5.5 Interfacing with the Command Line: Parameters to main( )

You may have noticed that the output from the utility program lint had a statement of the form

```
===============
(9)  warning: main() returns random value to invocation
environment
===============
```

This suggests that the function main can interact with its own environment – the operating system of the computer. The communication between the program and the operating system can go in two directions. If the program has an error such as division by 0, then the program communicates with the operating system and the program is halted. Communication in the other direction is done by means of command-line arguments.

In example 5.18, we present an example of a program that has command-line arguments. Notice the form of the arguments to main( ). These arguments are character strings that are put into the program by an interface between the command shell, which is part of the operating system, and the running program.

Example 5.18

```
#include <stdio.h>

main(int argc, char *argv[] )
{
    int i;

    puts("The arguments to this function are:");
    for (i = 0; i < argc; i++)
        printf("%s\n",argv[i]);
    printf("\n");
}
```

151

This is an important experiment. Type in this program and run it. If your executable program was named a.out (which is the default name for executable files under the UNIX operating system), then your output would be the character string

    a.out

on a line by itself. (The corresponding output in computers running under MS/DOS would be the character string

    progname

assuming that the executable file was named progname.) If you typed in the line

    a.out Fred Marie Harry Computer Science types

the output would be

    a.out
    Fred
    Marie
    Harry
    Computer
    Science
    types

with each string of characters printed on a line by itself. The command-line arguments in the first run of the program were

    a.out

In the second run of the program, there were the seven command-line arguments listed previously. The value of argc was 1 in the first run and 7 in the second run. The value of argc is always at least 1 since the name of the executable file (a.out in this example) is always counted as a command-line argument. The other command-line arguments are stored in argv[]. (On systems running under MS/DOS, the output would be identical except for the name of the executable file.)

This example shows that the command line, which included the name of the executable file and other character strings, was processed by the operating system and the information was given to the program. This is useful when we wish to pass arguments to a C program; we will do this many times in Part II.

The next example shows how we can read in a command-line argument as a string of characters (the only way to get commands from the operating system) and change it into an integer.

Example 5.19

```
#include <stdio.h>

main(int argc,char *argv[])
{
   int i,lim;
```

```
    lim = atoi(argv[1]);
    for(i=1;i <= lim;i++)
       printf("%d\n",i);
}
```

Type in this program and test it with several different arguments. It gives the correct answer if you type in a command line such as

```
    a.out 2
    a.out 23
```

or something similar. It also gives a correct output (nothing) if the command line is

```
    a.out c
```

where c can be any character. However, there is a serious error if you simply type the command line

```
    a.out
```

The program terminates ungracefully with a core dump. One of the exercises at the end of this chapter suggests a way of fixing this problem. The program is not well written from the standpoint of defensive programming since it can fail unpleasantly when presented with only minor errors in input. The exercise illustrates an extremely important principle of programming (especially C programming): be sure that possible errors in interfaces do not cause the program to crash. This warning applies both to interfaces to a human user entering data and to regular processing in the program.

The best way to write this program defensively is to insert some defensive code immediately after the type declarations. We will use the fact that the variable argc keeps track of the number of command-line arguments. We can use the argument count to exit if there are not enough arguments. This allows the program to terminate gracefully rather than dump the in-core memory into a file.

The defensive code is

```
    if (argc == 1)
       {
       printf("Error - not enough arguments\n");
       exit(1);
       }
```

This code allows the termination of the program by using the exit( ) function, which is called with an argument of 0 to indicate that no abnormal action should be taken by the operating system. A call to exit( ) always terminates the program.

5.6 Two-Dimensional Arrays in C

The title of this section is somewhat misleading in that C does not actually allow two-dimensional arrays. A two-dimensional array is an object composed of elements of the same type that is organized so that any element can be accessed by using the starting position of the array (which is known to the compiler) and the two indices that describe the position of the desired element. Every two-dimensional array must have the same number of elements in each row; the number of elements in each column must also be the same although it does not have to be the same as the number of elements in each row. The term "row" means the index for the first dimension, and "column" means the index for the second dimension. For example, a two-dimensional array with 4 elements in the first dimension and 5 elements in the second dimension has a total of 20 elements and is said to be a 4 by 5 array; that is, it has 4 rows and 5 columns. One such two-dimensional array is shown in example 5.20 in which we use the common representation in which rows extend horizontally and columns extend vertically.

Example 5.20

```
 2  4  6  8 10
12 14 16 18 20
22 24 26 28 30
32 34 36 38 40
```

The elements of this two-dimensional array are all of the same type. The element 22 is in the position described by the indices

```
row = 2
column = 0
```

since the C language begins indexing arrays at index 0.

The data structure represented in example 5.20 is common in computer science. How can we represent this idea in C if the language does not allow the use of two-dimensional arrays? We can by using one-dimensional arrays, each of whose elements is also a one-dimensional array. Thus the 20 numbers in example 5.20 can be represented by the data definition

```
int arr[4][5] ;
```

which says that arr is an array of 4 elements, each of which is an array of 5 elements, with the last-mentioned elements all being of type int. The element 22 is found by using the indices appropriately so that the value of arr[2][0] is equal to 22.

Once an array is defined and storage space is allocated to it, the only effect of not having two-dimensional arrays allowed in C is that the elements in an array called arr must be accessed using the form arr[i][j] instead of the form arr[i,j], which is common in many other languages. The expression arr[i,j] has an entirely different meaning in C using an obscure concept called the "comma operator"; the value of the expression arr[i,j] is arr[j], which is certainly not what we intend. We saw the comma operator earlier in this book and its use was complex. You should follow this warning:

Use the form arr[i][j] instead of arr[i,j] for accessing elements of two-dimensional arrays.

The array of example 5.20 is stored in row-major form; that is, the index that changes first is the second or column index. Figure 5.2 shows the way that this particular array is stored, with the beginning of the array at the bottom of the picture.

For ordinary, rectangular arrays with both dimensions fixed, there is no essential difference between the two methods of having two-dimensional arrays being represented either as a single entity or as a one-dimensional array of one-dimensional arrays as in C. There is a distinct advantage to the C method if the array size is not known at compile time. An examination of the storage indicated in Figure 5.2 suggests that the critical need is for the C compiler to know the number of elements in a column. The actual picture of memory is represented more accurately in Figure 5.3.

The storage for the first five ints would be exactly the same if we used the statement

```
int arr[][5] ;
```

since the only thing that we must know is the size of an arbitrary element of the array. The elements of the array arr are one-dimensional arrays of five ints each, and thus the storage allotted for any element of arr must be precisely the space needed for five expressions of type int.

The two notations

```
int arr[][5];
```

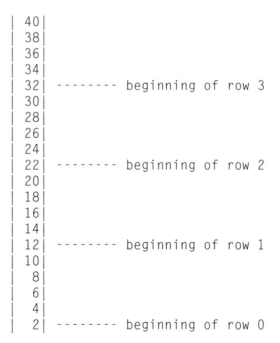

Figure 5.2 Storage of a two-dimensional array of fixed size

and

```
int arr[4][5];
```

are not the same. The reason for this is precisely the same reason that there was a distinction made between declarations and definitions in C arrays earlier in this chapter. The first notation says to the compiler that there will be a block of memory that will contain storage for an element whose size is the total size needed to store five ints. Nothing is guaranteed for the storage of any additional blocks of five ints. Attempting to store additional blocks of five ints might work fine or might overwrite the data from some other variable. The second notation says that we are to set aside enough storage for a total of 20 ints. We will return to this point in Chapter 8 when we discuss pointers.

Strictly speaking, the first notation int arr[ ][5] does not declare a two-dimensional array. It declares a pointer to an array whose elements are themselves arrays of five ints.

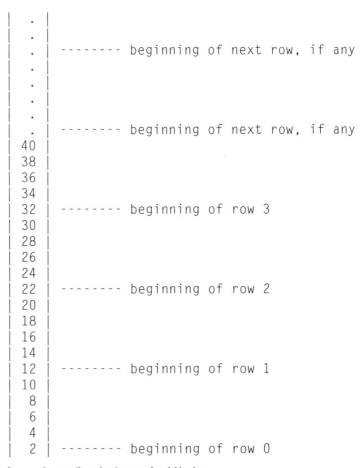

Figure 5.3 Storage of a two-dimensional array of variable size

A two-dimensional array can be initialized using the same construction used for one-dimensional arrays. It is probably easier to group the rows together in order to make the assignment of elements to their proper positions easy to understand. Examples 5.21 and 5.22 show alternative methods of declaring and initializing two-dimensional arrays that represent the values of coordinates of a pentagon. The pentagon is described as a polygon with six vertices. Six vertices are used since the data must interface with a graphics function that will draw the pentagon as a sequence of line segments. Having six vertices with the first and last identical ensures that the pentagon is a closed figure. The vertices are given as a two-dimensional array of dimensions 6 by 2. The first dimension indicates that there are six vertices and the second indicates 2 coordinates per vertex; we expect the first coordinate to correspond to the x coordinate and the second to correspond to the y coordinate.

Example 5.21 Initialization of two-dimensional arrays: readable form

```
float pentagon1[6][2] =
        {
        {0.0, 0.0},
        {1.0, 1.0},
        {2.0, 2.0},
        {10.0, 10.0},
        {0.0, 10.0},
        {0.0, 0.0}
        };
```

Example 5.22 Initialization of two-dimensional arrays: unreadable form

```
float pentagon2[6][2] = { 0.0, 0.0, 1.0, 1.0, 2.0, 2.0,
10.0, 10.0, 0.0, 10.0, 0.0, 0.0};
```

To summarize, there are four major things to remember about the treatment of two-dimensional arrays in C:

(1) Elements of the array must be accessed by the [row][column] rather than the [row,column] notation.
(2) The number of elements in each row of the array must be the same, but the number of rows need not be specified. However, no space is allocated if the number of rows is not specified, and unpredictable results can occur. Thus this omission of the leading dimension of an array is useful only within the context of an argument to a function.
(3) The elements in the array must have the same type.
(4) The array may be initialized using the construction

>   arr[row][column] = { { first row separated by commas },
>   {second row separated by commas},
>
>   .
>
>   .
>
>   {last row separated by commas} } ;

It is important to understand the way that two-dimensional arrays are stored in C programs. The address of the element arr[i][j] is obtained by using the expression

START + (i * NUMBER_OF_COLUMNS + j) * sizeof(arr[0][0])

where START is the address of the first element arr[0][0].

Higher-dimensional arrays can also be simulated in C. The method is the same as for two-dimensional arrays: write the array as an array of elements, each of which is itself an array of lower dimension. For example, a declaration for a three-dimensional array of floating point numbers, with the array name of arr and with N values in the first dimension, M values in the second dimension, and P values in the third dimension is

```
float arr[N][M][P];
```

The same array with a variable number of elements in the first dimension can be declared by something like

```
float arr[][M][P];
```

As was the case for two-dimensional arrays, every range of values for each of the indices, except for the first dimension's indices, must be specified so that the compiler can store the proper size elements. Omission of the first dimension is only appropriate if the array is an argument to a function.

5.7 Reading from Files

In Chapter 3, we saw a simple program to read input from files. We can use the ideas of the previous section to allow somewhat more flexible programs that can read their input from a command line. Example 5.23 shows how this can be done. It presents a template that should be used whenever a program reads data from a file whose name is specified on a command line. It is only a slight modification of the program of example 3.6.

Example 5.23

```
#include <stdio.h>

main(int argc, char *argv[])
{
  FILE *fp;
  int c;

  if (argc == 1) /* no file name on the command line*/
    {
    puts("Error - not enough arguments");
    exit(1);  /* exit with an error code          */
    }
```

```
else          /* file name was present on command line*/
  {
  fp= fopen(argv[1],"r");
  while ((c = getc(fp) ) != EOF)
    printf("%c",c);
  fclose(fp);
  }
}
```

Notice the way that the command-ine argument is passed to the function fopen( ). The name of the file is read from the second command-line argument. This argument is then passed to fopen and the correct file is opened for reading. If the name of the executable file is program1, then the command line

```
program1 file_name
```

allows the data to be read in from the input file named "file_name."

This code provides a useful template for reading input data from files. Equally as important is the defensive programming included in the check of the number of arguments. Without the check and smooth exit when the argument count is 1, that is, when the only argument on the command line is the name of the executable file, the program would crash with a core dump. This defensive programming technique is typical of programs that use command-line arguments.

Note: We could have used putc( ) instead of the printf( ) function to display the output.

For more information about reading from files, read Chapter 11.

5.8 Recursion Removal (Optional)

We now show another use of stacks. In example 5.24, we show the program that we wrote in Chapter 4 to find the factorial of a positive integer using recursion. It is presented here to show the use of a stack to hold objects of the same type that we will use in the following two examples.

Example 5.24

```
#include <stdio.h>

/* recursive factorial program */
int fact(int i);
```

```
main(void)
{
  int i;

  printf("Please enter a positive integer\n");
  scanf("%d",&i);
  printf("The factorial of %d is %d\n",i,fact(i)) ;
}

int fact(int i)
{
  if (i == 1)
    return 1;
  else
    return (i* fact(i-1));
}
```

The next example (example 5.25) demonstrates the use of a stack to simulate the action of recursive function calls. There is an algorithm for formally removing recursion from a program; one version of this algorithm is presented in [Horowitz and Sanhi, 1976]. We present the result of using their algorithm here. (The lowercase Roman numerals in the comments refer to the rules in Horowitz and Sanhi; you may ignore them if you wish.) The push( ) and pop( ) functions are similar to those used before and are omitted here.

Example 5.25

```
#include <stdio.h>

/* program developed by a recursion removal algorithm */
int fact(int i);

main(void)
{
  int i;

  printf("Please enter a positive integer\n");
  scanf("%d",&i);
  printf("The factorial of %d is %d\n",i,fact(i)) ;
}


/* ---------------------------------------*/
/* recursion removed from fact------------*/
/* ---------------------------------------*/
```

```
int fact(int n)
{
  int top, address;
  int stack[30], dummy_fact;                    /* i */

  top = 0;
  dummy_fact = 1;

  L1 :  if (n == 1)                             /* ii */
    if (top == 0)
      return(1);
    else
      {
      n = pop();            /* pop n off stack  xi */
      push( n * dummy_fact);/* push n*fact(n-1) xii */
      goto L2;
      }
    else                          /* n is not  1 */
      {
      push(n);                    /* iii */
      push(2);                    /* iv */
      --n;                        /*  v */
      goto L1;                    /* vi */
      L2:    dummy_fact = pop();  /* dummy_fact= n! vii */
      }

if (top == 0)
  return(dummy_fact);
  else
    {
    address = pop();            /* pop address   x */
    n = pop();                  /* pop n off stack  xi */
    push( n * dummy_fact);      /* push n*fact(n-1)  xii */
    goto L2;                    /* xiii   */
    }
} /* end fact */
```

This is an example of a poorly written function. It is difficult to follow because of the numerous goto statements that alter the flow of control. (This is the only program in this book that uses the goto statement and labels such as L1 and L2.) The comments refer to the steps in the recursion removal algorithm presented in Horowitz and Sanhi. As they point out, the algorithm frequently produces poor code. A slightly better version of the code is obtained if we simplify the function fact to have the form in the next example. (See Horowitz and Sanhi for some suggestions for how to improve the code obtained by using their algorithm for removing recursion from a program.)

Input: The input parsing routines should be able to interpret requests to print the contents of either memory or the disk. An input of 'p' means that the simulated memory is to be printed while an input of 'P' means that the disk is to be printed.

Data Movement: Movement from memory to disk and from disk to memory is determined by specifying the track index and sector index on the disk and the memory block index in memory for each block. The track index is in the range 0..NUM_TRACKS – 1. The sector index is in the range 0.. NUM_SECTORS – 1. The memory block index is in the range 0..NUM_MEM_BLOCKS – 1.

Note that there is a lot of leeway in the specifications given so far for this project. All of the lower-level decisions such as how the disk and memory are to be organized, how to error check, or how to implement the parsing of input are left to be determined during the design of the system.

5.10 Software Engineering Project: The Next Prototype

The design involves decisions about the following functions:

```
disk_to_mem(int mem_loc,int track, int sector)
```

Parameters are of type int. The first parameter represents a memory location in the range 0..NUM_MEM_BLOCKS – 1. The second parameter represents a track number in the range 0..NUM_TRACKS – 1, and the third parameter represents a sector number in the range 0..NUM_SECTORS – 1. This function will move a block of data that is specified by a track and a sector number to a memory location specified by the parameter mem_loc.

```
mem_to_disk(int mem_loc, int track, int sector)
```

Parameters are of type int. The first parameter represents a memory location in the range 0..MEMSIZE – 1. The second parameter represents a track number in the range 0..NUM_TRACKS – 1, and the third parameter represents a sector number in the range 0..NUM_SECTORS – 1. This function will move a block of data that is specified by a memory location to a disk block that is specified by a track number and a sector number.

```
print_disk(void)
```

Prints the contents of the array simulating the disk. Details are given later.

```
print_mem(void)
```

Prints the contents of the array simulating memory. Details are given later.

We have several choices here depending on the organization of the disk and memory. One solution is to have one-dimensional arrays for both the simulated memory and the simulated disk. The corresponding declarations are

```
MEMSIZE = NUM_MEM_BLOCKS * BLOCKSIZE;
DISK_SIZE = NUM_TRACKS * NUM_SECTORS * BLOCKSIZE ;
int data
int track , sector;  /* track and sector parameters */
int mem[MEMSIZE];    /* a one- dimensional array */
int disk[DISK_SIZE];
int mem_loc;
```

If we use this organization, then we will have to impose the disk and memory structures upon the program commands as they execute. This organization does not support the availability of high-level structures in the C language.

If we wish to preserve the block structure, one alternative is to design the disk as a two-dimensional array and to require that the memory organization should be in the form of a one dimensional array.

```
int data
int track , sector; /* track and sector parameters */
int mem[MEMSIZE];       /* a one-dimensional array */
int disk[NUM_TRACKS][NUM_SECTORS];
int mem_loc;
```

This causes us one problem – the disk is wrong! We don't have any way of indicating the contents of a block. Life is easier in a language such as Pascal in which we could declare the type of element on the disk to be a block of data. We will be able to do a somewhat similar thing later when we learn about structures and typedef construction in Part II of this text. For now, we can't use this organization.

If we use a three-dimensional array for the disk, then we will be able to access every disk element directly. Clearly we should use a similar arrangement for the organization of memory, so we could have memory declared as a two-dimensional array. In this organization, the structure of a block of data is relatively unimportant, since it has been incorporated into the disk itself. This is the organization that we will use for this project.

```
int data
int track, sector; /* track and sector parameters */
int mem[NUM_MEM_BLOCKS][BLOCKSIZE];
int disk[NUM_TRACKS][NUM_SECTORS][BLOCKSIZE]
int mem_loc;
```

What are the ramifications for the rest of the design? If we consider the disk as a three-dimensional array, then we can use the first two parameters to act as identifiers of blocks and use the third dimension as a counter for indexing the elements in the block. The simulated memory can be handled in a similar manner using the first parameter to identify the block and the second one to act as an index of the block elements. Because of the modular way that the program has been written, no changes need to be made to the main program or to the functions get_data( ) or opening_message( ).

The functions print_mem() and print_disk() are the easiest to implement, so we consider them first. They require no parameters, and the disk and memory organizations make them easy to design. In fact, the coding of these two functions is so simple that we can do it right now. To conserve space, we have not repeated the documentation of these two functions since it has not changed from Chapter 4.

The original functions were stubbed in and looked like

```
print_mem(void)
{
  printf("In print_mem\n");
}


print_disk(void)
{
  printf("In print_disk\n");
}
```

The printf( ) statements can be removed, and the simple loops to allow us to print the contents can be inserted easily.

```
print_mem(void)
{
  int i, j;

  for(i=0; i < NUM_MEM_BLOCKS; i++)
    {
    for (j = 0; j < BLOCKSIZE; j++)
      printf("%d",mem[i][j]);
    printf("\n");
    }
}

print_disk(void)
{
  int i, j, k;

  for(i=0; i < NUM_TRACKS; i++)
    {
    for (j = 0; j < NUM_SECTORS; j++)
      {
      for (k = 0; k < BLOCKSIZE; k++)
        printf("%d",mem[i][j][k]);
      printf("\n");
      }
    printf("\n");
    }
}
```

This is somewhat minimal in that there is no appropriate heading for the output. This might be marginally acceptable for a system in which the output is written to a file, but it is not at all appropriate for an interactive system. The formatting of output should be done at a later stage since it is not yet critical to the design. We will not consider it at this time.

It is now time to look more closely at the structure of memory and the disk. We have a situation something like that shown in Figure 5.4, assuming a value of 10 for BLOCKSIZE and that the value of NUM_MEM_BLOCKS is at least 9.

An element in memory is then found by directly specifying the block_number and the offset from the start of the block. For example, if the value of BLOCKSIZE is 10 and the value of NUM_MEM_BLOCKS is 10, then the last element in memory can be found by specifying a value of 9 for the block_number and a value of 9 for the offset. The next-to-last element has a block_number of 9 but an offset of 8, and so on.

We can relate the value of the variable mem_loc that we have previously used to the values of the block_number and offset by the formulas

```
mem_loc = block_number * BLOCKSIZE ;
block_number = mem_loc / BLOCKSIZE;
offset = mem_loc % BLOCKSIZE;
```

Note that the values of MEMSIZE or NUM_MEM_BLOCKS do not figure into these formulas. Note also that the location of a particular memory element is found by adding the offset of the element from the starting position in the block to the value of mem_loc.

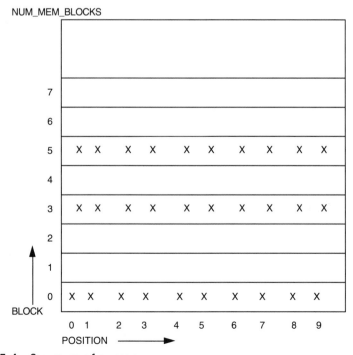

Figure 5.4 Structure of memory

What about the three remaining functions, put_in_memory( ), mem_to_disk( ), and disk_to_mem( )? In each case, we need to make a decision about where the block of data should be placed. There are several ways of doing this.

Consider the problem of placing a block of data into memory. We need to be able to find an available place for the insertion of a new block. There are two situations that we need to consider: one or more blocks available or nothing available.

If one or more memory blocks are available, then we have a situation something like that of Figure 5.5. In Figure 5.5, an upper case X indicates that the memory location is already in use while a blank space means that the space is available for insertion of data. Recall that we are assuming that data is transferred in blocks and not as individual memory locations.

There are three commonly used methods of inserting blocks into memory; they are known as "first fit," "best fit," and "worst fit." In the first-fit method, we start at the beginning of memory and ask for the first available block that is large enough for the data to be inserted. In the best-fit method, we look at all available spaces and insert our data into the one with the closest fit so that as little room as possible is wasted. In the worst-fit method, we again look at all the available spaces and choose the one that still has the largest excess space; this is done with the idea of keeping large contiguous spaces intact. All of the methods have advantages and disadvantages depending on the timing and

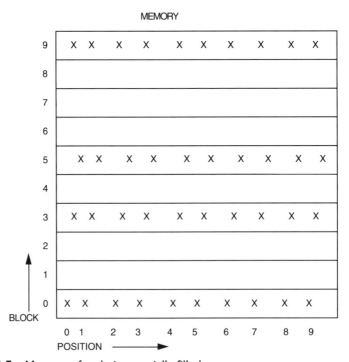

Figure 5.5 Memory after being partially filled

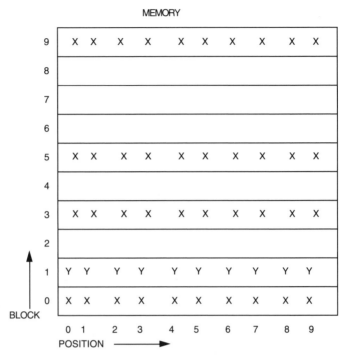

Figure 5.6 Results of the first-fit method

nature of requests for memory space. The results of using these three methods on the insertion of data of the form

Y Y Y Y Y Y Y Y Y

into the memory configuration that was previously displayed in Figure 5.5 are shown in Figures 5.6, 5.7, and 5.8.

Since the specifications did not address the nature of the memory placement method, we are free to choose the first-fit method since it is the simplest to code. Our documentation will therefore include this method. Since the terms first-fit, best-fit, and worst-fit are commonly understood by computer professionals, we will simply use the term first fit in our documentation.

We still have to consider the disk. We will use the same method of first fit to find available blocks, but with a slight difference. We will choose to fill up the disk by filling up all blocks on the first track, then all blocks on the second track, etc. On each track, we will fill up the sectors in increasing numerical order. This is the first-fit method applied to both the tracks and sectors, in order.

This takes care of the situation when there is room in memory for the storage of the desired data. If there is not room, then we have three choices. We can terminate the program with an appropriate error action. We can continue the program execution by swapping the block of data from memory to the disk and thus free up the memory block. The

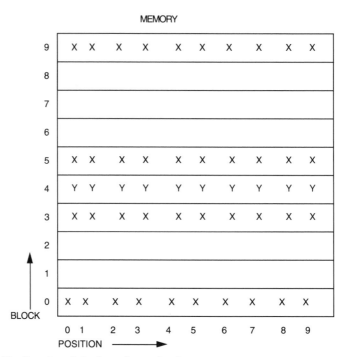

MEMORY

Figure 5.7 Results of the best-fit method

third option is unacceptable: we continue execution of the program in an error state. Options 1 and 2 are used in many computer systems. We will arbitrarily choose the second option if memory is full; that is, we write a memory block of data onto the disk.

A similar problem occurs when the disk is full. In this case, we have no place to put extra data and so we select the first strategy of terminating execution of our program with an appropriate error action.

Everything looks fine from the point of view of how to access blocks of data on the simulated disk or simulated memory. However, there are some things that we have overlooked. For example, we need to have some mechanism of determining if a block of space in memory or on the disk is available. We have to store such information somewhere and access it somehow. Finally, we have to know the state of the simulated disk and memory initially; that is, we have to initialize the system.

Real operating systems store information on what space is available in memory in what is historically called a free list or free vector. We will use an array to store the information for memory; this array will contain as many entries as there are blocks in memory, NUM_MEM_BLOCKS. Recall that the dimension of the simulated memory is MEMSIZE, which is the product of NUM_MEM_BLOCKS and MEMSIZE. Similarly, the availability of blocks on the disk is kept in a two-dimensional array. Thus we need the two new data declarations

```
int free_mem_list[NUM_MEM_BLOCKS];
int free_disk_list[NUM_TRACKS][NUM_SECTORS];
```

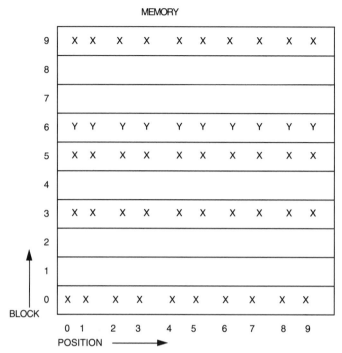

Figure 5.8   Results of the worst-fit method

in order to keep a record of the available blocks. If a block is available, then we should have a 0 in the corresponding "list"; if the block is in use, then we should have something else such as a 1 in the appropriate place.

We now know enough to do the design. We will follow the general principle of using a function to encapsulate an action that is repeated. The two functions put_in_memory( ) and disk_to_mem( ) require us to find an available memory block. Therefore we will define a new function find_mem_block( ). This function uses the first fit algorithm for obtaining a free block. We have to check the array called free_mem_list. The algorithm seems simple:

```
mem_block_number = 0
do
    {
    test free_mem_list[mem_block_number]
    mem_block_number ++
    }
while free_mem_list[mem_block_number] != 0
```

This works perfectly if there is a free block. If none is available, then we would continue searching until we exceed the amount of memory allotted to our running program. The correct algorithm tests for failure also:

```
mem_block_number = 0
do
   {
   test free_mem_list[mem_block_number]
   mem_block_number ++
   }
while (free_mem_list[mem_block_number] != 0) &&
                 (mem_block_number < NUM_MEM_BLOCKS);

if (mem_block_number == NUM_MEM_BLOCKS)
   printf("Error - no available memory blocks\n");
```

We will need to perform a similar search for free blocks on the disk. For the disk, the algorithm is

```
track_number = 0;
sector_number = 0;
do
   /* search each track, one sector at a time */
   do
      {
      /* search a complete track */
      test free_disk_list[track_number][sector_number];
            sector_number] ++;
      }
   while ( free_disk_list[track_number][sector_number] != 0 )
         && (sector_number < NUM_SECTORS);

   track_number ++;
   sector_number = 0;

while (free_disk_list[track_number][sector_number] != 0 ) &&
                 (track_number < NUM_TRACKS) ;

if (track_number == NUM_TRACKS)
   printf("Error - no available disk blocks\n");
```

It is time to take stock of our progress. We have designed a fairly elaborate system for moving data blocks to and from memory. Let us suppose that we have actually coded the program to carry out the algorithms and data structures in the design. How do we know that our software is correct? We have already seen algorithms that had some obvious omissions. Even the simple first-fit algorithm that was first given in this session had an error of omitting a test for the simulated computer memory having no free memory blocks.

In the language of the waterfall model of the software life cycle, the software is now in the testing and integration phase. Since we are following the rapid prototyping model of the software life cycle, we are simply continuing the process of testing, evaluating, and rewriting a prototype software system. In each model, we are faced with the same problem: how do we know that our software works? There are two common approaches to this problem: the *white box* and *black box* methods.

In the black box method, the code for various functions is tested by trying a set of inputs that are intended to produce expected results. The inputs and the expected outputs are determined by reading the specifications of the functions, but not by reading the code. This is frequently done by someone other than the programmer. This method requires knowing the results expected to be computed by every function. This is probably best done after the code has passed all the white box tests.

White box testing requires careful reading of the code. This method is based on the observations that many of the errors in software are caused by not testing all possible cases in selection statements or by being off by one in the indexing of either an array or a loop. The method requires that each branch of a switch or if-else statement be tested. While this does not guarantee that each possible program path will be executed, it does ensure that essential test comparisons will be made. Thus each input will be tested in the functions that get input or send information to and from the disk. The simulated memory and disk will be tested for inputs both when they have room and when they don't.

It is important to note that we really cannot do exhaustive testing of any major software project because of the complexity of the system. For example, there are NUM_MEM_BLOCKS possible memory blocks. The number of possible combinations of memory block availability includes

1 case of no blocks available,

NUM_MEM_BLOCKS cases of exactly one block available,

NUM_MEM_BLOCKS * (NUM_MEM_BLOCKS – 1) / 2 cases of exactly two blocks,

and so on for a total of 2 raised to the power NUM_MEM_BLOCKS possible groupings of memory alone. The number of possible disk block combinations is exponential in the number NUM_TRACKS + NUM_SECTORS, and the total number of combinations to be tested is astronomical. It is quite common to have systems that are so complex that complete testing would require centuries.

Summary of Chapter 5

The C language has very strong support for the array data structure, which allows elements of the same type to be combined into a larger structure. Arrays in C may be comprised of elements of any data type.

Array elements may be accessed by using the name of the array (and thus its starting location in memory) and the index of the element. In C, array indices start from 0. Arrays in C may be initialized as an aggregate or by using assignment statements for the entries of the array. All arrays, whether static, external, or automatic, may be initialized.

Character arrays in C may be treated in two ways. One method is to consider only arrays of the same size and to pad any shorter representation by padding with blanks. Another method is to terminate the character string by a special null byte that contains the escape sequence \0. Using this special byte terminates the array.

is a constant whose value is 80. A line is defined as a sequence of characters that is either ended by a newline character or is MAXLINE characters long. If the input has a sequence of more than MAXLINE characters without a new-line character, then this sequence is to have a new-line character placed within the output sequence and the rest of the sequence is to continue from the place after the insertion.

8. Write two C functions called bin_to_dec( ) and dec_to_bin( ) that will convert binary (base 2) integers to decimal (base 10) and vice versa. The input to the function bin_to_dec( ) is to be an array of characters, each of which is either 0 or 1. The array of characters might be something like

```
0101011
```

and this is to be interpreted as a binary number. The value returned by the function bin_to_dec( ) should be of type int. For the function dec_to_bin( ), the input and output types should be reversed. Test these functions by creating an appropriate main program.

9. Write a C program that will read in pairs of integers and add them. The input will be integers that are entered in the binary format. This should be done somewhat differently from the previous problem. In this problem, the input will be in the form

```
char first[], second[];
```

and first and second will be arrays of characters with each entry in the array being either 0 or 1. Assume that the input can fit on one line and hence the maximum size of the input arrays is 80. The addition will be done in binary format and you will have to write the actual routines to add $0 + 0$, $0 + 1$, $1 + 0$, and $1 + 1$, placing the results of each addition in the appropriate position and carrying any excess to the next position. Your program should be iterative; that is, it should not use recursion.

The output of this addition should be a variable named sum that is also a representation of a number in binary form. That is, the result will be in the form

```
char sum[]
```

The output array can hold up to 81 entries because of the carry; be sure to allocate enough room.

10. Perform the same task as in exercise 9, except that your program should use recursion.

11. Perform the same task as in exercise 9, except that your program should multiply the two inputs.

12. Perform the same task as in exercise 10, except that your program should multiply the two inputs.

13. Write a function called stringlength. This function will have as input parameter an array of characters terminated by a '\0' and will return an integer that represents the length of the string.

14. Write a function called stringcopy. This function will have as input parameters two arrays of characters, each of which is terminated by a '\0'. It will copy the entire contents of the second string into the first string and will work regardless of the lengths of the two input strings. This function has no return value.

15. Write a function called stringcompare. This function will have as input parameters two arrays of characters, each of which is terminated by a '\0'. It will return the value 0 if the two strings are identical (identical lengths and contents), 1 if the first is less than the second (using the numerical encoding of the character set), and −1 if the second is less than the first.

16. This exercise involves writing a C program that emulates the behavior of a classic program in the artificial intelligence community, the Eliza program that was designed by Jerome Weitzenbaum at MIT. The program was intended to act like a "nondirectional analyst" who never answered a question but responded instead with a new question related to the patient's last response. A sample session might go something like this:

Analyst: How are you feeling?
Patient: I am tired today.
Analyst: Has anything happened recently to make you tired?
Patient: No. Do you think I look tired?
Analyst: Why do you think you look tired?
Patient: I have looked tired since childhood.
Analyst: Tell me about your childhood.
Patient: I had a happy childhood.
Analyst: Really? Why are you so unhappy now?

The original program simply used string matching techniques to look for patterns in the input. Write a simple program to do something similar. Your program should parse the input into separate words and look for the appearance of one or more key words in the patient's description. To limit the size of the program, limit the patient to 100 responses and match from a list of 20 key words that you choose. Use a binary search on the key words.

17. Write a C program to implement a cross-reference tool. The input will be a C program that does not use structured data types. The output will be a listing in alphabetical order of the identifiers in the program and the lines that they appear on. Each appearance of an identifier is to be counted. For example, an input file such as

```
main()
{int j, i;
i ++;
i=i; j = i;
}
```

will have output similar to

```
IDENTIFIER    LINE
     i        2,3,4,4,4
     j        2,4
```

18. Write a C program that will change an arbitrary switch_statement with all its options into a collection of if-else or else-if statements.

19. Write two C functions ftoa( ) and atof( ). The first function, ftoa( ), has as input a floating point number and will produce an ASCII string that is identical in appearance to the original input number. The function atof( ) changes an ASCII string to an equivalent floating point number.

20. Write a C function that will compute the powers of 2 from 0 to 100. The function should perform its arithmetic on strings of characters instead of on integers since raising 2 to the larger powers will exceed the size that is allotted for integer arithmetic on most computers.

21. Write an algorithm that efficiently computes the sine of an angle. The input to this function is an angle that is to be given in degrees. The computation is to be done as follows:

- The angle is to be converted to an angle in the range 0.. 359 that has the same sine as the given angle. Be sure to allow for the possibility that an input angle might be negative.
- The converted angle is to be converted again to an equivalent angle in the range 0..90 where the sine of the new and old angles may differ but the absolute values are identical.
- The new angle has its sine determined by looking at the values of the sines of the angles from 0 degrees to 90 degrees.
- These angles between 0 and 90 degrees have had their sines computed and entered into a table. You are to create this table at the beginning of the program.

Perform an experiment to test the speed of your function as compared to the standard function sin( ) in the standard C math library.

22. Repeat the previous problem for a function called cosine.

23. The functions might be sped up somewhat by reducing the size of the arrays of sines and cosines of angles from the range 0..90 to the range 0..45 by using the trigonometric identity

$$sin(A) = cos(90 - A)$$

Before coding, indicate if this is likely to be of any use.

24. Implement a collection of functions to operate on queues. Recall that a queue follows the principle of first in – first out. Implement your queue data structure as an array of MAXQUEUE number of ints, where MAXQUEUE is (temporarily) initialized to 100. Write functions to insert into the queue, delete from the queue, and test for the queue being empty. Use two variables named "front" and "rear" to access the front and rear of the queue, respectively. Recall that we insert at the rear of the queue and delete from the front of the queue.

Software Engineering Exercise

25. Complete the coding of each of the functions indicated in the discussion of our software engineering project. Test each of these functions. After you have tested each of these functions separately, test the entire system.

CHAPTER 6

Summary of Part I

6.1 A Case Study

My first experience programming in the C language was at a large federal installation. My task was to develop a prototype graphics interface display using a commercially available windowing system. This was before the Apple Macintosh, X Windows, Microsoft Windows, GEM desktop manager, and other graphics interface systems were popular. Hence there were no standards to guide the applications software development process. There were several conflicting standards for graphics development and there were some doubts about the feasibility of using personal computers to replace expensive graphics terminals.

The objective of the project was to demonstrate the feasibility of using personal computers as display devices. The code for the project was approximately 5,000 lines long and consisted primarily of loops to display multiple copies of similar data. It made many calls to existing graphics functions to control the window display and to represent certain two- and three-dimensional objects as was necessary. The program was developed on a personal computer using none of the UNIX or other computer software development tools that assist in program development. There were no debugging tools available. The compiler was primitive by modern standards in terms of compilation speed.

This program used only the C constructions that have been presented in Part I. I avoided some of the problems with arrays that we saw in Chapter 5 by making sure that I always used exactly the correct number of array elements each time that I needed them for calling a subroutine. In order to use the mouse on this system, it was usually necessary to check the bits that were generated by the pressing of the mouse buttons. This set

Exercises

1. Look at the 10 most recent programs you have written in languages other than C. Evaluate how well each of these programs adheres to the principles of software engineering.

2. Look at the 10 most recent programs you have written in languages other than C. Evaluate each of them to determine what percentage of the code could have been written using the C constructions that we have studied so far in this text.

3. Write an essay describing how three computer languages that you are familiar with support the principles of software engineering.

4. Write an essay comparing the methods that three computer languages that you are familiar with use for passing variables to and from subprograms. Be sure to discuss the advantages and disadvantages of each method.

5. Study a copy of the report of the ANSI standards committee's report on the ANSI version of the C language. Write a set of predictions about any problems that this new standard is likely to cause with regard to the large amount of existing C code written in Kernighan and Ritchie or other dialects of C.

Part II

CHAPTER 7

Advanced Program Structure

In this chapter, we consider some features of the C programming language that encourage good software engineering practice. Goals of software engineering include having correct, easily modified programs that can be produced ahead of schedule and with reasonable cost. The most common model of the software development cycle is the "waterfall model" in which the software life cycle is divided into the five phases of specification, design, code, testing and integration, and maintenance. The interaction among the five phases in the waterfall model is shown in Figure 7.1.

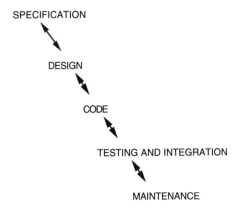

Figure 7.1 Interaction among the phases of the waterfall model

In this model, any changes in any one stage of the software life cycle can only affect the previous stage and the remaining stages. There have been many analyses of the costs attributed to the individual stages of the life cycle; they indicate that important software written with the expectation of a long lifetime has 50% or more of the total cost in the maintenance stage.

Note that this waterfall model is different from the rapid prototyping model that we have used in the discussion of our major software engineering project. The waterfall model assumes that the system can be well specified long before the coding phase begins.

Software engineering is the application of engineering methodology to the software development process. The basic principles of software engineering are listed in Figure 7.2.

Items 1, 5, and 6 are major topics in a course in software engineering. They often use techniques such as formal walkthroughs of the specifications and code. For more details, see the references or any standard text on software engineering.

Note that these principles of software engineering are independent of the model that is used for software development; both the waterfall model and the rapid prototyping model, as well as other popular models, have these same principles.

Previously, we briefly discussed documentation of code and some of the requirements of good coding style. Most companies have an accepted style that all programmers are supposed to use. You will learn the required style of the company by looking at a company style manual and by examining samples of code written by employees.

This chapter will focus on items 2 and 3 since these concepts are reasonably well supported by the C programming language.

1. Understand the specifications of the problem.

2. Write the code in modular form, using few global variables and minimizing side effects.

3. Whenever possible, reuse code that has been previously written and well tested.

4. Properly document the code.

5. Require all programmers working on a project to use the same software development methodology, style, and notation so that they may communicate.

6. Use a formal mechanism for testing software.

Figure 7.2   The basic principles of software engineering

7.1 Separate Compilation

Separate compilation means that the program may consist of several C source code files. The idea is to group those functions and declarations that either use the same data type or perform similar operations together into a single file. This file can then be used in other programs.

For example, suppose that we have written a C program that uses two functions called push( ) and pop( ) to manipulate a stack of integers. We wrote such functions in chapter 5 when we used them as part of a program to emulate a desk calculator. Suppose that we now want to use these same two functions to manipulate a stack of integers that is to be used in a program to simulate the availability of memory addresses. There are several possible ways to organize this new program.

If all the original C source code was contained in one source file, then we could decide that it would be easier to retype the two functions push( ) and pop( ) as part of the source code file of the new program. This does not require us to learn anything new about C and is therefore an appealing method to some beginning programmers, especially those who are poor typists. This is clearly a waste of resources and provides an opportunity for errors to be included in the copied functions even though they were not present in the original version.

We could also decide to recopy the required code from the original by making a copy of the original code onto a new file whose name indicates the use to which the new program will be put. We then can edit the new file and delete all the code that is not relevant to the functions that we wish to copy. This is better than the first method in that we are less likely to have typographical errors. However, we are wasting a large amount of disk space in storing several copies of the same code. It is also possible that not all of the code to be reused is located in the same place in the file so that not all of the portions of the code will be present in the newly edited file.

The first two methods for reusing code require the programmer to know precisely which functions are in which files. This can only be determined by a reading of the code, at least at the level of reading the documentation of the program. A better method is to design the code in advance to be sufficiently modular so that it can easily be incorporated into programs as needed. This is the way that the C libraries for input/output, mathematical computations, and graphics are organized. As an example of how a file can be broken up, consider the following simple situation.

The program in example 7.1 is written as if it were contained in a single file. In example 7.2, the program in example 7.1 is reformed into two separate files. The two programs are identical in function; only their physical format has been changed by separating the program into two files. Notice the way that we have included the function prototypes for all the functions in file1.c, since all of the functions are either defined or called by other functions in this file.

Example 7.1 A sample program in a single file

```
void do_input_stuff(void);
void do_analysis_1(int i);
void do_analysis_2(void);
void do_output_stuff(void);

main(void)
{
  int i = 1;

  do_input_stuff();
  do_analysis_1(i);
  do_analysis_2();
  do_output_stuff();
}

void do_input_stuff(void)
{--- lots of code ---}

void do_analysis_1(int i)
{--- lots of code ---}

void do_analysis_2(void)
{--- lots of code ---}

void do_output_stuff(void)
{--- lots of code ---}
```

We will not follow our coding conventions for indentation of blocks of code and bodies of functions in the examples that show files side by side in order to indicate program decomposition into separate files.

Example 7.2 The program of example 7.1 broken into two files

```
FILE1.c                          FILE2.c

void do_input_stuff(void);
void do_analysis_1(int i);       void do_analysis_1(int);
void do_analysis_2(void);        void do_analysis_2(void);
void do_output_stuff(void);

main(void)
{
int i = 1;                       void do_analysis_1(int i)
do_input_stuff();                {--- lots of code --}
```

```
do_analysis_1(i);
do_analysis_2();
do_output_stuff();                      void do_analysis_2()
}                                       {--- lots of code --}

void do_input_stuff(void)
{--- lots of code ---}

void do_output_stuff(void)
{--- lots of code --- }
```

Notice that in example 7.2 the only function prototypes that we have placed in the file file2.c are those of the functions that are actually used in that file. This seems to make the program slightly easier to understand than having a long list of function prototypes at the beginning of a source code file when many of the functions are not actually used in the particular file. No harm would have been done if we had included all the function prototypes in the beginning of both files.

You may have noticed that there is another way to treat the function prototypes when the program of example 7.1 is separated into multiple files. We can group all the appropriate function prototypes into a file that consists only of function prototypes and then include this in each source code file using the C preprocessor. This has the advantage of reducing the amount of typing necessary and also often reduces the potential confusion about precisely which functions are included in a file, since this information is somewhat hidden. The program now contains three files: file1.c, file2.c, and a header file that we have named prototype.h. This is an easy solution that works quite well in simple examples like this one. We will consider more complex organization of function prototypes later in this chapter.

The new code is shown in example 7.3. Note the use of the double quotes around the name of the include file prototype.h to indicate that it is a user-defined file and should be searched for in the same directory as the rest of the source code.

Example 7.3 The program of example 7.1 with an include file for function prototypes

INCLUDE FILE prototype.h

```
void do_input_stuff(void);
void do_analysis_1(int i);
void do_analysis_2(void);
void do_output_stuff(void);
```

```
FILE1.c                             FILE2.c

#include "prototype.h"               #include "prototype.h"
main(void)
{
int i = 1;                          void do_analysis_1(int i)
```

```
do_input_stuff();              {--- lots of code --}
do_analysis_1(i);
do_analysis_2();
do_output_stuff();             void do_analysis_2()
}                              {--- lots of code --}

void do_input_stuff(void)
{--- lots of code --}

void do_output_stuff(void)
{--- lots of code --}
```

In any event, an easy way to compile the two files together into a single executable file is either to type

```
cc file1.c file2.c
```

which compiles the two source code files into two object files and then links them together into a single executable file, or by compiling file1.c first, creating its object file, and forming the executable file by compiling file2.c and then linking to the object file file1.o as in

```
cc -c file1.c
cc file2.c file1.o
```

This works for the standard C compiler on many computer systems running UNIX; the compiler on your computer system may be slightly different. Experiment – try this for the simple example 7.2 and notice the messages that appear on the screen as the compiler compiles each source code file. The executable code works in precisely the same way as when the functions were included in the same file. This works perfectly and easily for any program that follows the format of the decomposition of example 7.2 in which either all the communication between functions is by means of parameters or else no communication between functions is present at all. There are several difficulties that occur when there are variables that must be accessed but these variables are not used as parameters; we will discuss these difficulties in section 7.4.

7.2 The make Utility

In the previous section, we discussed how to break up a C source code file into several files. What happens when there are a number of files in your program and you keep making changes to one of the files? As you saw when trying example 7.2, each of the source code files was recompiled and then the two files were linked together. This seems like a waste of time. What we want is some intelligence in the compiler to be able to recognize that the only files that need to be recompiled are those that changed after the last linking of the compiled files was done. The make utility program is exactly what we need to do this. The make utility is a standard utility available under the UNIX operating system; it is also included with Turbo C and many C compilers for personal computers.

The make utility uses a file created by the programmer, which is generally called a makefile or Makefile, to interpret a set of instructions for the compiler. The instructions in the makefile tell the make utility that the program is to be created from a set of source code files by compiling them and linking the object files together, perhaps with certain libraries also linked together. The makefile thus tells the make utility about the dependencies of the program and the various source and object files. A call to make results in the creation of the executable file, assuming that all goes well in the compilation and linking process.

The power of make becomes apparent if there is a change in any of the source code files making up the program (or if the source code is ported to another system). In order to create a new executable file after changing one of the source files, we simply type

```
make executable_name
```

The make utility then checks the time stamps on the source code files and the executable file whose name is specified in the makefile. If any source code file has a time stamp later than that of the executable file, or if the executable file does not exist, then the only source code files compiled and linked again are those that are necessary for the system. Unchanged source code files (those with a time stamp earlier than the executable file) are not recompiled; only their object files are relinked. This can be a great time saver and can also save a lot of typing.

The syntax of the make utility is slightly unusual and is different on different systems. In this section, we will give some examples of makefiles from two different UNIX systems. The ideas presented here will be helpful even if your system uses a different syntax.

The first makefile is taken from an AT&T 3B2 computer running AT&T System V UNIX, version 3.2. It uses the instructions in the makefile as follows. The executable file is named complex and is obtained from the object files (the files whose names have the extension .o). The object files are created by using the corresponding C source code files (the files whose names have the extension .c).

Warning: make is very sensitive to one particular syntax: the cc command on line 2 of the makefile MUST be preceded by a tab rather than any collection of blanks.

Example 7.4 shows how the executable file complex is obtained from the three source code files called extra.c, y.tab.c, and lex.yy.c.

Example 7.4

```
complex: extra.o y.tab.o lex.yy.o
        cc extra.c y.tab.c lex.yy.c -o complex -ll
```

The make utility interprets the makefile as follows:

(1) The three C source code files on line 2 (after the tab) are compiled using the -o option of this compiler. This creates three object files, namely extra.o, y.tab.o, and lex.yy.o. Check your manual for the meaning of this or other options in your system.

(2) The three object files are then linked together with the appropriate library. In this example, the library used is the lex library which is denoted by the -ll at the end of line 2.

The strange names of the files y.tab.c and lex.yy.c were not given by me. They are the names that are produced by the UNIX utilities lex and yacc and which are used to create parts of a compiler which will be able to do arithmetic with complex numbers.

This makefile is created using any standard editor. After the makefile is created, it is used by the UNIX make utility by simply typing the command

```
make complex
```

The next example is somewhat similar. It is currently being used as part of the development of a prototype compiler for the language Ada as part of a research project. It also uses the UNIX utilities lex and yacc. Since the executable file called ada was expected to have errors and need considerable testing, the second line required compilation with the -g option and using the DEBUG action available in the lex library. Note that the format for the rest of the file is somewhat different from the format of example 7.4 in that we use the object files (with the .o extension) on line 2 and show the relation of the object files to the corresponding source files on lines 3 and 4 of the makefile. Both methods are correct; use the one that seems most sensible to you.

Example 7.5

```
ada: lex.yy.o y.tab.o
        cc -lg lex.yy.o y.tab.o -o ada -ll
lex.yy.o:        lex.yy.c
y.tab.o :        y.tab.c
```

(The files lex.yy.c and y.tab.c in this example are different from the ones used in example 7.4.)

Here is an example from a SUN 3 computer running a version of UNIX. It creates an executable file called icec using five object files and two libraries, curses (for high-level, device-independent control of the screen display) and m (for the math library). The program was 2,632 lines long. The libraries are linked in the -lcurses and -lm statements. Note that the syntax on line 2 is slightly different from the examples using the AT&T System V UNIX version of make in terms of the placement of the name of the executable file.

Example 7.6

```
icec  : main.o parse.o icecopt.o demos.o complex_ops.o
        cc -o icec main.o parse.o icecopt.o demos.o
complex_ops.o -lcurses -lm

main.o : main.c
parse.o : parse.c
icecopt.o : icecopt.c
demos.o : demos.c
complex.o :complex.c
```

Many implementations of make for C compilers running on personal computers have slightly different syntax. Check the manual for your version of make if none of the formats shown in the examples in this section seems to work.

7.3 The Use of make and Projects in Turbo C

In this section, we describe the use of the separate compilation facility in Turbo C. In keeping with our goal of avoiding machine- and compiler-specific features, we have not generally discussed special features of any implementation of C. The Turbo C separate compilation facility will be discussed here because it is somewhat different from the standard UNIX make utility and these differences make it impossible to get started using separate compilation in Turbo C.

Turbo C has a menu-driven user interface. The easiest way to get separate compilation to work in Turbo C is to create what Turbo C calls a "project." A project file has the three-character extension ".prj" and consists of the names of the C source code files that make up the system that you are creating. For example, the system developed in example 7.2 would be encoded in a project file whose contents are

```
FILE1.C
FILE2.C
```

(Recall that DOS uses upper case for filenames and does not distinguish between upper and lower case. We are using uppercase names for clarity.) The two files would be created using the Turbo C editor or another text editor.

Once the two source code files are created, the system can be created by using the call to project, followed by a call to the compilation facility available in the menu. The program can be executed by using the "run" option in the menu. Of course this can be made faster by selecting the "make" menu option.

The separate compilation system in Turbo C was efficient and was sophisticated enough to recompile only those source code files that were changed if any of the source code files in the system were edited.

The menu-driven system for separate compilation was easy to learn and could be used easily without reading the manual. There was no syntax to learn, which is a big advantage. However, you should know the principles of the make utility even if you do all your work in Turbo C or similar software development systems.

7.4 Scope Rules for Programs in Several Source Files

It should be clear that splitting a C program into several source code files can make the process of writing software easier, especially if the make utility is available. However, there are some new difficulties that arise if we write a program over several C source code files. They are all related to the scope of variables; that is the portion of the program in which these variables are visible to other functions. The scope rules are extensions of the scope rules that we saw in Chapter 4. For clarity, we repeat those rules here.

1. If the variable is defined inside a function, then its scope is that function. Static variables retain their values on successive function calls while automatic variables do not. Neither is available outside the defining function.

2. If the variable is defined outside every function, then it will be available to any function defined from that point to the end of the file.

3. If the variable is defined outside every function, then it can be made available to any function in the file by declaring the variable to be extern in the function that wishes to use it.

4. The C language does not permit a function to be defined inside another function. That is, a function cannot contain another function body within its own body of code.

Figure 7.3 Scope rules for programs consisting of a single file

There are three possibilities for the scope of variables in a C program if the program is contained in a single C source file. The rules are listed in Figure 7.3.

Since the rules consider only the relationships between variables and functions contained in a single source code file, all these rules are valid even if the program is contained in several source code files. In order to extend the rules to programs with several source code files, it is necessary to distinguish between a declaration and a definition of a variable.

There is no problem with variables that are first declared inside functions. The two functions in example 7.7 have declarations of variables named count. These two variables are completely separate and have no relation to any other variable named count regardless of where that name appears in the program. The variable flag is external to each of the functions in the file. In addition, flag is visible to every function in the file from the point where it is first defined until the end of the file. In order to make the variable flag visible to the function f( ), which appears earlier in the file, we added a statement to the body of the function f( ) which declared flag to be external to the function.

Example 7.7

```
void f(void)
{
int count;
extern char flag;

C_statements;
}

char flag;
```

```
void g(void)
{
int count = 0;

C_statements;
}
```

The statement

```
        char flag;
```

which occurred outside of every function is a definition of the variable flag. It tells the C compiler that the variable flag is of type char and that space should be allocated for it. On the other hand, the statement

```
        extern char flag;
```

appearing within the function f( ) tells the compiler to look for a definition of the variable flag elsewhere. This statement is called a declaration because it tells the compiler the properties of the variable such as its size and type. It differs from a definition in that no storage space in memory is allocated in a declaration. This distinction is important – if we always allocated space, then we would be accessing two different memory locations. If no space was ever allocated, then we would not be able to use the variable. This line of reasoning helps explain the way that C treats external variables in programs that use more than one source file.

Suppose that we wish to use a variable in several files. We must have at least a declaration of the variable indicating the type and size in each file in order to be able to use the variable properly. We must have precisely one place where the variable has had space allocated; that is, where the variable is defined. Example 7.7 shows how to use the qualifier extern to have access to variables that are outside of all functions in a file. In examples 7.8 and 7.9, we show two different methods of how to access the variable flag if the program is composed of two source files. There is a header file named header.h whose contents are shown below.

Example 7.8

```
prototype.h:

void f(void);
void g(void);
```

```
file1.c:                        file2.c:

#include "prototype.h"          #include "prototype.h"
```

```
f()                              char flag ;
{                                void toy(char a,char b)
int count;                       {
extern char flag;                char a,b ;
C_statements;                    f();
g();                             }
}

                                 main(void)
                                 {
extern char flag;                char a = 'a', b = 'b';
                                 flag ='Q';
                                 toy(a,b);
g()                              }
{
int count = 0;
C_statements;
}
```

In example 7.8, the variable flag is declared in the source code of file1.c. It is declared to be extern inside the function f( ) and declared to be a character defined in another file in the statement between the functions f( ) and g( ). The definition of the variable flag occurs at the beginning of file2.c before any function is defined so that flag is visible throughout file2.c. In example 7.9, there is only a single declaration of the variable flag in file1.c and a single definition of flag in file2.c.

The two source code files use the same header file as before.

Example 7.9

```
prototype.h:

void f(void);
void g(void);
```

```
file1.c:                         file2.c:

#include "prototype.h"           #include "prototype.h"

extern char flag;
f()                              char flag ;
{                                void toy(char a, char b)
int count;                       {
C_statements;                    char a,b ;
g();                             f();
}                                }
```

```
g()                              main(void)
{int count = 0;                  {
C_statements;                    char a = 'a', b = 'b';
}                                flag ='Q';
                                 toy(a,b);
                                 }
```

There are many other ways to arrange the definition and declaration of a variable such as flag. Experience shows that it is better to have all definitions and declarations of external variables at the beginning of the file and not to have the visibility of variables depend on the scoping rule that an external variable defined in a file is visible from the point of definition to the end of the file. If a file is to be used with several other files when being used as a component file in more than one program, then it should be as easy to read as possible. Its purpose should be relatively clear without reading all the code in the file. Thus any use of external variables in another file should be indicated at the beginning of the file.

The situation is identical if we wish to use functions that return values whose type is not int. In example 7.10 we show some code from the file math.h which is to be included in C programs that access the math library. Don't worry if you don't know all of the functions in the file; the important thing is that they use the words "extern double" in front of the names of the functions to communicate their type. Again, function prototypes are all that we need (in addition to the actual object code for the library functions when we link them to the rest of the program). Example 7.10 shows declarations of some of the functions in the math library.

Example 7.10 Some of the function prototypes in math.h

```
extern double fabs(double), floor(double), ceil(double);
extern double fmod(double), ldexp(double), frexp(double);
extern double modf(double), sqrt(double), hypot(double);
extern double sin(double), cos(double); tan(double);
extern double asin(double), acos(double),atan(double);
extern double atan2(double), exp(double), log(double);
extern double log10(double), sinh(double), cosh(double);
extern double tanh(double);
```

Recall that any program that uses these functions needs to have the statement

```
#include <math.h>
```

and must be linked to the appropriate library.

You need to be careful about the use of user-defined header files. If they only contain constants and descriptions of variable types, then they should be included in all files that need them.

One additional comment on the use of external variables and functions is in order. We can use both the words extern and static to describe a variable or function such as

```
extern static int alpha;
extern static float func(float);
```

These external and static variables and functions are known only within the source file in which they are defined and cannot be referenced in any other source file. This deliberate prevention of communication means that we can develop programs using different files and not worry about having two functions or variables causing errors because they have the same name.

7.5 Advanced Documentation and Commenting of C Programs

Documentation refers to the textual information about the program describing the design and implementation. It is usually done by a collection of comments within the code itself. Many software companies require that additional documentation be available in a separate document. In this section we describe typical documentation that might be included within the code when a single program extends over several source code files. As you might imagine, using multiple files creates extra demands on the programmer or programmers writing the software.

A programmer working as part of a programming team must be especially careful to make sure that the functions, variables, and data that he or she uses in one file do not have any unexpected effects on functions, variables, or data that are in files written by other programmers. Thus each C source file in a program requires extra documentation. In addition, the documentation of the logical structure of the program must be accompanied by a complete description of the physical structure of the program; that is, of the placement of functions into files.

I must admit to having somewhat of a hard-line attitude about the subject of documentation. I have seen too many programs that were impossible to decipher and that had strange bugs. One of the hardest bugs to find was in a program that worked perfectly on a personal computer on the second floor but would not work on the third floor. The program would not even compile, getting a message that there was not enough memory available. When I did more testing, I found that even a tiny program such as the first one in this chapter was too large to compile. The actual problem was that the computer on the third floor had a memory expansion card that was not understood by the code-generation portion of the compiler that I was using. The computer on the second floor did not. I could have isolated this problem more quickly if the documentation had included a summary of the environment in which the program was developed. The summary of the environment would include the computer, operating system, compiler, terminal type, etc., that are used in the program.

Here is a portion of a program header that includes all of this information. It includes discussion of the manner in which portions of the code that are not portable are used so that the program can be easily modified.

Example 7.11

```
/*-------------------------------------------------------*/
/*                                                       */
/*       Programmer   :         Ronald J. Leach          */
/*       Location :             Systems & Computer Science*/
/*                              School of Engineering     */
/*                              Howard University         */
/*                              Washington, D.C. 20059    */
/*       Language :             C (std C compiler)        */
/*       Operating System :     SUN UNIX v4.0.1           */
/*       Environment   :        SUN 3/60                  */
/*                         16 MB memory                   */
/*                         427 MB disk capacity           */
/*                         Open Windows v3.1              */
/*-------------------------------------------------------*/


/*-------------------------------------------------------*/
/*       The structure of the program is as follows :    */
/*                                                       */
/*                         main                          */
/*                        /  |  \                        */
/*                       /   |   \                       */
/*                      /    |    \                      */
/*                     /     |     \                     */
/*                    /      |      \                    */
/*                   /       |       \                   */
/*              demos     icecopt     parse              */
/*                                       \               */
/*                                        \              */
/*                                  complex_ops          */
/*                                                       */
/*                                                       */
/*  main.c contains the main menu, opening and           */
/*  closing messages. The main menu will be displayed    */
/*  in a panel; options are chosen by a mouse.           */
/*  All the options except for the quit option are       */
/*  linked to functions defined in other files.          */
/*-------------------------------------------------------*/
```

Every program should have this level of documentation at a minimum. To save space, this will not be given in this book. However, you should include it in all your programs. In the interest of conserving paper, we will provide only those comments necessary for understanding the programs.

Software systems that consist of multiple source code files should be placed in a directory by themselves. Many actual systems are so complex that they extend over several directories. A simple file in ASCII format that briefly describes the organization and contents of the directories is very helpful. Such a file is often called a README file.

7.6 Libraries

As we described in Chapter 6, many C software systems consist of a relatively small number of C functions written especially for the problem at hand together with a large collection of library functions. (We are using the term software system instead of the term program since we wish to be able to think about larger amounts of code than before.) The library functions used in a program can be provided with the compiler, such as the standard ANSI C libraries, as part of an applications system such as graphics libraries, user-defined libraries, or some combination of these. We have already seen examples of how to use the math library in Chapter 4 and how to incorporate the use of libraries into makefiles in some of the earlier examples in this chapter. We now briefly describe some of the issues used when developing a user-defined library.

What makes a function a good candidate for inclusion in a user's library? Generally, a function must be modular in design, be needed more than once in a variety of situations, have a simple, well-defined interface, and must be extremely well documented and tested.

The need for modular design, multiple uses for the function, and a well-defined interface is fairly clear. The other requirements are somewhat less obvious and so we discuss them in more detail.

The whole point of library software is that it is usually considered to be reliable. That is, the library functions are presumed to be carefully tested and to cause no problems in programs that use them. It is as if library functions are considered to be off-the-shelf software components that can simply be fitted into the programs that need them. These functions are subjected to far more severe testing than is typical for other functions or even programs that are used once and then thrown away.

Once one or more functions are subjected to the extensive testing necessary for library functions, they must be documented. The documentation here must be more extensive than the internal documentation of source code files. There should be some external documentation, at least at the level of one or two pages describing the specifications of the interface and action of each library file. This documentation can be stored electronically if you will be the only user of the library functions that you create. There must be additional documentation if the library functions are to be used by others. Creating a manual page can also be helpful for on-line documentation systems.

If there are only a few user-defined library functions, then they can be placed in one file, or at worst a small number of files. In more complex software systems, it may be more sensible to organize the user-defined library functions into several directories, grouped by functionality.

We generally wish to separate the source code from the compiled object code and from other related artifacts of these library functions by placing them in separate directories. The following is a reasonably effective method of organizing the various features of any user-defined library.

- Determine logical groupings of the library functions into directories. Use this logical organization consistently for storage of all aspects of library organization.
- Create appropriate header files for all function prototypes and place them into directories using the hierarchical organization as appropriate.
- Compile each of the library functions from the appropriate source code and place the resulting object files into directories using the hierarchical organization as appropriate.
- Create appropriate on-line documentation for each of the new library functions and place them into directories using the hierarchical organization as appropriate. This may be superseded by an existing standard for documentation such as that provided by the UNIX *man* utility.
- Place the source code for each of the library functions into an appropriate directory. Use only read-only permissions if possible to protect the integrity of the source code. This may not always be provided to purchasers of commercial products.

7.7 Software Engineering Project: Changed Requirements

Let's summarize the state of our project. We have completed the discussion of specifications and design for a system that can process commands that move data within a system that simulates a computer's disk and memory. We have begun to make some inroads into the coding and testing of this system. In the next chapters we will change the specifications to allow for a more elaborate data structure – the file.

A file is a collection of data that is stored somewhere. How we organize the structure of a file is up to us as long as we meet the needs of a user of the system. We won't discuss this any more at this point but will return to it in the next few chapters. For now, we just want to be flexible enough to incorporate future design changes.

We are already starting to notice some potential problems. Without even thinking about additional structure for files or other future enhancements, we have more than 250 lines of code. Since it seems to work correctly now, it doesn't make sense to keep recompiling the same code whenever we add a feature. Why not use a makefile?

The new requirement is: design the software so that it can be easily changed when new features are added. A formal requirement about the details of the amount of code placed into separately compiled files is beyond the scope of this book. However, the goal is clear. We discuss the ramifications in the next section.

7.8 Software Engineering Project: The Next Prototype

The most natural way to group the files for separate compilation is to use the functionality as a guideline. The new design calls for us to have five files named

```
main.c
print.c
disk.c
memory.c
move_data.c
```

The physical grouping of the functions has been set in the specifications. Our tasks for the project now are

- Declare/define external variables so that communication can occur.
- Create a makefile.
- Document the physical structure of the program.

The system is getting complicated enough so that the constants such as MEM_SIZE or NUM_TRACKS should be grouped together. We could choose to define them in one file and to declare them in all other files. It is a more common practice to group them into a "header file" and then include this file in all source code files. It makes the program slightly larger but makes the dependency easier to understand. I like this organization for constants.

The header file looks something like the following:

```
/*  header file for disk simulation project  */

#define NUM_MEM_BLOCKS 10
#define NUM_TRACKS 50
#define NUM_SECTORS 10
#define BLOCKSIZE 10
```

Each of the five files

```
main.c
print.c
disk.c
memory.c
move_data.c
```

will now have the statement

```
#include "header.h"
```

at the beginning. Note the use of double quotes instead of the '<' and '>' that are used for system-defined include files such as stdio.h; this is a user-defined header file.

A makefile should be created using the principles given in this chapter. It also needs some form of commenting. The standard way to do this is to include comments in the makefile. Comments in a makefile begin with a pound sign '#' in the leftmost position of a line. If the executable file for this system is called d_sim, then the makefile might look something like:

```
# makefile for disk simulation program
# the executable file is named d_sim
d_sim: main.o print.o disk.o memory.o move_data.o
        cc main.c print.c disk.c memory.c move_data.c -o d_sim
```

The system requires additional documentation that is incorporated to include a description of the physical structure. The additional documentation might look something like:

```
/*        FILE: main.c                               */
/*                                                   */
/*        File contains the main functions for a system  */
/*        to simulate a computer's memory and disk.  */
/*                                                   */
/*        This file contains the function(s)         */
/*                          .                        */
/*                        .                          */
/*                      .                            */
/*        Other files in the system are:             */
/*                      .                            */
/*                      .                            */
/*                      .                            */


/*        FILE: print.c                              */
/*                                                   */
/*        Contains functions to print contents of a  */
/*        simulated disk and memory.                 */
/*        This file contains the function(s)         */
/*                      .                            */
/*                      .                            */
/*                      .                            */
/*        The functions in this file are called by   */
/*        main() in the file main.c                  */
/*                      .                            */
/*                      .                            */
```

Note that we have added no new functionality to the system by the actions of this and the previous section. It has taken some time to perform the separation and to write the new documentation. The benefits will be clear only when the system grows considerably in size and complexity. It will.

Note also that our life could have been easier if we had known about separate compilation at the beginning of the software development process.

Summary of Chapter 7

C allows, and in fact encourages, the separation of programs into multiple source code files. The files may be compiled separately and linked later. This is a major feature of the C language and is one of the advanced ways in which C supports good software engineering practice by encouraging modularity at a higher level than just functions.

There are several software development tools available for management of separately compiled files. Among the more popular are the UNIX make utility and Turbo C's project facility. The syntax and semantics of these tools vary from system to system.

The scope rules for multiple files are an extension of the scope rules for single files, with the additional feature that external static expressions have their scope limited to the file in which they are defined and cannot be accessed, even if there is an extern declaration in another file.

Exercises

1. Consider the two files below, each of which constitutes an attempt to write a portion of a C program. The line numbers are included for your reference and are not part of the program itself.

```
        file_1.c                          file_2.c

1 int i= 1;                       static int c = 0;
2 main()
3 { int imin, imax;              do_more_stuff()
4 imax = imin;                   float a,b;
5 do_stuff(imin,imax);          char ch = 'p';
6 }                              y = still_more();
7                                }
8 int j;                         double y;
9                                still_more()
10 do_stuff(int i,int j)          {}
11 {
12 i = i + 5; j = 0;
13 do_more_stuff(i, i+j);
14 }
```

(a) Show in the program where the left brace { must be placed in the function do_stuff in file_1.c and in the function do_more_stuff in file_2.c in order to make the program compile. Also, insert the function prototypes correctly.

(b) What is the scope of the variable i on line 1 of file_1.c ?

(c) What is the scope of the variable j on line 8 of file_1.c ?

(d) What is the scope of the variable y on line 8 of file_2.c ?

(e) What is the scope of the variable a on line 4 of file_2.c ?

(f) What do we need to write in file_1.c to make the variable j visible to the two functions do_stuff and main of file_1.c? List all changes that we need to make in file_1.c.

(g) Write a makefile to compile the program in these two files into a single executable file. The executable file will be called goodies.

2. Write a C program that will perform the same computation as the program of example 1 but that will be composed of three C source code files. Write a makefile for this program.

3. Consider the calculator program that was discussed in Chapter 5 both in the text of the chapter as well as in some of the exercises. Decompose the program into three separate files. The first file is to be named stackops.c and is to contain all the functions for stack operations. The second file is to be called eval.c and is to contain all the functions necessary in order for the evaluation of the expressions. The third file is called main.c and is to have all the functions necessary for input and output of expressions and for the user interface. The file main.c also contains the main( ) function. Any global constants or data type declarations should be included in a fourth file named global.h, which is to be included in each of the other three files using the #include instruction to the C preprocessor.

4. The make utility can handle a variety of automatic programming utilities not just C programs. If you have the make utility available on your system, experiment to see how this can be used for aiding in the compilation of Pascal language or other programs.

5. The make utility can handle many problems. It can keep track of changes to different C source code files that make up a program. What happens if the C source code files depend upon a header file? Perform an experiment to see what happens in the following two situations. First situation: the make file does not have explicit mention of the include file global.h and the header file is changed without recompiling. Second situation: the make file does explicitly mention the header file.

Software Engineering Exercises

6. Separate the program into the five files that were indicated previously in this chapter. If the make facility is available, then write the makefile for the system. Include the extra documentation for the new source code files. Then compile your system (using the make command if it is available) and make sure that the system runs correctly. List the changes that you had to make in order to have separate source code files.

7. Determine an appropriate grouping of user-defined library functions for this exercise.

CHAPTER **8**

Pointers

In this chapter we will study pointers and how they are implemented and used in C. Pointers are addresses of memory locations. The subject of pointers and their implementation is introduced in section 8.1. In section 8.2, we discuss the relationship between pointers and arrays and how C integrates these concepts into a single idea. The remaining sections of the chapter discuss applications of pointers. They will be used extensively later in this book when we discuss structured data types in C. As a result of our study of pointers, we will obtain some insight into the popularity of C as a language for systems programming.

8.1 Definition of a Pointer

The term *pointer* in C means a memory address or location. The contents of the location could be any variable or constant and could be of any type whatsoever. Figure 8.1 shows a fragment of contiguous memory locations beginning at address 8000.

Pointers are of little value unless we are able to specify the contents of a memory location and how these contents are to be interpreted. We also need to be able to access any specific memory location that we have used. We will need two operations to manipulate pointers in C: the "address operator" which is denoted by '&', and the "contents operator" which is denoted by the symbol '*'.

The contents operator '*' is used to represent the actual value that is stored in a memory location. Thus if ptr is a pointer to a memory location that contains an integer variable, say 8002, then the expression *ptr refers to the contents of that location (8002 in this case) and would be used in a manner similar to

```
*ptr = 7;
```

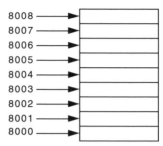

Figure 8.1 Some contiguous memory locations

or

```
int_value = *ptr;
```

In the first case, the integer 7 is stored in the memory location pointed to by the variable ptr, which is 8002 in our example. In the second case, the variable int_value is assigned as its value the contents of the location pointed to by ptr. If these two statements were executed in a C program that had allocated the right amount of storage for the pointer ptr, then the contents of the location pointed to by ptr would be 7 and the value of the variable int_value would also be 7. Sample code to do this might look like

```
int int_value, *ptr;
```

The declarations indicate to the compiler that ptr is a pointer to an int; that is, an address whose contents are to be interpreted as an integer. The compiler would reserve enough contiguous memory space starting at location 8002 for the storage of this int; the actual number of bytes reserved depends upon the compiler and the underlying hardware. For short, we say that ptr is a pointer to int. Of course, int_value is also an int.

You should recall that the function scanf( ) in Chapter 3 used the symbol '&' when reading in variables. This was our first use of the "address operator" although we did not call it that at the time. The purpose of the ampersand symbol '&' in that function was to be able to read the input data into locations in memory that were pointers to the desired variables.

The address operator '&' is essentially the inverse of the contents operator, which we denoted by '*'. For example, a statement such as

```
*ptr = int_value;
```

means that the contents of the location ptr are to be assigned the value of the expression int_value. The related statement

```
ptr = &int_value;
```

means that the value of the pointer ptr has been changed to be the address of the variable int_value. There is one exception to the use of this inverse relationship. It is incorrect to write a C statement such as

```
ptr = &7;        /* wrong !! */
```

because 7 is a constant and does not have an obvious address. In general, we cannot take the address of any constant expression. Constants have their values and locations pre-assigned by the compiler, and these locations cannot be changed by the programmer during program execution.

It is possible to apply the address and contents operators to any types of variables that can be stored in memory. Since register variables are considered by the programmer as being stored in special hardware registers, C compilers do not allow either of these operators to be applied to register variables. In fact, this is prohibited by the original Kernighan and Ritchie C language manual.

You should be aware that it is very easy to get into serious trouble using pointers since you are actually addressing memory locations. The reason for the difficulty is that the operating system and the compiler treat the memory of the computer as a linear array of objects and the fact that you expect a certain order to be imposed on this linear array is not really relevant. Programs cannot arbitrarily access memory locations that are either reserved to the operating systems for its own use, or assigned to other programs in multi-user systems. Chaos would result if we allowed indiscriminate memory access without some degree of control.

Consider the program shown in example 8.1. This program shows how the C programming language gives information that is not usually available in higher-level programming languages. We can actually see where the compiler stores information about the location of variables, as in the information provided in the output of the second and third printf( ) statements. This information is not usually important to a casual user or to an applications programmer, but would be useful to a compiler writer.

Example 8.1

```
/*  A dangerous use of a pointer.   */
/*  The pointer is uninitialized.   */

#include <stdio.h>

main(void)
{
  int *ptr ;

  printf("The value of ptr in decimal is %d\n",ptr);
  printf("The address of ptr in decimal is %d\n",&ptr);
  printf("The address of ptr in octal is %o\n",&ptr);
  printf("The contents of the address of ptr is %d\n",
         *&ptr);
}
```

Example 8.1 has the output (on one computer)

```
The value of ptr in decimal is 0
The address of ptr in decimal is 251657856
The address of ptr in octal is 1677777200
The contents of the address of ptr is 0
```

This example shows how a pointer can be misused. In the first statement of the program, a variable named ptr was declared to be a pointer to a variable of type int. The variable ptr was not defined and no value was given to it. The compiler generated a place for the variable ptr to be stored, namely in memory location 251657856 (which is 1677777200 octal). The first line of the output shows that at least in this case, we have the value 0 in the memory location 251657856. Unless we are doing systems-level programming, we are not usually interested in the actual value of the memory address but are interested in the contents of that address and in how to access these contents. In particular, trying to access arbitrary memory locations usually causes an error message from the operating system. Adding the single line

```
printf("The contents are %d\n",*ptr);
```

to the program in example 8.1 causes the error message

```
Segmentation fault (core dumped)
```

to be printed for exactly the same reason that we got this while trying to print data other than strings using the %s control specification – we were attempting access to a memory area that we shouldn't and didn't have access to.

We have already seen several situations in which pointers can cause difficulty. It is reasonable to ask why pointers are important, given these problems. We haven't seemed to need them up to this point and we have been able to perform all of the operations of a language such as FORTRAN that does not allow the use of pointers.

Pointers have two common uses. The first one is for the dynamic allocation of computer memory locations as a program runs rather than preassigning memory at compile time. This is the sense in which pointers are used in this chapter. The other common use of pointers is to access complex data structures and will be discussed later in this book. Pointers can be used as arguments to a function, thereby giving the function access to the data that is pointed to by the pointer. This is the way that experienced C programmers get around the C language only allowing the passing of arguments to functions by value.

In applications programming in which we are not concerned with the actual addresses of data, the proper use of a pointer is to use a high-level model of pointers and the objects to which the pointers point and to leave the actual calculation of memory addresses to the operating system. The high-level view of pointers is shown in Figure 8.2.

We need a method of communicating to the operating system just how large an area of memory we need for the storage of our data objects. In the memory configuration shown in Figure 8.2, storage of an object the size of object 1 is clearly possible in the available space above where object 2 is stored. However, there is not enough room for a second object that is the size of object 2 in that space, so storage of a second object the size of object 2 must take place elsewhere.

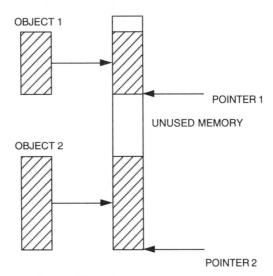

COMPUTER MEMORY

OBJECT 1

OBJECT 2

POINTER 1

UNUSED MEMORY

POINTER 2

Figure 8.2 A view of two objects in memory

One method of communicating our space needs to the operating system is to use a special C function named malloc( ). The function malloc( ) is used to allocate a space in memory for an object that is pointed to by the desired pointer. Its return type is "pointer to void." The syntax that must be used with the function malloc( ) is shown in example 8.2.

Example 8.2

```
#include <stdio.h>
#include <stdlib.h>
main(void)
{
   int *ptr ;

   ptr = (int *) malloc(sizeof(int));
   printf("The value of ptr is %d\n",ptr);
   printf("ptr is stored in address %d\n",&ptr);
   printf("The contents of ptr are %d\n",*ptr);
}
```

The output from this example is shown below; your output will probably be different since your computer will have a different memory usage.

```
The value of ptr is 142896
ptr is stored in address  251657856
The contents of ptr are 0
```

213

```
int *ptr ;

ptr = (int *) malloc(sizeof(int));
printf("The pointer is %d\n",ptr);
printf("The address of the pointer is %d\n",&ptr);
*ptr = 7;
printf("The contents of the pointer are %d\n",*ptr);
}
```

Example 8.3 has the output

```
The pointer is 142896
The address of the pointer is 251657856
The contents of the pointer are 7
```

Use this example as a template for the creation of pointers to variables of various types and for the initialization of their values.

C has other storage allocation utilities that are used less frequently than malloc( ). The most common such function is calloc( ) which is used to allocate space for the storage of arrays. Unlike memory allocation with malloc( ), initialization of the allocated space can be assumed to be performed by calloc( ). Thus a call to calloc( ) will always take longer than a loop that repeats a set of calls to malloc( ) (to allocate the same total amount of space because calloc( ) always sets the data stored in its allocated memory to 0).

A typical use of calloc( ) might be

```
int_array_ptr = calloc(NUM_ELEMENTS, sizeof(int));
```

for allocation of memory for an array of ints.

The functions malloc( ) and calloc( ) allocate memory regions that are accessed by the pointers returned by these functions. Of course there is a reverse operation. The function free( ) whose syntax is

```
free(ptr)
```

deallocates a memory region pointed to by the pointer ptr.

The structure of the region pointed to by ptr in a call to the function free( ) and the type of variable that ptr was originally declared to point to must be the same or else confusion can result. It is not clear what happens if the two do not match; different compilers treat this mismatch differently. The lint utility can be very helpful in detecting this type of typing error in your programs.

8.2 Pointers and Arrays

Pointers and arrays are closely related in C. In fact, the original Kernighan and Ritchie C language reference manual [1978] introduced these concepts in the same chapter. For clarity, we have separated the discussion of these two concepts. It is now time to consider them together. To help us to better understand how these two concepts are related, consider how an array of objects is stored in a typical procedural programming language such as C, Pascal, Ada, FORTRAN, or BASIC. The first element in the array is accessed by knowing its location in memory and the size of the object. Other elements in the array are located by locating the first element and adding an offset to the address of the first element. The offset depends upon both the index of the element and the size of an arbitrary object in the array. These quantities are related by the following formula:

```
address of element "i" in array "a" =
      of the first element in the array "a"
      + (size of an element of the array "a") * i
```

Formula 8.1

This formula is correct for languages such as C and BASIC where array index values begin at 0. In a language such as Pascal where array index values normally begin at 1, the value of i in the product on the right-hand side should be replaced by the expression i – 1. More complicated formulas are necessary if the starting index is something else, as might be the case when a subrange type is used for enumeration of array indices in a language such as Pascal.

It is essential to note that this formula holds regardless of the size of the elements in the array. That is, the formula is valid for arrays of floating point numbers, for arrays of characters, for arrays of integers, etc. The size of an element is incorporated into the formula by the compiler.

In Chapter 5, we learned how to address the element with index "i" of an array "a" by the notation a[i]. It ought to be clear that there is another way of doing this based on computing addresses – we can add an offset to the first element; that is, we can add an integer to a pointer. This second method would even be easier if the language permitted the automatic inclusion of the size of an element into the computation so that all we need to do is know the index. C provides precisely this language support.

Figure 8.3 shows the locations of the first few elements in three different arrays. Each of these arrays is assumed to have its first element in memory location 8000. The computer is assumed to store character variables in a single byte, integer variables in four bytes, and floating point variables in eight bytes.

The C compiler knows the size of each of the standard data types: int, char, long, short, unsigned, float, and double. It can also be told the size of the structured data types that we will see later in the text. The method of computing the element indexed by "i" in the array "arr" is to use the expression

```
*(arr+i)
```

which is interpreted as follows:

- arr is the name of the array.
- When arr is used in an arithmetic expression, the location of the first element of the array arr is used. Thus arr is now treated as a pointer to the first element of the array arr.
- The result of the arithmetic computation arr + i is a pointer that is computed by using formula 8.1.
- The contents operator * is used to determine the actual object that is stored in the array in index i.

217

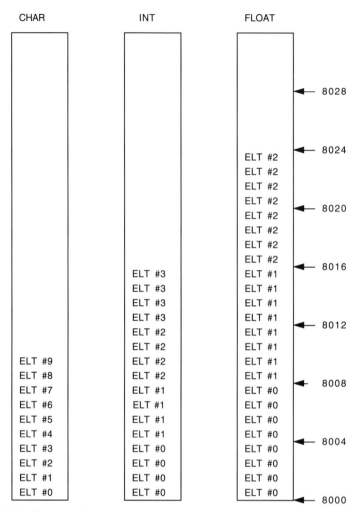

Figure 8.3 Storage of several arrays with different elements

The two expressions

```
*(arr + i);
```

and

```
arr[i]
```

are thus completely equivalent for array elements.

Consider the program in example 8.4:

Example 8.4

```c
#include <stdio.h>

main(void)
{
  int i;
  float a[11];

  for(i=0;i <= 10;i++)
    {
    a[i] = 2.0*i;
    printf("%f\n", a[i]);
    }
}
```

It gives the output

```
0.000000
2.000000
4.000000
6.000000
8.000000
10.000000
12.000000
14.000000
16.000000
18.000000
20.000000
```

The program shown in example 8.4 has precisely the same output as the program given in example 8.5.

Example 8.5 Same output as example 8.4

```c
#include <stdio.h>

main(void)
{
int i;
  float a[11];

  for(i=0;i <= 10;i++)
    {
    a[i] = 2.0*i;
    printf("%f\n", *(a+i));
    }
}
```

Examples 8.4 and 8.5 differ only in the C source code representation of the expressions to be printed; the compiler's internal representation of them is identical. In the first case, we printed the contents of the element indexed by i in the array. In example 8.5, we printed the contents of the location that was pointed to by the expression a + i. This is typical in C; array elements may be accessed by using either the form

```
array_name[array_index]
```

or the form

```
*(array_starting_position + array_index)
```

where we have used the contents operator *. The two forms of array access are completely equivalent in C. In fact, most C compilers change the expression

```
array_name[array_index]
```

to the form

```
*(array_starting_position + array_index)
```

when generating code for programs. Thus there are two different ways for C programs to describe array access.

Why are there two ways of describing array access in C? Which way is better? These are two reasonable questions. The answers are relatively straightforward. Since the C compilers usually use the pointer form, it will not affect either the time of compilation or the time for execution of the program, at least for one-dimensional arrays. The pointer form is designed so that fast array access can be made. The other form that uses the a[i] notation is much clearer and easier to use than the pointer form, especially for those programmers new to the language or to the topic of pointers. You should be able to use and understand both methods since their use is common in C programs.

Consider the declaration

```
char *argv[];
```

that is often used in C programs that use command-line arguments. This format uses an array of character pointers to represent the arguments. An alternate method is to use the declaration

```
char **argv ;
```

which means that argv is a pointer to a pointer to a character. We saw this notation in Chapter 5. This is not an especially good notation, because it obscures what we really want – each of the command-line arguments to be treated as a separate string of characters, each with its own character pointer. The "inner pointer" is equivalent to an array of characters.

Incidentally, *argv[ ] means an array of character pointers and not a pointer to an array of characters. The precedence table in Appendix 5 requires that

```
*argv[]
```

be interpreted as an array of character pointers rather than as a pointer to an array of characters. The [ ] appears higher in the precedence table than does the * and hence the [ ] is performed first. Thus we have an array of something; the something in this case is pointers to characters.

8.3 Pointer Arithmetic

In the previous section, we performed operations of the form a + b where a was a pointer and b was an integer. In this section we discuss the range of allowable operations on pointers and show some of the typical problems that can occur in pointer arithmetic. In general, operations can be performed if one of the operators is a pointer and the other is an integer, but not in other cases. Consider the C statements

```
1      int *ptr;
2      int i = 1;
3      char c = 'a';
4      float f = 123.456;

5      ptr = ptr + i;
6      ptr = ptr + c;
7      ptr = ptr + f;
```

All of the statements except the last are valid in the C programming language. Statements 5 and 6, which involve an assignment of the value of ptr, are valid since they use only pointers and integers (char variables are converted to type int as we saw in Chapter 4). The last statement is not correct and will not even compile; the error message is

```
operands of + have incompatible types
```

and there is an additional warning message (at least on my computer) of the form

```
warning:illegal combination of pointer and integer,op =
```

indicating that we have made an assignment that might cause problems (assuming that the code would have been compiled correctly).

Example 8.6 shows some of the results of pointer arithmetic. You may get different messages from your compiler since we did not allocate space using malloc in this example. Of course, different systems will produce different output, or even error messages, because of differences in computer memory usage.

Example 8.6

```
#include <stdio.h>

main(void)
{
  int a[];
  int b[10];
  int *d;
  char *c;
  float *f;
```

```
arr + 7
```

is 251657732. Thus the difference between the two expressions is 280. It is reasonable to ask how this difference was computed.

In Chapter 5, we learned that two-dimensional arrays in C are actually implemented as one-dimensional arrays whose elements are also one-dimensional arrays. Thus arr is actually an array of 10 elements, each of which is a one-dimensional array that contains 10 floating point numbers. The formula for the sum of arr and 7 is thus

```
starting location of the array arr
+
7 * (size of an arbitrary element of arr)


=


starting location of the array arr
+
7 * (size of an element in the ONE dimensional array)
  * (number of elements in the ONE dimensional array)


=

251657452  + 7 * 4 * 10

= 251657732
```

since the computer used for this program stores floating point numbers in four successive bytes. The same reasoning can be used to understand the result of the printed value of &arr[2][5]. Of course the value of arr[2][5] is correctly printed. This describes the first four printf( ) statements.

The next three results are somewhat surprising at first glance since they seem to say that the array has only 0 for its elements in spite of the initialization that was performed earlier in the program. However, they merely indicate that arr is an array whose elements are 10 one-dimensional arrays of 10 floating point elements each and that the contents of the locations arr and arr + 2 cannot be interpreted sensibly by the compiler according to the specification %f of the printf( ) statement.

The next statement shows the contents of the element in the last assigned row and column of the array arr and is a good example of how not to use the contents operator (*) with two-dimensional arrays. (Recall that array indices in C begin at 0.)

Finally, the last statement shows how to use the contents operator to locate an address of an array element. The expression *arr[9] is parsed as being the contents of element number 9 in the array arr; that is, as the one-dimensional array of 10 floating point numbers ranging from 90.0 to 99.0.

Example 8.8 shows a subtle difficulty that can occur in using arrays in C, even in as simple a program as one that performs a sequential search of an array. The program in example 8.8 was run on two different computers with very different results. The difficulty is caused by the way that C treats pointers.

Example 8.8 A subtle error in pointer access

```
/* code has a subtle error */
#include <stdio.h>
#define NUM_ELEMENTS 100

main(void)
{
  int i,  key;
  int arr[NUM_ELEMENTS];

  puts("Please enter the key to be searched for");
  scanf("%d",&key);
  for(i=0;i <= NUM_ELEMENTS;i++) /* the error is here */
    arr[i] = 300 + i;
  i=0;
  while (i < NUM_ELEMENTS )
    {
    if (arr[i] == key)
      {
      printf("The key is found in position %d.\n",i);
      break;
      }
    else
      i++;
    }
  if (i == NUM_ELEMENTS)
    printf("The key %d is not in the array.\n",key);
}
```

The error is extremely difficult to spot, at least without the comment showing where it occurs. To make matters worse, the program worked correctly on one computer but on the other computer always gave the output

```
The key 400 is not in the array.
```

even if the value entered for key was 324, which is obviously present in the array.

What happened in this example is that the compiler generated very tightly written code to minimize the use of storage. The array arr was intended to be placed in NUM_ELEMENTS contiguous memory locations, each of which stored an integer variable. The integer variables i and key were to be stored immediately after the memory area where the array arr was stored. Notice that the for-loop will execute NUM_ELEMENTS + 1 times since array indices begin at 0 in C. The body of the assignment portion of the loop will thus be executed NUM_ELEMENTS + 1 times. The statement

```
a[i] = 300 + i;
```

is equivalent to

```
    *(a + i) = 300 + i;
```

and this statement will be executed NUM_ELEMENTS + 1 times. This will place the number 400 (= 300 + NUM_ELEMENTS) in the next location after the area that was set aside for the array arr. Since the compiler used the next memory location for the storage of the variable key, the value of key read in was overwritten by the value of the extra array element. This explains the constant output of the statement that 400 was not in the array, at least on one computer. Note that in example 8.8, the comparison being made in the linear search can be written as

```
    if  (*(arr + i) == key)
```

using pointer arithmetic instead of the explicit array notation. The correct program using array addressing is given in example 8.9; compare it with the program in example 5.3.

Example 8.9 Correct code for a sequential search

```c
/* sequential search - pointer notation for array access */
#include <stdio.h>
#define NUM_ELEMENTS 100

main(void)
{
   int i,  key;
   int arr[NUM_ELEMENTS];

   puts("Please enter the key to be searched for");
   scanf("%d",&key);
   for(i=0; i< NUM_ELEMENTS; i++)
     *(arr + i) = 300 + i;
   i=0;
   while (i < NUM_ELEMENTS )
     {
     if ( *(arr + i)  == key)
       {
       printf("The key is found in position %d.\n",i);
       break;
       }
     else
       i++;
     }
   if (i == NUM_ELEMENTS)
     printf("The key %d is not in the array.\n",key);
}
```

Incidentally, we can speed up the sequential search by removing one of the comparisons in the loop. The idea is to use a sentinel of

```
arr[NUM_ELEMENTS] == key
```

and have the while-loop condition be

```
while (1)
```

as in the code fragment

```
while (1)
  {
  if (*(arr + i) == key)
    {
    printf("The key is in position %d\n",i);
    break;
    }
  else
    i++;
  }
if (i == NUM_ELEMENTS)
  printf("The key %d is not in the array\n");
```

The presence of the sentinel means that the loop will always terminate. This is the fastest way to perform a sequential search.

8.4 Storage Access: A Case History

The function malloc( ) is used for memory management. It is reasonable to ask how efficient this operation is. The advantage of pointers is that space need not be preassigned for the storage of various data types when the program is compiled. Instead, pointers may be initialized to point to memory locations that are used only when needed and released when not needed.

Consider the storage of 1,000 variables of type int. These variables must be declared before they are used. If these variables are to be needed at the beginning of the program, they must also be defined; that is, memory must be set aside for their storage. On a computer with a 32-bit integer size, this means that 32,000 bits or 4,000 bytes will be used for storage of these integers. This is a fairly substantial amount of space that is wasted if many of the variables will never be used. A related storage problem occurs when only a few of the entries in the array are nonzero. In the next chapter, we will discuss some methods that may be used to conserve space in data storage.

In this chapter, we consider how array accesses can be sped up by using pointers instead of the obvious arr[i][j]. The example discussed is fairly well known in the technical literature. One example of the use of these ideas is the research paper by Meyer [1988]. The problem occurred in the analysis of an algorithm to decompose a matrix into the product of two matrices, each of which is triangular.

To understand more clearly the problem that Meyer solved, consider examples 8.10 and 8.11 in which we show two of his functions used to compute the determinant of a square matrix in which all elements are 0 other than those on the diagonal.

Example 8.10

```
#define SIZE 17

/*-------------------------------------------------------------*/
/*    function to compute the determinant of a diagonal     */
/*    matrix using the array representation                  */
/*-------------------------------------------------------------*/

double det1(double data[SIZE][SIZE])
{
  double det = 1.0;
  int i;

  for (i = 1; i < SIZE; i++)
    det *= data[i][i];
  return det;
}
```

Example 8.11

```
#define SIZE 17

/*-------------------------------------------------------------*/
/*    function to compute the determinant of a              */
/*    diagonal matrix using pointer arithmetic              */
/*-------------------------------------------------------------*/

double det2(double *data )
{
  double det = 1.0;
  int i;

  for (i = 1; i < SIZE; i++)
    {
    det *= *data;
    data += SIZE + 1;
    }
  return det;
}
```

The function in example 8.10 is very straightforward. It simply uses the array access mechanism to find the successive diagonal elements and to store their product into the variable det. When all of the diagonal elements have been processed, the value of det is returned. The loop is entered SIZE times, with each iteration requiring a multiplication plus the time for an array access to locate the element data[i][i]. C compilers use the formula

```
START + (i * NUMBER_OF_COLUMNS + j)*sizeof(arr[0][0])
```

that we gave in Chapter 5. Here START denotes the address of the first element of the array. Using a compiler with a poor code generator, the function of example 8.10 requires two additional integer multiplications as well as two additional integer additions for the array access. A better code generator rewrites the expression for array access as

```
START + (i * sizeof(arr[0][0]) * NUMBER_OF_COLUMNS) +
j * sizeof(arr[0][0])
```

which can be reduced to

```
START + (i * TEMP) + j * sizeof(arr[0][0])
```

by performing one of the multiplications outside of the loop so that it is not constantly repeated. Since the value of sizeof(arr[0][0]) is nearly always a power of 2 for floating point arithmetic, this multiplication can be done by a fast shifting of the bits making up the integer i. Even this higher quality code requires the use of one additional multiplication, one shift, and two additions. The additional arithmetic operations are integer operations and so they might be somewhat faster than floating point operations on some computers.

The function in example 8.11 appears quite strange at first glance. It differs from the function of example 8.10 in two places: the function parameters and the body of the loop. In the function header, the parameter data is declared as a pointer to a double-precision value

```
double *data;
```

This means that the value stored in the location corresponding to START is to be interpreted as a double-precision value. Therefore any pointer arithmetic that uses this location and an integer as its operands produces a result that is a pointer to a double precision location, as we saw earlier in this chapter. The second statement

```
data += SIZE + 1;
```

is a compact C statement that takes the current value of the pointer data and adds to it the value of SIZE + 1. The result of this value, which is also a pointer, is now stored as the value of the pointer named "data." (It might appear that we have changed the location of the array values; this is not the case, because C only passes a copy of the value of the variable data to the function det2( ). This operation takes a single addition, since the value of SIZE + 1 as well as the value of sizeof(arr[0][0]) can be determined at compile time.

The first line of the loop

```
det *= *data;
```

is also easy to understand once you separate it into individual tokens. (The order of operations can be checked by looking at the precedence table in Appendix 5.) The first asterisk is part of the token "*=" and so the statement could have been written

```
det = det * (*data);
```

The function

```
strlen(string)
```

returns the length of the string by starting at the location pointed to by the string and counting until we reach the null byte \0 terminating the string. The actual implementation of the strlen( ) function might be something like

```
while ( *(string + i) != '\0' )
        i++;
```

This is occasionally written more succinctly as

```
while ( *(string + i) )
        i++;
```

I think the more explicit comparison of the contents of the string to the null byte is easier to understand.

8.7 Pointers to Functions

This section might be a little difficult to understand at first reading. It is reasonable to ask why anyone would want to use such a strange construction, even if it were available in a programming language. Certainly languages such as Pascal, FORTRAN, and BASIC have no such facility.

Consider the function whose rule of operation is "add 1 to the value of the input parameter and then square the result." We can write the action of this function as the composition

```
result = f(g(x)),
```

where f( ) might be the squaring function (whose rule is "square the value of the input parameter") and g( ) might be the function whose rule is "add 1 to the input parameter." In this case the composition of the two functions would be "add 1 to the input value and then square the result." For most languages, this is easy to do for a single value of the input such as in the loop

```
for (x = 0; x <= 1.0; x += .01)
        printf("%d",(x+1)*(x+1));
```

Note that in this example, we have only computed individual values using the rules of the function and have combined the results in a single statement.

Perhaps a better example might be

```
for (x = 0; x <= 1.0; x += .01)
        printf("%d",f(g(x)));
```

where f( ) and g( )are defined by

```
float f(float x)
{
      return x*x;
}


float g((float x)
{
      return x + 1;
}
```

Even in this example, what we have is the passing of values of a function g( ) at specific values of the input x to another function f( ) by computing the value of u = g(x) and then passing the value of u to f( ) as an input.

A language that has pointers has the ability to change the values of parameters to functions simply by changing the contents of the location accessed by the pointer. If the language allowed pointers to functions, then it might be possible to pass functions as parameters to other functions such as is done in mathematical functions that have rules or that describe their action such as "find all real roots of the function," "find the maximum value of a function," or "compute the definite integral of a function over a given interval," where the function on which we perform these actions is not fixed. This is not passing a function to another function in the sense of communicating a rule. We need the notion of pointers to functions to be able to do this.

A nonmathematical example of the use of this idea occurs in the UNIX system call function signal( ) that is used for communicating the existence of certain events such as the termination of a process, an interrupt from a keyboard, etc. The syntax for the signal() system call is

```
int (*signal(int sig, int (*fcn) () ) )  ()
```

On the next few lines we have separated the declaration of the signal( ) system call into several lines for clarity.

```
int (*signal (
        int sig,
        int (*fcn) ()
        )
        )
        ()
```

The first line indicates that the value returned by signal is of type "pointer to a function whose return type is int," with the rest of the declaration to follow. The second line is simple. The third line indicates that the second argument is also a pointer to a function whose return value is int.

The system call using the signal function in UNIX is quite complex and will be discussed here only at a very high level in this and the next two paragraphs. The only thing that you need to know at this time is that such a construction using pointers to functions is used in certain nonmathematical programs.

When an event of a certain sort occurs, such as overflow of a register, division by 0, etc., a signal is sent by the operating system. The signal has been been given a pre-determined integer value in the operating system header file signal.h. A typical signal for these arithmetic faults is SIGFPE, which is a mnemonic for "signal floating point exception." The user's program should have a statement in it such as

```
... signal( SIGFPE, signal_catcher) ...
```

that indicates that a detection of this particular signal has been made by the operating system and that the program should take appropriate action. The appropriate action is to do what the programmer wishes to do, assuming that he or she has anticipated this error state and has previously included the signal catcher function in the program. If there is no signal handler in place, then the operating system generates a signal SIGKILL, which always terminates the program, and a message such as

```
Floating Point Violation

Bus Error - Core dumped

EMT Violation - Core dumped
```

or similar is given to the user.

Here is another example. You are probably familiar with the concept of a window system in which one or more processes run in different windows. The choice of an active window is often made by a mouse or other pointing device. The movement of the mouse causes an interrupt of the CPU in order to have the mouse's movement translated into movement of a "mouse cursor" on the screen. The positioning of the mouse cursor on a window and the pressing of a button on the mouse are events that must be interpreted by the display system. The event might mean that a window is to be closed, hidden from view by another window, placed in front of other windows that partially cover it, changed in size, or changed into some other form such as an icon. Each of these possible actions can be chosen according to the state of the mouse cursor and button. The pressing of the mouse button sends a signal, usually SIGINT, that is "caught" by a "signal catcher" function that is accessed by a pointer. How does the display system decide what to do? It looks at the function pointed to by the signal-catching function. The design of a signal-catching function can be quite complex and is best left to an advanced monograph on the UNIX operating system.

We now turn to the discussion of another use of pointers to functions. Mathematical examples of pointers to functions are somewhat simpler to understand than the use of the signal system call in UNIX. As an example, we consider the problem of writing a function to obtain the maximum and minimum values of an arbitrary function defined on an interval. We will do this with a function called max( ) that gets its information by using pointers to other functions.

What information do we need? We must know the rule describing the function and the endpoints of the interval that we are interested in. The program is given in example 8.11. It includes a subtle error in the function max() that we will discuss later.

Example 8.12

```
#include <stdio.h>
#include <math.h>

/* function prototypes */
double max(double a, double b, double tol,double (*gptr)());
double f(double x);

main(void)
{
  double a, b, tolerance;
  double maxval;   /* for value returned from max()    */
  char choice;

  printf("Enter the endpoints of the interval\n");
  scanf("%lf %lf",&a,&b);
  printf("Enter the accuracy of the calculation\n");
  scanf("%lf",&tolerance);
  printf("Enter the choice of function\n\n");
  printf("sin(x)  ..... 1\n\n");
  printf("exp(x)  ..... 2\n\n");
  printf("2 x -3  ..... 3\n\n");
  printf("------------->");
  getchar();
  choice = getchar();
  printf("The choice was %c\n\n",choice);
  switch (choice)
    {
    case '1':
      maxval = max(a,b,tolerance,sin);
      break;
    case '2':
      maxval = max(a,b,tolerance,exp);
      break;
    case '3':
      maxval = max(a,b,tolerance,f);
      break;
    }
  printf("The maximum value of the function
  is%lf\n",maxval);
}
```

```
/*-----------------------------------------------------------*/
/*  FUNCTION TO FIND THE MAXIMUM OF ANOTHER FUNCTION    */
/*  THE INPUT IS A POINTER TO ANOTHER FUNCTION AND      */
/*  THREE FLOATING POINT VARIABLES                      */
/*  ARGUMENTS:                                          */
/*  double a,b --- endpoints of the interval            */
/*  double tol --- accuracy of divisions of the interval */
/*  double (*gptr) () --- pointer to a function         */
/*-----------------------------------------------------------*/

double max(double a, double b, double tol, double (*gptr)())

{
  double x, ymax;

  printf("The address of the function is %ld\n", (*gptr)());
  ymax = (*gptr)(a);
  printf("%lf\n",ymax);

  /* be careful of round-off errors */
  for (x= a; x <= b; x += tol)
    {
    printf("%lf\n",(*gptr)(x));
      if  ((*gptr)(x) > ymax)
        ymax = (*gptr)(x);
    }
  return ymax;
}

/* user-defined function   */
double f(double x)
{
  return 2.0 * x - 3.0;
}
```

A portion of the output from three runs of this program is given below:

Example 8.13 First run of the program of example 8.12

```
Enter the endpoints of the interval
      0.0
      3.0
      Enter the accuracy of the calculation
      0.1

      Enter the choice of function
```

```
      sin(x)  ..... 1

      exp(x)  ..... 2

      2 x -3  ..... 3

      ------------>1

    The choice was 1

    The address of the function is 14
    0.000000
    0.000000
    0.099833
    0.198669
    0.295520
    0.389418
    0.479426
    0.564642
    0.644218
    0.717356
    0.783327
    The maximum value of the function is 0.783327
```

Example 8.14 Second run of the program of example 8.12

```
Enter the endpoints of the interval
0.0
1.0
Enter the accuracy of the calculation
0.1
Enter the choice of function

sin(x)  ..... 1

exp(x)  ..... 2

2 x -3  ..... 3

------------>2
The choice was 2

The address of the function is 1072693248
1.000000
1.000000
```

```
1.105171
1.221403
1.349859
1.491825
1.648721
1.822119
2.013753
2.225541
2.459603
The maximum value of the function is 2.459603
```

Example 8.15 Third run of the program of example 8.12

```
Enter the endpoints of the interval
0.0
1.0
Enter the accuracy of the calculation
0.1
Enter the choice of function

sin(x)  ..... 1

exp(x)  ..... 2

2 x -3  ..... 3

------------>3
The choice was 3

The address of the function is -1073217536

-3.000000
-3.000000
-2.800000
-2.600000
-2.400000
-2.200000
-2.000000
-1.800000
-1.600000
-1.400000
-1.200000
The maximum value of the function is -1.200000
```

There are many features of this program and its output that need discussion. The first observation is that we have used the mathematics library and therefore need to include the standard header file math.h in our program. Although it is not clear from the code, the compilation required the mathematics library to be linked by using a command such as

```
cc toy.c -lm
```

As we discussed in Chapter 4, your system might require different commands to perform this linkage.

The first part of the code prior to the switch statement is relatively clear and straightforward. Note the declaration of the functions max( ) and f( ) as having returned values of type float so that the compiler can link properly. The interesting features occur in the switch statements that contain the calls to the function max( ).

The function max( ) is called three times corresponding to the three choices of the switch statement. There were four parameters in the first call to max( ); a, b, tolerance, and sin. The parameters a, b, and tolerance were defined in the first line of the function main( ). Where was sin declared or defined? Since the program worked, the compiler must have understood the meaning of sin (at least in this context). The three characters "sin" are the name of a C function that is not defined in the program proper but in the standard math library that was included using the header file. In a similar manner, the call to max( ) with the parameter exp is also known to the compiler in the same way.

The third call to max( ) that could have been selected as an option in the switch statement is slightly different in that the symbol "f" is not in the standard math library but instead is in the set of functions already declared in the program.

Each of the three possible calls to max( ) includes the name of a function. In order to communicate the rule describing the function to max( ) and not simply give values returned by the function, max( ) had to include in its heading a statement such as

```
float (*gptr) ();
```

and a similar syntax was used in the evaluations of values of the function that was passed to max( ). The reasoning is that the name of the function is known to the compiler when the calling statement is encountered. However, inside the function max( ) itself no such knowledge is available. C expects that every argument to a function is either an expression or a pointer; the only operations allowed on functions are calling them or using their address. Since the address of the function is used in this example, each function call will make use of the contents of the function that is stored at the desired address. Thus we used statements such as

```
ymax = (*gptr)(a);
```

in this example instead of something like

```
ymax = g(a);
```

The second notation is more like standard mathematical notation. The idea behind using the second notation is that we are replacing the contents of the function pointer gptr by the function that is pointed to. It actually made no difference which of the two notations was used; use whichever one seems easier for you.

The use of pointers to functions as parameters is likely to cause some problems in portability. Not all C compilers implement this correctly. In addition, the changes in ANSI standard C will have quite an effect on the syntax of function calls with functions as parameters; see Appendix 6 for additional information.

You should also expect the UNIX utility program lint to complain about the use of pointers to functions. The output from lint on two different UNIX systems is given in examples 8.16 and 8.17. (In example 8.16, the function _filbuf( ) is a system function that is called by our program writing to a memory buffer; we are not usually aware of the existence of such low-level system functions, and we should certainly ignore their presence in lint's output.)

Example 8.16 First lint evaluation of the program of example 8.12

```
max, arg. 4 used inconsistently toy.c(50) :: toy.c(30)
max, arg. 4 used inconsistently toy.c(50) :: toy.c(32)
max, arg. 4 used inconsistently toy.c(50) :: toy.c(34)
_filbuf returns value which is sometimes ignored
printf returns value which is always ignored
scanf returns value which is always ignored
```

Example 8.17 Second lint evaluation of the program of example 8.12

```
toy.c
===============
(38)  warning: main() returns random value to
invocation environment


===============
name used but not defined
sin         toy.c(30)
exp         toy.c(32)
name declared but never used or defined
cos         toy.c?(14)
tan         toy.c?(14)
(all other functions in math.h were also mentioned )
function argument ( number ) used inconsistently
max( arg 4 )        toy.c(50) :: toy.c(30)
max( arg 4 )        toy.c(50) :: toy.c(32)
function returns value which is always ignored
printf          scanf
function returns value which is sometimes ignored
getchar
```

Using pointers to functions can provide your programs with considerable power to do things that would be impossible in other languages. However, issues such as portability, strangeness of syntax, and possible type-matching problems such as those shown by lint indicate that this language feature be used sparingly in C programs, especially for the beginning programmer.

The program of example 8.12 was tested on two different computers. Output was the same on both machines (including the location at which the functions sin( ) and exp( ) were stored). Note that the two programs each gave incorrect answers for the maximum value of the function f( ); this is due to both roundoff and truncation errors in the storage of the binary equivalents of decimal results. It is not so clear that the answers for the other functions are also incorrect; however, they are incorrect and for the same reason. If you don't believe this, count the number of values computed in the function max( ). It is clear that the right-hand endpoint is never evaluated. The code can be corrected by replacing the for-loop in max( ) by

```
for (x= a; x < b + tol; x += tol)
```

This change forces the value of the function to be computed at the right hand endpoint. This is a typical problem caused by the computer performing inexact decimal computation because of roundoff and truncation errors. For more information about the typical inaccuracies of numerical computation on computers, see the references.

8.8 Passing Parameters by Reference

Now that we understand pointers, we can discuss passing parameters by reference. We mentioned the concept in Chapter 4 when we found out that C only supports the method of passing parameters by value. Recall that passing parameters by value means that only a copy of the value of the parameter is passed to the function and this copy is destroyed upon exit from the function.

When a function is called with a set of parameters, the compiler begins the execution of the machine code for the function by making a copy of the values of the parameters. The function is free to use its copy of the parameters in any way that it wishes. After the function finishes execution, it destroys the copy of the parameters, and the original set of values of the parameters is the same as the set of values of the parameters after the call to the function. This is called passing parameters by value and is the only way that parameters can be passed in C.

Thus the function swap( ) defined by

```
swap(int a, int b)
{
    int temp;

    temp = a;
    a = b;
    b = temp;
}
```

doesn't actually change the values of a and b, since only local copies of the values of a and b are changed by swap( ).

The easiest way to interchange the variables is to pass pointers as in

```
swap(  int *a, int *b)
{
    int *temp;

    *temp = *a;
    *a = *b;
    *b = *temp;
}
```

What we are actually doing is changing the value of a copy of a memory address. The copy and the original refer to the same address, but the contents of this address are changed. This is the same idea as your giving me a copy of your address on a piece of paper, my painting your house green, and then tearing up the piece of paper. My copy of your address is destroyed, but the house is now green.

Here is another example of a situation where passing parameters by reference is useful. Suppose that we wished to sort an array by using a function to provide the sort. We probably don't want to allocate temporary storage for the sorted array in the calling function and thus want the returned array to be stored in the same memory location as the original array. The array would be passed by reference; that is, as a pointer to the place where the data is stored.

An example of this approach is the standard C library function qsort( ), which uses this method of passing parameters. There are four parameters to this library function: a pointer to the array to be sorted, the number of elements in the array, the size of each of the array elements, and a user-defined function for performing comparisons between the individual array elements. The syntax of this function is

```
void qsort( void *arr_ptr, size_t num_elements,
        size_t element_size,
        int compare( const void *, const void *)
        );
```

The first argument is the address of the array to be sorted (with an explicit void so that the function works independently of data types). The second and third arguments are the sizes, which are unsigned ints. The last argument is a function of return type int that takes two arguments: pointers to the array elements being compared.

This last function argument must be a function that is written by the programmer. The name of this function can be anything but must agree with the character string used for the argument to the library function qsort( ). It can be as simple as comparing two ints with

```
int compare (const void * xptr, const void * yptr)
{
  if (* xptr < *yptr)
    return 1;
  else
    return 2;
}
```

comparing two character strings with

```
int compare (const void * first, const void * second)
{
  return (strcmp( first, second);
}
```

or allowing a comparison of some user-defined data types, depending on the wishes of the programmer.

Notice the high level of abstraction and portability exemplified here. The sorting is done independently of the data types of the elements in the array to be sorted. This ability to have a single sorting function that works on any abstract data type is a major software engineering feature of the C programming language. It greatly improves the utility of sorting routines. A general-purpose sorting routine of high quality (it runs fast and does not blow up on unexpected data distributions) is extremely useful in reducing programmer effort. We will meet abstract data types again in the next chapter.

8.9 Functions with a Variable Number of Arguments

This is probably as good a time as any to mention the ability of C to have functions with variable numbers of arguments. There is a header file named varargs.h that provides access to the standard library functions that allow variable arguments. A moment's reflection reminds us that printf( ), scanf( ) and main( ) can all take a variable number of arguments. The use of command-line arguments also requires that main( ) be allowed to have a variable number of arguments.

A function that uses the variable number of arguments feature will have to have some way of determining the beginning and the end of the list of variable arguments as well as moving to the next argument on the list. Such a function will have a format similar to that of the following:

```
#include <varargs.h>
/* prototype */
return_type var_arg_function(arg_type arg1, ...);
```

```
/* other stuff here */

return_type var_arg_function(arg_type arg1, ...)
{
var_args_list  start; /* start list for variable argument */

/* other variables */

var_arg_start(ap, arg1);

/* other part of function using var_arg(ap, arg_type)    */
/* var_arg() helps move to the next argument in the list */

var_end(ap); /* end list of variable arguments           */

/* rest of code goes here including return value, if any  */
}
;
```

There are some issues here that need additional discussion. The need for appropriate header files and having a function prototype should be very familiar by now. There is one part of the syntax here that might be overlooked. We have previously used three dots (...) in some examples as a notation in order to indicate to you that there is more source code than what we have written explicitly. The three dots in the function prototype in this example and the function definition are used to indicate to the compiler the need for a variable number of arguments.

The use of the functions var_arg_start( ) and var_end( ) delimit the portion of the code that requires a variable number of arguments.

This feature of C is described in the ANSI C standard, but is not available in most earlier dialects of the C language or even in all current versions. You should probably expect some portability problems if you use this feature. There is a large amount of testing necessary when using the variable number of arguments feature of C.

You might find it convenient at times to have a smooth way of parsing command-line arguments if you write software that has many options. The function getopt( ) is available on many C compilers and is especially common on some AT&T-based UNIX systems. However, it is not generally available on C compilers for personal computers.

Here is an example of the use of getopt( ) in a software system that was used to analyze a set of C source code files. The command -line of the software system included the name of the executable file ("measure"), a set of options (including 'a', 'A', 'c', 'C', 'd', 'g', 'h', 'm', and no option specified at all, which meant that all options were selected by default), and a list of input files to be analyzed by the software. The user of the system was allowed to enter command-lines such as

```
measure -d file1.c
```

and

```
measure -c file2.c file3.c
```

with single options,

```
measure -d -h file1.c

measure -c -m file2.c file3.c

measure -d -C -m file1.c

measure  file2.c file3.c
```

with multiple options that were flagged with minus signs, and

```
measure -cdm file2.c file3.c
```

where multiple options were allowed to be flagged by a single minus sign. The syntax for our use of a call to getopt( ) in this software system was

```
while (( option = getopt(argc, argv, "hcmdCAag") )
                    != EOF )
  {
  switch (option)
    {
    case 'a :
    case 'A' :
      ANSIoption = TRUE;
      break;

            .
            .
            .

    }
  }
```

Note that this code fragment uses a while-loop to check for each one of the arguments being present. Note also the use of EOF to check for the end of the argument list.

8.10 Software Engineering Project: Changed Requirements

In this project, you will use the routines written in previous versions of the project to move blocks of data to and from a simulated disk. The purpose of the project is to incorporate a file system and an access method on the simulated disk.

The file system will be a simple hierarchical one as follows:

- The root of the file system is called root, which is a directory.
- There are three subdirectories of root: bin, etc, and usr. Each of these subdirectories is also a directory.
- The directory bin contains the files: mail, make, time.
- The directory etc contains the files: fsck, halt, ttys.
- The directory usr contains the files: comp, uter, prog, rams.

Table 8.2 Possible storage of blocks and files

FILE	BLOCK	TRACK	SECTOR
1	0	5	6
1	1	5	7
1	2	5	8
1	3	5	9
1	4	5	0
1	5	6	1
1	6	6	6
1	7	6	6
1	8	6	3
1	9	6	4
1	10	6	5
1	11	6	6
1	12	6	7
1	13	6	8
1	14	6	9
2	0	7	0
2	1	7	1
.	.	.	.
.	.	.	.
.	.	.	.

determine what to do if the files grow too large for the space allocated for them. Also, space may be wasted if we use contiguous storage of files that do not fill up the allotted space completely. On the other hand, if we allow files to be stored noncontiguously, that is, if we allow the files to be stored in pieces, then we will need pointers to the various disk blocks that begin new segments of the file. Noncontiguous storage also requires a more complex table to store file locations. For simplicity, we will allow space to be wasted and in our specifications we will require that all files be stored contiguously. If a file exhausts the space allocated for it, then we will have to search the disk to find an available space. If no such space is available, then we will take some type of error action; the nature of the action will be determined later.

In summary, we have the following new specifications about file access

- The file allocation method will be sequential access.
- The files will be stored contiguously.

Table 8.3 Possible storage of blocks, files, and data elements

FILE	UNIT	BLOCKS	DATA ELEMENTS	TRACK	SECTOR
1	1	0 - 9	0 - 99	7	5
1	2	10-14	100-149	10	2
2	3	20-29	200-299	12	7
.	.	.	.	.	.
.	.	.	.	.	.
.	.	.	.	.	.

It is now time to specify directories. We choose to do this the way that the UNIX operating system does – by using a construction called "i-nodes" and "i-numbers." An i-number is a number assigned to a file that serves as an index into an array of i-nodes. The i-node contains information about the file such as location on disk (track, sector) and size. In the UNIX operating system, it contains additional information about the ownership of the file, access permissions, times of modification, etc. For simplicity we will ignore this additional information that is usually stored in an i-node. Surprisingly, an i-node associated with a file does not contain the name of the file.

The only way to access a file by name is by reading the contents of a type of file called a directory. A directory stores, in computer-readable form, pairs of data about the files in that directory. The pairs are of the form

(name of file, i-number)

and are the only way of accessing the file by using its name. In order to find a file named "filename" we have to go through the following steps.

(1) Get request for file "filename."
(2) Find location of current directory.
(3) From directory, find the i-number.
(4) Find place where (i-node, i-number) pairs are stored.
(5) Read i-node and find where on disk the file is stored.
(6) Go to place on disk where file is stored.
(7) The files that we will be able to access are those mentioned earlier.

These steps should be added to the functional specification of the file system. In addition, we will need to specify those places that the software is required to store certain information. Since other functions of the file system need to use this information, we will place it in the specifications for the system.

Our system has 14 files with the following organization:

i-number	file type	contents	
1	root directory	bin	2
		etc	3
		usr	4
2	bin directory	mail	5
		make	6
		time	7
3	etc directory	fsck	8
		halt	9
		ttys	10
4	usr directory	comp	11
		uter	12
		prog	13
		rams	14

```
     5           mail           ordinary   data
     6           make           ordinary   data
     7           time           ordinary   data
     8           fsck           ordinary   data
     9           halt           ordinary   data
    10           ttys           ordinary   data
    11           comp           ordinary   data
    12           uter           ordinary   data
    13           prog           ordinary   data
    14           rams           ordinary   data
```

We have to specify the size of the files mail, make, time, fsck, halt, and ttys. We will fix each of them to have exactly eight characters in the file. The contents of the file mail will be "mailmail," the contents of the file make will be "makemake," the contents of the file time will be "timetime," etc.

This is a sufficient amount of specification for us to be able to design the file system simulation as an addition to our system.

8.11 Software Engineering Project: The Next Prototype

We now consider a prototype system that includes file system simulation. In order to describe the (i-number, i-node) pairs, we have to determine where the information should be stored. The typical solution is to have the information stored on the disk in adjacent tracks; we will begin on track 0 and continue in increasing order. How much room do we need for the storage of information on each file? Our simplified version of an i-node contains both track and sector numbers and a size. We will add one more item to this storage, the i-number. This is four integers and will fit into a single block of data.

The first 10 i-numbers correspond to fixed-size files in our system (root, bin, etc, usr, mail, make, time, fsck, halt, and ttys) and the last 4 (comp, uter, prog, and rams) can vary in size. Of course in a real system, the usr directory could grow as more users are added to the system. The first file, root, is a directory file and contains three pairs of information: three characters plus i-numbers. Since root is the most critical directory file, it will be placed as close to the beginning of the disk as possible. It will follow a more important file – the one where the file structure information is kept.

The first thing stored on the disk will be the table that tells us where the i-nodes are listed. The i-number, i-node table is stored at the start of the disk since it will be accessed most often. We need a track and sector for each of the 14 files. This is a total of 3 times 14, or 42 integers. Of course this would be larger if we were to allow more files to be created. We can fit all 42 integers into 5 blocks. To make computations easy and to keep some extra space for expansion, we will reserve the entire first track for the i-number, i-node table.

The i-node table is stored in track 0 in sectors 0 through 4, with the remaining sectors 5 through 9 on track 0 unused. The contents of the i-node table look something like Table 8.4.

Table 8.4 Possible i-node table

i-number	TRACK	SECTOR	(NAME OF FILE)
1	1	0	root
2	1	1	bin
3	1	2	etc
4	1	3	usr
5	1	4	mail
6	1	5	make
7	1	6	time
8	1	7	fsck
9	1	8	halt
10	1	9	ttys
11	2	0	comp
12	2	1	uter
13	2	2	prog
14	2	3	rams

Access to a file via its i-node is quite indirect. Suppose that you as a user wish to look up something in the file comp. The current directory is searched for the existence of the string "comp." The entry in the directory that corresponds to this is the i-number of the file comp. The next step is searching the i-number, i-node table at the beginning of the disk for the location of the i-node of the file comp, which in this case is in track 2, sector 0. We then move to track 2, sector 0 on the disk and look at the data that is stored in the i-node. From the i-node, we find the location of the file on the disk. This is triple indirection!

Why is this triple indirection? We found the i-number from a search of the current directory. We found the location of the i-node corresponding to the file in the i-number, i-node table. We finally find the file's location on the disk by reading the contents of the i-node.

We have left space for possible expansion of the i-number, i-node table by not using all of track 0. We also ought to leave room for expansion of the set of i-nodes. Let's agree to leave the rest of track 2 unused. The storage of the files on the disk should begin in track 3. Of course, the first file to be stored on the disk is the start of the directory – the root directory.

The root directory requires the use of nine characters, three spaces for separation of the characters, and three integers for the i-numbers. We ignore for the moment the problem of mixing characters and integers on the disk. This means that we need to have a total of 15 single bytes, since the integers can be represented in a single byte. This will fit into two blocks. Let us reserve two blocks for the contents of the root directory and for the other three directories bin, etc, and usr. This takes a total of eight blocks for the first four files (i-numbers 1, 2, 3, and 4).

The rest of the files now can be entered onto the disk in the indicated order. In the exercises, you will be asked to continue this project.

Summary of Chapter 8

Pointers are addresses of data in computer memory. They can be used to access objects and to allow the operating system to allocate memory dynamically.

There are two basic operations that can be performed on pointers: the contents operator * and the address operator &.

Pointers are used extensively with arrays. There are two notations that can be used interchangeably to access the elements of an array

```
arr[i]
```

and

```
* (arr + i)
```

Pointers can be used with space allocation functions such as malloc( ) and calloc( ). In order to allocate space using malloc( ) or calloc( ), we must know the size of the object and its type so that we know how large the object is and how much space must be reserved.

We need to use a cast operator such as in

```
float_ptr = (float *) malloc(sizeof(float) );
```

Pointers are appropriate for the treatment of character strings. A character string is passed as a command-line argument using the construction

```
main(int argc,char *argv[] )
```

in which the interface to the command interpreter of the operating system automatically places a termination byte \0 at the end of each string in a command-line argument. In order to use functions such as atoi( ), strlen( ), strcmp( ), and others, we must be sure to pass the arguments as character pointers and to have the string terminated by a termination byte \0.

Pointers are the only way to simulate passing parameters by reference in C.

Exercises

1. In the exercises at the end of Chapter 5, we considered a function named stringcompare( ) that took as input two arrays of characters and returned a value of type int that was obtained by the following rules:

0 if the two arrays were identical,

-1 if the first array was less than the second (in lexical order),

1 if the second array was less than the first (in lexical order).

Rewrite this function using inputs that are pointers to characters, instead of being of the form

```
char first[], second[];
```

Test your function carefully. What changes did you have to make? Compare this function to the function strcmp( ) available in the standard C input/output library.

2. In this problem, you will compare the efficiency of the two functions to compute the determinant of a square matrix that were given earlier in this chapter in examples 8.10 and 8.11.

    (a)   Create a square matrix whose entries in the first row begin 0.0, 1.0, 2.0, etc., and continue increasing by 1.0 as the column index increases. All of the other rows should have the same contents as the first. (This should mean that the value of the determinant will be 0.) As a start, use the value 17 for SIZE.

    (b)   Write a program that incorporates the two functions that were presented in the examples. The program should be able to call either of the two functions without waiting for a user to make a choice. In order to do this, use command-line arguments in your program as we discussed in Chapter 5. If the name of the executable code is experiment, then the program will call the first determinant function det1( ) if the command-line is

    experiment a

    and will call the second determinant function det2( ) if the command-line is

    experiment b

    (c)   Measure the amount of time that the two versions need to run and compare the difference. If the difference is too small to measure, or if you are using a watch instead of a system clock, increase the value of SIZE. Make a chart of the value of size compared with the times that the two versions need for various values of SIZE in the range 10 to 60.

    (d)   To get an even better estimate of how the program is spending its time in the evaluation of which functions, use a profiler if one is available on your system. Profilers are available on most UNIX C compilers, among others. To use a profiler on a UNIX system, simply compile the program with the -p option:

```
cc -p file.c
```

    and run the program. Each time the program completes successfully, a file named mon.out is created. This file contains the various functions called (both user-defined and low-level system functions) as well as the time that is spent executing each function.

    (e)   A final test can be made of your compiler. Make a copy of your source code and edit both copies so that only one of the determinant functions appears in each. Compile each version and compare the sizes of the executable codes. If they are identical, then it is likely that your compiler generates very good and very fast executing code. (Very bad is also possible but you should hope for the best.) Now recompile each of the programs using an optimizing option if one is available. Compare the size of each new executable file with the previous one. If you have sufficient time, repeat part c of this problem.

10. The next program is an example of poor programming practice. It is based on an actual program that was used to control the display of a moving object. The main consideration at that time was speeding up the program as much as possible. That is your objective here. Some of the code was the actual code used in the first attempt to perform the desired action. I added a few nasty features to slow the program down. Try to find as many ways as possible to speed up the code. You should concentrate on minimizing the number of floating point operations. There are at least nine separate improvements that can be made.

Note: The functions move_to( ) and draw_to( ) were actual graphics functions; use the ones given here to simulate the time that such functions take.

```
#include <stdio.h>
#include <math.h>

#define PI 3.14159

static double old[3][3] =
    {
    {0.0, 0.0, 0.0},
    {0.0, 0.0, 0.0},
    {0.0, 0.0, 0.0}
    };
static double new[3][3] =
    {
    {1.0, 0.0, 0.0},
    {0.0, 1.0, 0.0 },
    {0.0, 0.0, 1.0}
    };
static double trans[3][3]=
    {
    {0.0, 0.0, 0.0},
    {0.0, 0.0, 0.0},
    {0.0, 0.0, 0.0}
    };

static double x,y,z,theta = PI, phi = PI,psi = 2* PI ;

/* function prototypes */
void get_angles(void)
void move_to(double x,double y,double z);


main(void)
{
    int i,j,k,    count,p,q,r,s,t,u,v,w,a,b,c,d,e,f,g,h,l,m,n,o;
```

```
    for (count =1; count <= 500; count ++)
      {
      get_angles();
      get_transformation_matrix(theta,phi,psi);;
      for(i=0 ; i <= 3-1; i ++)
        {
        for (j = 0; j <= 3-1;  j++)
          {
          new[i][j] = 0.0;
          for(k =0; k <=3-1; k++)
            new[i][j] = new[i][j] + new[i][k]* trans[k][j];
          new[i][j] = (new[i][0]*0.9 +new[i][1]*0.9 +
                          new[i][2]*1.2) / 4.60;

          /*   next line verifies that output is correct */
          /*   remove it when you check for time         */
          printf("%d %f\n",count,new[i][j]);

          x = new[0][0];
          y = new[0][1];
          z = new[0][2];
          }
        }
      if (count %2 == 0)
        move_to(x,y,z);
      else
        draw_to(x,y,z);
  }                  /* end of count loop */
}                        /* end of main */


/*---------------------------------------------------------*/
/* A poor simulation of a random number generator --   */
/* note the range of values of theta, psi, and phi     */
/*---------------------------------------------------------*/

void get_angles(void)
{
  static int i;
  float result = PI;

  if ( i == -1)
    i =1;
  theta = result /(i+6);
  phi = (theta)/( i +2);
```

```
      psi = (((psi))/(i + 4));
      i = i + 1.000;
}


/*-------------------------------------------------------*/

get_transformation_matrix(double theta,double phi,
            double psi)
{
int i,j,k ;
/* a lot of matrix multiplication */

trans[0][0] = cos(theta);
trans[0][1] = sin(theta);

trans[1][0] = - sin(theta);
trans[1][1] = cos(theta);
trans[2][2] = 1.0 ;
trans[0][1] = trans[0][1] * cos_phi;
trans[0][2] = trans[0][1] * sin_phi + trans[0][2] * cos_phi;
trans[1][1] = trans[1][1] * -sin_phi;
trans[1][2] = trans[1][1] * sin_phi;
trans[2][1] = trans[2][2] * -sin_phi;
trans[2][1] = trans[2][2] * cos_phi;
trans[0][0] = trans[0][0] * cos_psi + trans[0][2] *sin_psi ;
trans[1][0] = trans[1][0] * cos_psi + trans[1][2] *sin_psi ;
trans[2][0] = trans[2][0] * cos_psi + trans[2][2] *sin_psi ;
trans[0][2] = trans[0][0] * -sin_psi + trans[0][2] *cos_psi;
trans[1][2] = trans[1][0] * -sin_psi + trans[1][2] *cos_psi;
trans[2][2] = trans[2][0] * -sin_psi + trans[2][2] *cos_psi;
}


/*-------------------------------------------------------*/
/* don't change this function                            */
/* It does nothing but simulate the cursor moving time */
void move_to(double x,double y,double z)
{
  int i;

  for (i=1;i <= 10000;i++)
          ;
}
```

```
/*----------------------------------------------------------*/
/* don't change this function                               */
/* It does nothing but simulate the cursor moving time */
draw_to(double x,double y,double z)
{
  int i ;

  for (i=1;i <= 10000;i++)
         ;
}
```

11. Write a program to profile another program. This means that you will be able to tell approximately how much time your program spends executing the functions in the program or executing various blocks of code that you think are important. The idea is to compute the time before and after the functions or the specially chosen blocks of code are entered and exited. The organization of a profiler for the C program of exercise 10 might collect times before and after the functions move_to( ), draw_to( ), get_angles( ), get_transformation_matrix( ), and the innermost loop of main( ) are executed.

You will have to use the system clock in order to write this program. In the UNIX C compiler, you can simply incorporate the statement

```
system("date");
```

within your program at the various places.

Using the Turbo C compiler on an MS/DOS-based personal computer, we can access the system clock using a function gettime( ) and a structured data type called time. We will study structured data types in more detail in Chapter 10. For now, simply use the code sample as a template to include in your program.

```
#include <stdio.h>
#include <dos.h>

main()
{
  struct time start, end;

  gettime(&start);
  printf("starts at %0.2d:%0.2d:%0.2d:%0.2d\n",
      start.ti_hour, start.ti_min,
      start.ti_sec, start.ti_hund);
  gettime(&end);
  printf("ends at %0.2d:%0.2d:%0.2d:%0.2d\n",
      end.ti_hour, end.ti_min,
      end.ti_sec, end.ti_hund);
}
```

12. The output from the program of exercise 10 is quite messy since it records the time for each call of a function and each entry into a block of code separately. A much better output can be obtained by keeping track of the total time elapsed from the output from each function or block of code entered and then sorting the result in decreasing order of execution. The output of the profiler available in the UNIX operating system on the program given in exercise 10 is

%time	cumsecs	#call	ms/call	name
21.9	8.04	1	8039.79	_profil
16.3	14.02	400	14.95	_draw_to
15.6	19.76	400	14.35	_move_to
11.9	24.14	138240	0.03	Fmuld
6.7	26.62	96972	0.03	Faddd
5.7	28.70			mcount
3.8	30.08			d_exte
3.6	31.39	59314	0.02	Fcmpd
2.1	32.18			d_usel
2.1	32.96	1	779.98	_main
1.8	33.64	87200	0.01	Fstod
1.8	34.29			d_rcp
1.1	34.68	28800	0.01	Fdtos
0.8	34.98	2400	0.12	Fdivd
0.6	35.21			_Fdsinapprox_
0.6	35.43			_FFcosd_
0.5	35.63			_cos
0.5	35.80			_Fdcosapprox_
0.4	35.96	800	0.20	get_transformation_matrix
0.4	36.11			d_norm
0.3	36.23	3200	0.04	Ffltd
0.3	36.35	12294	0.01	Fsubd
0.3	36.45			_FFsind_
0.2	36.53			_sin
0.1	36.57			__vsind
0.1	36.60	812	0.04	Fintd
0.1	36.63			Fscaleid
0.1	36.66			d_pack
0.1	36.68			Fstatus
0.1	36.70			__vcoshd
0.1	36.72	800	0.03	_get_angles
0.0	36.73			Fcoshd
0.0	36.74			Fsind
0.0	36.75			Fund
0.0	36.76			V_switch
0.0	36.76	12	0.00	Fanintd
0.0	36.76	1	0.00	_exit
0.0	36.76	1	0.00	_finitfp_
0.0	36.76	1	0.00	_on_exit

Note that several low level system calls are included in this output. Your output should not include any information on these low level operations and should be made simpler by eliminating three of the fields of the input. It should also remove the initial underscore in the function listing.

```
%time     name
 16.3     draw_to
 15.6     move_to
  2.1     main
  0.5     cos
  0.4     get_transformation_matrix
  0.2     sin
  0.1     get_angles
```

13. Rewrite the calculator program of example 5.6 to handle infinite precision integer arithmetic. The elements on the stack are pointers to characters, with the (implied) characters consisting of 0's and 1's and terminated by a '\0'. Restrict the arithmetic operations to + and −.

14. It is often a good idea to check the performance and accuracy of system-supplied functions. This exercise will suggest how to do this for the standard library function qsor( ).

(a) Write a program to initialize an array of 1,000 entries of size int. The entries are to be randomly selected using the standard library function rand( ).

(b) Find the time needed for the initialization. You might wish to use the functions in the standard library that can be accessed by the header file time.h; however, a watch will probably suffice.

(c) Sort this array using the standard library function qsort( ).

(d) Compute the times for steps a and c.

(e) Write a quicksort function and use it to sort the array in part a.

(f) Compare the time for steps a and e with the times for steps a and c.

(g) Repeat the experiment for array sizes of 10,000, 100,000, and 1,000000. Which is faster, your routine or the library one?

15. Use the construction in the book as a template to write a C function that will take a variable number of arguments and that will print the arguments. Assume that the arguments are all of type char. You may use putc( ) or putchar( ), but do not use the printf( ) statement.

Software Engineering Exercises

16. Initialize the disk with the file organization that was discussed in the text. Use integers only on the disk and represent the name of each file by some sort of integer code. The reason for this integer encoding of file-names is that we cannot have mixed types of elements in the array; array elements must all be of the same type (in this case, they are of type int).

17. Write a set of specifications for using the random access method of file access.

18. Write a set of specifications for using the indexed sequential access method of file access.

19. What effect will the choice of a different file access method have on the amount of disk space needed for tables needed for file locations? What will be the effect on the disk in terms of wasted space?

CHAPTER 9

Structured Data Types

The subject of this chapter is the support of the C language for the writing of programs that allow the data to have specific structure associated with it. The idea is that the data should be organized in such a way as to support the fundamental actions on the original problem that the computer program was intended to solve. The idea is based on Nicklaus Wirth's [1976] famous dictum:

ALGORITHMS + DATA STRUCTURES = PROGRAMS.

C allows the typical data structure of an array as do nearly all common procedural programming languages. C also allows for the inclusion of several related pieces of information, which may be of different types, to be grouped into a variable of a single data type so that either each piece can be accessed separately or the combination may be accessed as a complete entity of some structured data type. This combination is familiar to Pascal programmers as the record construction.

As with most variables in C, we must do three things. We must declare the variable; that is, we must tell the compiler how the actual memory of the computer that is used for storage of the structured data is to be interpreted. We must define the variable; that is, we must actually set aside the right amount of memory for this data. Finally, we must access the data; that is, we must be able to assign values to the various pieces of the structured data type and be able to use these values.

9.1 Structs

We begin our study of structured data types by an example. Suppose that we wish to make a telephone directory of frequently called numbers. This directory must keep the following information about its entries: name, telephone number, and address. One approach to this problem that might be used by a programmer who is only familiar with languages such as FORTRAN or BASIC that do not support structured data types is to use only those techniques that we learned in Part I of this book. Three separate arrays would be used for storage of the names, telephone numbers, and addresses, respectively. We would set aside a fixed amount of space for the storage of each name and address, say 20 characters for storage of the name and 50 characters for storage of the address. The three arrays might be called NAME, TELNO, and ADDR. The determination of the telephone number of John Smith would involve looking through the array of names for the entry "John Smith," finding its index, and then using this index to find the corresponding entry in the array of telephone numbers. This method is not very intuitive and requires an additional array access to find the number.

A better approach is to store all of the data (name, telephone number, address) in a single entry in an array of such entries. We need all of the entries in the array to have the same type so that we can access them. The type of the entry is a structured type that we will call tel_entry. The syntax for this structured data type is

```
struct tel_entry
    {
    char name[20];
    int telno;
    char  address[50];
    };
```

Let us examine the syntax and semantics of this statement. The key word "struct" indicates that the next token, in this case "tel_entry," is the name of a data type of some structured data. The structure is indicated by the portion of the code between the next two right and left matching braces. In this case, the portions of the structured type are an array of 20 characters, an integer for the telephone number, and an array of 50 characters for the address. This is the first step in using the structured variable – we have told the compiler how storage is to be allotted for this data type. We haven't yet told the compiler to allocate this space when we want to assign actual values to the data. In fact, what we have done is the equivalent of a declaration such as "the next variable is of type int." In each case, we have told the compiler that the data has a certain format but no space has been used yet.

There are two distinct ways that we can indicate to the C compiler that a variable has this structured type. The two methods are illustrated by the code fragments in examples 9.1 and 9.2. In example 9.1, the variable named entry is defined in the same statement in which the structured data type tel_entry is defined. In example 9.2, the structured data type tel_entry is defined in a statement before the variable entry is defined, and therefore the type of this variable must be included in its definition. Note the use of the C reserved word struct twice in example 9.2. The second occurrence of the word is necessary in example 9.2 because there is no data type called "tel_entry" in C. The "struct tel_entry entry" informs the compiler that the variable "entry" is of this structured type.

Example 9.1 One method of declaring structured variables and their types

```
struct tel_entry
    {
    char name[20];
    int telno;
    char  address[50];
    } entry ;
```

Example 9.2 Another method of declaring structured variables and their types

```
struct tel_entry
    {
    char name[20];
    int telno;
    char  address[50];
    } ;
struct tel_entry entry ;
```

The remaining problem for us is the method of accessing the values of this struct variable. We can access the portions name, telno, and address of the structured data type in exactly the same way that we would access them if they were not part of a structured type. Thus we can make the assignment of 5551212 to the variable telno, which is a portion of a struct and is of type int. We can also access any of the characters in the arrays name or address by referring to them by their position. We need to be able to communicate with the compiler that the variables that are portions of a structured type are associated with that type. C uses a dot '.' to separate the struct from one of its component parts. For example, we can make assignments such as

```
entry.telno = 5551212;
```

which assigns the value of 5551212 to the telno portion of the struct named entry. If the name portion of the array name has been assigned the value "John Smith," then the value of entry.name[2] would be the character 'h'. Of course, we cannot make the assignment

```
entry.name = "John Smith"
```

because this type of assignment is not allowed for arrays in C; the problem has nothing to do with structured data types. With the data declarations that we have made, the only way to assign values to the name is to make the assignment character by character.

The general syntax for making an assignment to a portion of a structured data type is

```
structured_variable_name.portion = new_portion_value
```

This is allowable for any assignment that is possible without structured data types.

The next example illustrates that pointers can be used as a portion of a struct. We can improve somewhat on the organization of our data by replacing the definition of the data type tel_entry by

```
struct tel_entry
    {
    char *name;
    char *telno;
    char  *address;
    } entry ;
```

Note that we have represented the telephone number by a pointer to characters instead of as an int since we do not wish to perform any arithmetic on this information. A short program to illustrate this is shown in example 9.3.

Example 9.3

```
#include <stdio.h>

main()
{
  struct tel_entry
    {
    char *name;
    char *telno;
    char  *address;
    } entry;

  entry.name = "John Smith";
  entry.telno = "5551212";
  entry.address = "123 Fourth Street Anywhere USA 56789" ;
  printf("%s\n",entry.name);
  printf("%s\n",entry.telno);
  printf("%s\n",entry.address);
}
```

It has the expected output

```
John Smith
5551212
123 Fourth Street Anywhere USA 56789
```

Variables whose type is some structured data type have the same rights and privileges as simpler variable types: they can be included as part of more complex data structures. For example, an array of variables of the structured data type tel_entry can be declared by the C statement

```
struct tel_entry
  {
  char *name;
  char *telno;
  char  *address;
  } entry[];
```

This statement is identical in its structure to the C statement

```
int arr[];
```

in the sense that both declare an array of variables of a specific type. In the first case, the type is the structured type tel_entry, and in the second case the type is int. Additional information was needed to be given to the compiler in the first case because the compiler did not have tel_entry as one of its previously defined data types and thus could not determine the storage requirements for variables of this type.

Structured data types are commonly used in one of three situations. The first one is to store several pieces of related data in the same structured variable and to have many such variables stored in an array. We have already seen an example of this. The second common use is for the storage of related data in a structure that can be accessed indirectly through the use of pointers. The third common use is frequently a combination of the first two in that a structured data type is used for the implementation of an abstraction of some complex data object.

Before we describe a common use of pointers in conjunction with structured data types, a brief review of pointers is in order. The term pointer in C means a memory address or location. The contents of the location could be any variable or constant and could be of any type whatsoever.

The "contents operator" '*' is used to represent the actual value that is stored in a memory location. Thus if ptr is a pointer to a memory location that contains an integer variable, the expression *ptr refers to the contents of that location and would be used in the forms

```
*ptr = 7;
```

or

```
int_value = *ptr;
```

In the first case, the integer 7 is stored in the memory location pointed to by the variable ptr. In the second case, the variable int_value is assigned as its value the contents of the location pointed to by ptr. If these two statements were executed in a C program that had allocated the right amount of storage for the pointer ptr, then the contents of the location pointed to by ptr would be 7 and the value of the variable int_value would also be 7.

The "address operator" '&' is essentially the inverse of the contents operator that we denoted by '*'. For example, a statement such as

```
*ptr = int_value;
```

means that the contents of the location ptr are the variable int_value. The related statement

```
ptr = &int_value;
```

means that the value of the pointer ptr has been changed to be the address of the variable int_value. There is one exception to the use of this inverse relationship – it is incorrect to write a C statement such as

```
ptr = &7;        /* wrong !! */
```

because 7 is a constant and does not have an obvious address. In general, we cannot take the address of any constant expression. Constants have their values and locations pre-assigned by the compiler, and these locations cannot be changed during program execution.

We now consider how we can access the structured variable entry that we have used earlier in this section. There are several possible methods. The first idea is simply to use different variables for each of the different instances of the structured data type. A more appealing approach is to use a variable named entry_ptr (for "entry pointer") that points to the structured data type. For example, we could have the declarations

```
struct tel_entry
   {
   char *name;
   char *telno;
   char  *address;
   } *entry_ptr;
```

that tells the compiler that entry_ptr is a pointer to an object that has the structured data type tel_entry.

As we saw several times in Chapter 8, we cannot simply use a pointer after such a declaration as this. We need to allocate space for the data and make sure that the space will be interpreted correctly by the C compiler. As before, the system function malloc( ) will be used.

Recall that malloc( ) requires a parameter that represents the size of the data that is pointed to by the pointer and that malloc( ) always returns a pointer to a character. In order to have a pointer to the right kind of structured data, we will use malloc( ) as we did previously with a "cast" operation to ensure that the value returned is a pointer to the correct data type.

A sample program using malloc( ) and structured data types is shown in example 9.4 which has the same output as example 9.3. Note the use of the cast operation with malloc( ).

Example 9.4

```
#include <stdio.h>
#include <stdlib.h>

main(void)
{
  struct tel_entry
```

```
        {
        char *name;
        int telno;
        char  *address;
        } *entry_ptr;

    entry_ptr = (struct tel_entry *)
                    malloc(sizeof (struct tel_entry)) ;
    (*entry_ptr).name = "John Smith";
    (*entry_ptr).telno = 5551212;
    (*entry_ptr).address =
                    "123 Fourth Street Anywhere USA 56789" ;
    printf("%s\n",(*entry_ptr).name);
    printf("%d\n",(*entry_ptr).telno);
    printf("%s\n",(*entry_ptr).address);
}
```

The output is what is expected, namely the values of the various portions of the data in the struct.

The program has several syntactical features that need amplification. In the call to malloc( ), the type of the variable is used rather than the name of the variable. Thus we used struct tel_entry, which was the name of the structured type, rather than entry_ptr, which was the name of a pointer variable to such a structured type. The change from the type of the rvalue that was returned by malloc( ) ("pointer to void") to the type of the lvalue ("pointer to the structured type tel_entry") is done by the cast operation before the assignment.

The only difference is that the C compiler forces us to retype the word "struct" to remind us that tel_entry is a structured type.

The second feature that requires amplification is the use of parentheses in the last six lines of the program. The reason for this is the fact that there are two operators, '*' and '.', that are used on the left-hand side of the '=' sign in a statement such as

```
    *entry_ptr.name = "John Smith";
```

and that when the C compiler parses such a statement into tokens, it has to make a decision about which of the two operators is to perform its actions first. The choices are

```
    '*' first,
```

which means:

Take the contents of the pointer entry_ptr. These contents are a variable whose type is the structured data type tel_entry. Next perform the '.' operation on the contents which means look at the portion of the data that is referred to by the next argument, which is "name." This is precisely what we want, and the code is easily understood by using parentheses as we did.

and

```
    '.' first,
```

which means:

Take the contents of the variable pointed to by the pointer entry_ptr that is a pointer to a structured data type. Take the name portion (IF you can find it without an address being given) and then interpret this as the address of a memory location that is the beginning of the storage of the structured data type. This seems likely to cause serious errors, and in fact the result of the second choice is a disaster.

If we remove parentheses from just two lines in the program of example 9.4 and use the default operator precedence, the result is a collection of warnings.

```
#include <stdio.h>
#include <stdlib.h>

/* INCORRECT CODE - PROBLEM IN PRECEDENCE */

main(void)
{
  struct tel_entry
    {
    char *name;
    int telno;
    char  *address;
    } *entry_ptr;

  entry_ptr = (struct tel_entry *)
                 malloc (sizeof(struct tel_entry)) ;
  (*entry_ptr).name = "John Smith";
  (*entry_ptr).telno = "5551212";

  (*entry_ptr).address =
     "123 Fourth Street Anywhere USA 56789"; /* NO !*/

  printf("%s\n",(*entry_ptr).name);
  printf("%d\n",(*entry_ptr).telno);
  printf("%s\n",(*entry_ptr).address);     /* NO !  */
}
```

The warnings from one compiler are

```
"toy.c", line 13: warning: struct/union or struct/union
pointer required
"toy.c", line 13: warning: illegal combination of pointer
and integer,     op =
"toy.c", line 16: warning: struct/union or struct/union
pointer required
```

If we try to run this program, the output is the dreaded message

```
Segmentation fault (core dumped)
```

which indicates that we have tried to access a restricted memory location.

Decisions about which operation is to be performed first are made by the C compiler using the precedence table to which we have referred many times and which is found in Appendix 5. The actual rules are quite complex to remember and are often not easy to apply in practice. It is probably a lot easier to use parentheses since they never get you in trouble and make clear what usage was intended in the program. Complex situations such as structures containing structures require even more careful use of parentheses.

There is another commonly used notation that avoids the frequent use of parentheses to make sure that the correct order of precedence of operations is performed. It applies only when a structured data type is being accessed by a pointer. The idea is that a statement of the form

```
(*data_structure_pointer).portion_of_the_data
```

is replaced by the equivalent statement

```
data_structure_pointer->portion_of_the_data
```

That is, the parentheses have been removed and the '.' to indicate that we wish to access a portion of the data has been replaced by the '->', which indicates that the next token is the name of the portion of the data that is pointed to by the pointer before the '->'. Example 9.5 shows how this is used in a program that is completely equivalent to the program of example 9.4.

Example 9.5 The code of example 9.4 with changed notation

```
#include <stdio.h>
#include <stdlib.h>

main()
{
   struct tel_entry
      {
      char *name;
      int telno;
      char  *address;
      } *entry_ptr;

   entry_ptr = (struct tel_entry *)
            malloc(sizeof (struct tel_entry)) ;
   entry_ptr->name = "John Smith";
   entry_ptr->telno = 5551212;
```

```
        entry_ptr->address =
                "123 Fourth Street Anywhere USA 56789" ;
        printf("%s\n",entry_ptr->name);
        printf("%d\n",entry_ptr->telno);
        printf("%s\n",entry_ptr->address);
}
```

Look at the complete precedence table given in Appendix 5. Note how the

```
    ->
```

operator has an extremely high precedence and is left-associative. The high precedence for this operator is the reason for its utility.

We have seen a lot of new notation and several new concepts in this section. The next section includes several more complex examples of the use of structured data types.

9.2 Some Data Structures in C: Lists and Trees

In this section, we will show several examples of the use of the struct mechanism for the C implementation of structured data types. The intent is to show the typical ways in which the idea can be used. However, the C source code that we present will often be somewhat inefficient since our purpose is to illustrate a concept rather than to write commercial-quality code.

The first example in this section illustrates the way that the abstraction of a linked list can be implemented in C using the struct concept. Figure 9.1 shows the general form of a linked list. The nodes have two fields: a field called "info" that contains the data stored in the node and a field called "link" that contains a pointer to the next node in the list. Access to any node on the list can be obtained by starting at the head of the list and accessing subsequent nodes by moving along the links. We have described a singly-linked list in the sense that backward traversals of the list are not possible; we would have to start at the head of the list again if we have passed a particular node in our traversal.

Notice that each node of the linked list has two fields: an information field that contains the data to be stored in the node and a link to the next node, if any. Thus a link is a pointer to a node, which is a structured data type, and a node is a structured data type that is pointed to by a link, has a pointer to a node as one of its fields, and a field called "info" as the other. This type of arrangement where a pointer points to a data object that has a field that is of the same type as the pointer is frequently called a "self-referential" data type. The right-hand side of the diagram in Figure 9.1 indicates that the last link in the

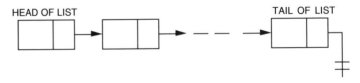

HEAD OF LIST   TAIL OF LIST

Figure 9.1 A linked list

list points to no object whatsoever. We say that the pointer of the last node is a "null pointer" or that it points to NULL.

In example 9.6, we show how to have a linked list of nodes whose contents are data of type int. In example 9.6, we consider the code to be made up of three sections: creating the list head; placing of data into the nodes of the list that is pointed to by the list head; and accessing the data in the list in the order in which the data was entered. In this example, we have a list of 10 nodes that contain data of type int. The data is initially obtained by reading an integer. This initial data is entered in the head of the list. The remaining nodes have contents that are 10 more than the previous node.

The list is terminated by a null pointer; this is implemented by defining NULL to be 0 and having the last pointer always point to NULL.

Example 9.6

```
/*  program to create and manipulate a linked list */

#include <stdio.h>
#include <stdlib.h>

#define NULL 0

/* data declaration */
struct node
  {
  int info ;
  struct  node *link;
  };

/*  function prototype */
void insert(struct node *list_head, int i) ;


main(void)
{
  int i;
  struct node *head, *p;

  printf("enter an integer\n");
  scanf("%d",&i);
  head = ( struct node *) malloc(sizeof( struct node));

      /* create list */
  head->link = NULL;
  head->info =i;

  insert(head,i);  /* insert into list pointed to by head */
```

The program in example 9.6 creates the list by first creating the node that represents the head of the list. Once this head node is created and the fields of the node are given the appropriate values (the correct int variable for the info field and the NULL pointer for the pointer field), the rest of the list is created by getting new nodes, linking them to the end of the list in the correct manner, and then putting the appropriate values in the various fields. The nodes in the list were created by the use of a call to the function malloc( ) that we have used so many times before. Notice how we passed the parameter head to the list insertion function insert( ); we minimized the interface between the two functions main( ) and insert( ) by using parameters instead of global variables. This is especially important in more realistic programs in which the insert( ) and other list management functions would probably be written in a separate C source code file.

The program also uses what is frequently called a "list walk." This involves the use of two pointers that are used to move down the list. The pointer, p, is initialized to point to the head of the list and always reflects the current node that we wish to operate on. The construction

```
while (p != NULL)
    {
    printf("info is %d\n",p->info);
    p = p->link;
    }
```

has the effect of testing at the top of the loop for the condition that the pointer p is NULL; thus this loop will not be entered if the list were empty. If the list were not empty, then the head would not be NULL and the loop would be entered at least once. Each time through the loop, the node pointed to by p is accessed and the pointer p is replaced by the pointer field of the node pointed to by p. The check for p being NULL at the top of the loop then prevents any attempt to run off the end of the list by trying to access the pointer field of a NULL pointer, which would always cause an error.

There is one last thing to notice about the design of example 9.6. The error checking for an empty list is enclosed in the function insert( ) rather than in the calling function main( ). This makes it much easier to use the function insert( ) again in other programs.

So far this chapter has considered the data structure of linked lists. In earlier sections of this book, we have considered the data structure of a stack. In the remainder of this section, we describe the last of the common structured data types in C: the tree. We will provide some examples of the implementation details of trees and compare the utility of several methods of storing and accessing data that is needed for a simple problem. There are two reasons for doing this. First, the novice programmer should see actual examples of how the typical abstract algorithms for using such structures might be implemented. Second, every C programmer needs to keep in mind the features that can be used to speed up programs, and some of these ideas come into play here.

For our purposes a binary tree can be defined recursively as:

A tree is either
 empty
or else
 an object consisting of a node and two other objects called subtrees, each of which is also a tree.

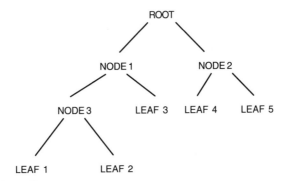

Figure 9.2 A small tree

The objects are considered to contain information, and the two additional objects described in the second part of the definition are called subtrees. Strictly speaking, the object that we have defined is called a binary tree since each node has at most two branches coming out of it. We will not consider more general trees in this book. Figure 9.2 shows a graphical representation of a tree with a single root node, four internal nodes (nodes 1, 2, and 3 and the root node), and five external nodes called leaves. The two nodes node 1 and node 2 are the roots of subtrees. The leaves are also the roots of subtrees, and these subtrees have no objects. Standard terminology describes nodes 1 and 2 as being children of the root and being siblings; node 2 is called a parent of leaves 4 and 5. The diagram follows the standard pattern of having the root of the tree at the top of the diagram.

We can use this recursive definition of a tree to describe the structure. It is convenient to use pointers to structured data types to implement this concept. Example 9.7 shows how this is done for a tree in which the information content is a single floating point number. Note the similarity to the way that the structure was declared recursively for nodes in linked lists.

Example 9.7 Declarations for a tree structure

```
struct TREE
   {
   struct TREE *left;
   float info;
   struct TREE *right;
   } ;
struct TREE *tree;
```

As before, malloc( ) is needed to create actual space for a tree.

```
tree = malloc( sizeof(struct TREE) );
```

Note that the structure of a TREE as shown in example 9.7 forces pointers to have certain non-NULL values if they are not leaf nodes. For example, the tree shown in Figure 9.2 has the value NULL for each of the pointers of the leaf nodes. The two pointer fields of root are pointers to node 1 and node 2, respectively.

A typical program that uses trees has two parts – the creation of the tree and the processing of the elements that make up the tree. The creation of the tree is usually the harder problem and so we discuss it first.

There are two possible methods for constructing a tree: constructing it from the leaves up or from the root down. To construct a tree from the root down, we need to create the root first. This requires a call to malloc( ) with the info portion declared appropriately. When more information is added to the tree, a search is performed to find the appropriate place for the data to be included. Once the tree root is created, the algorithm is

- Go to the root of the tree.
- Find the appropriate place for the new data relative to the existing root.
- The new place is below some existing leaf node.
- The pointer fields of the existing leaf node found in the previous step are currently set to NULL. Create a new node and set the appropriate pointer field of the existing leaf node to point to the new node. The new node is now a leaf node and the previously chosen leaf node is now an interior node of the tree.
- Place the data in the new node. Set the pointer fields of the new node to NULL to indicate that this new node is now a leaf node.

To construct a tree from the bottom up, we follow a different procedure. Again, the first step is to create the root, which we do by getting a node, marking its position in memory by a pointer, and setting its pointer fields to NULL. After creation of the root, the algorithm is

- Go to the root of the tree.
- Move down the tree to find the appropriate place for the new data.
- The new place is above the existing root node.
- Create a new root node.
- The pointer fields of the new root node found in the previous step are currently set to NULL. Set the left and right pointer fields of the new root node to the old root and to NULL, depending on whether we want the new root to be to the left or right of the old root.
- Place the data in the appropriate new root node.

Processing the elements that make up a tree is much easier since we can use the recursive structure of the tree to perform tree traversals similar in function to the list walk that we saw earlier. Since a tree is defined recursively, we can most easily traverse the tree using a recursive technique.

There are three possible natural orders in which we can traverse a tree from left to right. The three possible natural orders are

(1) post-order, in which the order at each node is left subtree first, then right subtree, then node
(2) pre-order, in which the order at each node is node first, then left subtree, then right subtree
(3) in-order, in which the order at each node is left subtree first, then node, then right subtree

To understand this terminology better, consider that the tree can have the arithmetic operation represented in the form:

```
+ 2 5
```

for pre-order tree traversal,

```
2 + 5
```

for in-order tree traversal,

and

```
2 5 +
```

for post-order tree traversal.

These can easily be implemented. For example, to traverse the tree in pre-order with the information that is stored in a node is acted on by a function called process( ) before the information in its children, we have the code fragment of example 9.8. In this and the next two examples, the initial call to the function is of the form

```
traverse(root);
```

since we are passing a pointer to the tree.

Example 9.8 Pre-order tree traversal

```
/* code for pre-order traversal of tree    */
/* using the function process() at each node */
traverse(struct TREE *tree_ptr)
{
   if (tree_pointer != NULL)
     {
     process(tree_ptr.info);
     traverse(tree_ptr.left);
     traverse(tree_ptr.right);
     }
}
```

The in-order traversal in which the order is left child, then parent, then right child is given in example 9.9.

Example 9.9 In-order tree traversal

```
/* code for in-order traversal of tree    */
/* using the function process() at each node */
traverse(struct TREE *tree_ptr)
{
   if (tree_ptr != NULL)
     {
     traverse(tree_ptr.left);
     process(tree_ptr.info);
     traverse(tree_ptr.right);
     }
}
```

The post-order traversal in which the order is left child, then right child, then parent is given in example 9.10.

Example 9.10 Post-order tree traversal

```
/* code for post-order traversal of tree     */
/* using the function process() at each node  */
traverse(struct TREE *tree_ptr)
{
  if (tree_pointer != NULL)
    {
    traverse(tree_ptr.left);
    traverse(tree_ptr.right);
    process(tree_ptr.info);
    }
}
```

Here is a common use of trees. Suppose that we have an expression that is to be evaluated and that the expression is given in postfix form; that is, every binary operator is written after its two operands. For example, the expressions

    2   3   +   5   *   8   -

and

    1   2   3   +   +   8   -

are in postfix form, but

    2   +   3   *   5   -   8

is not. (It is in infix form because each binary operator is between its two operands.) In the exercises you will be asked to transform expressions from infix to postfix form, as well as to perform other operations. For now, note that the postfix notation is unambiguous in the order of operations. We simply read across the list of tokens in a postfix expression and place all of the operands on a stack. When we encounter an operator, we simply pop the appropriate operands off the stack, perform the operation, and push the result onto the stack. This evaluation operation is quite simple.

We can do the same thing using trees. A tree can be created using the operators as internal nodes and the operands as leaves. Figure 9.3 shows a tree representation of the postfix expression

    2   3   +   5   *   8   -

which is equivalent to the infix form

    2   +   3   *   5   -   8

We should always write our programs by trying to adhere to the software engineering principles discussed earlier. This suggests that the operations on the tree (creation,

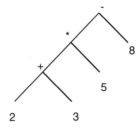

Figure 9.3 A tree representation for the postfix expression 2 3 + 5* 8-

insertion of a node, and deletion of a node) should all be in a separate file. The internal structure of the user's implementation of the tree data type should be made available to each function that needs it.

In practice, this means that the tree operations should be in a file named something like treeops.c and that the structure

```
struct TREE
    {
    struct TREE *left;
    float info;
    struct TREE *right;
    } ;

struct TREE *tree;
```

should be incorporated into a header file named tree.h or something similar. Thus the organization should be something like:

```
main.c
tree.h
treeops.c
other C files
```

and the make utility should be used to help with compilation.

See the exercises for more information on the use of trees and their applications.

9.3 Additional Data Structures in C: Queues

In this section, we consider the queue data structure. A queue allows for the insertion of data at the end of the queue and the removal of data from the head of the queue. The positions of the end and the head are kept in two variables that are called the front and the rear of the queue, respectively. The insertion and removal discipline of the queue is FIFO or first-in–first-out instead of the LIFO or last-in–first-out discipline of the stack. The first thing needed for manipulation of queues is the appropriate data structure.

Note that there are several ways in which a queue can be implemented. Also, the abstraction of being able to insert in a FIFO manner does not restrict us in the size of

281

the queue. This size can be fixed as in the case when the queue uses an array of fixed size for its elements or is virtually infinite, such as when a linked list with pointers and dynamic memory allocation of the nodes is used for storage of the objects in the queue. We demonstrate the implementation of queues using the fixed-size array for storage of the elements and discuss the other method in the exercises.

We should follow good software engineering practice, just as we did in the discussion of trees in the previous section. We will use header files for information that needs to be globally available, and we will hide other information about queue operations in a separate file named queueops.c, or something similar.

Example 9.11 shows the data structure for a queue whose elements are floating point numbers. In example 9.11, MAXQUEUE is a user-defined constant representing the size of the queue. The header file is called queue.h in this example.

Example 9.11 Possible declarations for a queue structure — file queue.h

```
/* header file queue.h for an array implementation of */
/* queues using a fixed-size array                     */

#define MAXQUEUE 1000

struct QUEUE
  {
  float info[MAXQUEUE];
  int front, rear;
  } ;
```

All operations on queues are based on certain primitive operations for inserting and deleting items from the queue and for determining if the queue is empty or full. Any C program using queues should have these primitive queue operations grouped together in a single file. This file should be incorporated into the executable program by using a make-file. Example 9.12 shows a file that includes the primitive operations for a queue. The file queue.h is a user-defined file that contains the data structure shown in example 9.11 as well as the constant MAXQUEUE.

Example 9.12

```
#include "queue.h"

/*************************************************/
/* inserts element after checking for full queue   */
/* if queue is full, error message is printed.      */
/*************************************************/

void insert(struct QUEUE queue, float element)
/* our queue has float elements    */
```

```
  {
  if (!full(queue))
    {
    queue.rear ++;
    queue.info[rear] = element;
    }
  else
    printf("Error - queue full -- cannot insert\n");
}


/*****************************************************/
/* deletes element after checking for empty queue   */
/* if queue is empty, error message is printed.      */
/*****************************************************/
void delete(struct QUEUE queue, float element)
/* our queue had float elements     */

{
  if (!empty(queue))
    {
    queue.front ++ ;
    queue.info[front] = NULL;
    }
  else
    printf("Error - queue empty -- cannot delete\n");
}



/*****************************************************/
/*   Tests for empty by comparing front and rear     */
/*   If front > rear then return 0                    */
/*   Otherwise, the function returns 1 indicating     */
/*   that there is at least one element in queue.     */
/*****************************************************/
int empty(struct QUEUE queue)
{
  if (queue.front > queue.rear)
    return 0 ;
  else
    return 1;
}
```

```
/**************************************************/
/*   tests for queue full by comparing front and  */
/*   rear indices.  If rear = MAXQUEUE then this   */
/*   function returns 0 indicating that the queue  */
/*   is full. Otherwise, the function returns 1    */
/*   indicating that room is available in the queue */
/**************************************************/

int full(struct QUEUE queue)
{
  if (queue.rear == MAXQUEUE)
    return 0
  else
    return 1;
}


/**************************************************/
/*   initializes the queue to have all its entries 0 */
/*   and to set the values of front and rear      */
/**************************************************/
void initialize(struct QUEUE queue)
{
  int i;

  for (i = 0; i < MAXQUEUE; i++)
    queue.info[i] = NULL;
  queue.front = 0;
  queue.rear = 0;
}
```

Note the high level of documentation provided in this file. Since such a file can reasonably be expected to be reused (that is, it will probably be included whenever queue operations are needed and the queue is implemented as an array), it will probably be used at a time when the person using the file does not recall the details of the code. This situation occurs frequently when software is written by a team of programmers. If you write these utility programs carefully and document them well, then you will be more productive in the long run because you can reuse code without having to debug it over and over again.

The test for the queue being empty or full depends on the positions of the front and rear pointers. The test for the queue being full is that there is no space in the array, and thus

```
rear = MAXQUEUE
```

The condition for the queue being empty is that the front and rear pointers satisfy the inequality

```
front > rear
```

Note that this implementation of a queue is wasteful in that it is possible for the entire array to be free of queue elements but for the function full( ) to return the value 0. This is possible if the entire queue fills up with elements and then each of the queue elements gets deleted in turn. After this set of actions, the values of front and rear are MAXQUEUE + 1 and MAXQUEUE, respectively, and therefore the queue is declared (incorrectly) to be full. This is a well-known problem in the implementation of queues. In our functions, it is caused by never decrementing the index front and thus always wasting space. We could always move all of the array elements forward in the event of a deletion of an array element. This agrees with the way that a line at a bank or grocery store moves but is very time-consuming because of the large amount of data movement required in many circumstances. Some of the exercises included at the end of this chapter are for implementations of queues that avoid this problem to some degree. In particular, the use of circular queues helps avoid some of this wasted space as does the pointer implementation.

There are other possible implementations for queues. For example, we can implement a queue as a linked list using two pointers instead of two integer indices to represent the front and the rear of the queue. A data structure for one possible implementation in this manner of a queue whose contents are integers is

```
struct QUEUE
    {
    int info;
    struct QUEUE *front, *rear;
    };
```

All the code in example 9.12 would have to be rewritten in order to implement queues in this manner. However, if the rest of the program interfaced with the queue only through the functions in example 9.12, then the rest of the program would be essentially unchanged, as long as the type of an object in the queue remains int.

Note that structures can be used in other contexts also. In example 9.13, we present a function that performs a binary search of an array of character strings. The strings are the reserved words of the Ada programming language, and the function was used in the development of a prototype Ada compiler. The input to the function is given in pointer notation.

Example 9.13

```
#include <stdio.h>
#include <stdlib.h>

static char *name;
    reserved_words[] =
        {
        "ABORT", "ABS", "ACCEPT", "ACCESS","ALL", "AND",
        "ARRAY", "AT", "BEGIN", "BODY", "CASE", "CONSTANT",
         "DECLARE", "DELAY", "DELTA", "DIGITS", "DO", "ELSE",
```

```
                  "ELSIF", "END", "ENTRY", "EXCEPTION", "EXIT", "FOR",
                  "FUNCTION", "GENERIC", "GOTO", "IF", "IN", "IS",
                  "LIMITED", "LOOP", "MOD", "NEW", "NULL", "NOT", "OR",
                  "OTHERS", "OUT", "PACKAGE", "PRAGMA", "PRIVATE",
                  "PROCEDURE", "RAISE", "RANGE", "RECORD", "REM",
                  "RENAMES", "RETURN", "REVERSE", "SELECT", "SEPARATE",
                  "SUBTYPE", "TASK", "TERMINATE", "THEN", "TYPE", "USE",
                  "WHEN", "WHILE", "WITH", "XOR"
              };


main(void)
{
   char key[80]; /* reserve space for the input of key */
   int low = 0;
   int high = sizeof(reserved_words);
   int mid;
   int c ;

   printf("Enter a string\n");
   scanf("%s",key);
   printf("The string was %s\n",key);
   while (low <= high)
      {
      mid =  (high + low)/2;
      if (( c = strcmp(reserved_words[mid], key)) == 0  )
         {
         printf("\n %s was in the array\n",key);
         return;
         }
      else if (c < 0)
         low = mid + 1;
      else
         high = mid - 1;
      }
   printf("The string %s was not in the array.\n",key);
}
```

The algorithm of example 9.13 is easily seen to be binary search.

Note that there is a standard library function called bsearch( ) that could have been used here. Its use would have replaced the while-loop of exercise 9.13 with a single function call. As in our previous discussion of the standard library function qsort( ) in section 8.8, the user must write a function with return type int to compare the two elements being compared. In this case, it seemed easier to write the few lines of code myself instead of writing the comparison function and invoking the library search. In other cases, it might be easier to use the library functions, especially if you are unsure of how to write a binary search.

9.4 User-Defined Data Types and typedef

One of the fundamental principles of modern software engineering is that data, as well as its implementation and the operations that can be performed on the data, should be abstracted and should be hidden from the programmer as much as possible. The purpose is to ensure that a programmer changing code in one part of a program doesn't cause errors in another part by accessing variables and data structures that should be hidden. This is especially important in software that is so large that it is written by a team of programmers since it is far too complex for any one individual to create; this applies to almost all commercial or government software. Hopefully, some of the code that you write will be so well written and so modular that it can easily be reused by incorporating it into programs other than the one for which it was originally written.

Since we have now seen all the major features of C (unions are a relatively minor feature and I/O is not part of the C language), it is reasonable to ask how well C supports meeting the goals of software engineering. Like most other programming languages, C encourages the decomposition of programs into smaller units. In the case of C, these units are functions and files. The scope rules of C encourage the hiding of data in files from functions in other files. It is conceivable that abstractions of data types can be supported by encapsulating all the relevant data structures and operations on the data structures in files and controlling the interface. The notion of an abstract data type is the basis of such "object-oriented" languages such as C++, which is a new language intended to allow objects as the fundamental structure. Most implementations of C++ allow the incorporation of C code. (The Ada language allows object-oriented programming by means of its "generic" features for data types and procedures also.) The idea of an object-oriented language is to create these objects by describing their properties as well as the transformations that can be made on the objects. The C language supports the ideas of information hiding to a limited extent but does not provide the level of abstraction available in object-oriented languages. It does allow user-defined data types.

Consider the example of a stack. The important feature of a stack is that the data on the stack is accessed on a LIFO (last-in–first-out) basis. The actual operations possible on a stack are pushing a data item on the stack and popping a data element off the stack. Except for performance issues, it is really not relevant to the programmer precisely how the stack is implemented. Thus we could implement the stack as an array, or as a linked list, or make use of some other possible underlying data structure. The details of the choice can be hidden from the rest of the program by placing the stack operations in a separate file. If we use only static variables and functions that are external to all functions in that file, then these variables and functions are hidden from functions and variables in other files. This provides some level of modularity.

The level of abstraction is not very high, however. If we wish to have a stack of integer values and a stack of pointers to characters, then we need to write two sets of nearly identical functions to handle the push and pop operations for each type of stack. This is wasteful and makes the code look ugly. A more serious problem is that the modularity and clean design of the program have been lost, because we need to have different names for the functions that act on different types of data. Thus we might need functions push_int( ) and pop_int( ) for stacks of integer variables, push_char( ) and pop_char( )

for stacks of character variables, push_char_ptr( ) and pop_char_ptr( ) for stacks whose data consists of pointers to characters, etc. The names are somewhat mnemonic and help the programmer to determine which of the functions should be used for any specific type of data. However, we still need a new set of stack functions for each new type of stack data.

The C reserved word typedef can be used in this type of situation to make the program somewhat less cumbersome. The idea is to rename types by using the typedef facility to suggest that the type of the data is easily changed. The next example shows how this syntax works. Instead of having a stack of integer data, we have a stack of data of type STACK_ITEM where the name of the type int in example 9.14 has been changed to STACK_ITEM for this data in example 9.15.

Example 9.14 Operations on stacks of integers

```
/*****************************************************/
/*     FILENAME : int_stack.c                       */
/*     THE FILE CONTAINS STACK OPERATIONS           */
/*     THE STACK IS IMPLEMENTED USING A FIXED ARRAY  */
/*     THE ELEMENTS OF THE ARRAY ARE INTEGERS       */
/*     FUNCTIONS IN FILE:                           */
/*         push()                                   */
/*         pop()                                    */
/*                                                  */
/*     FILE WRITTEN: JULY  14, 1975                 */
/*     PROGRAMMER: A. B. SEE                        */
/*     MODIFIED BY: HU ISHE                         */
/*     MODIFICATION DATE: FEBRUARY 29, 1993         */
/*****************************************************/


#define MAXSTACK 20              /* max. items in stack */
int top = -1;
int stack[MAXSTACK];            /* array of integers    */

/* pushes an argument onto stack                        */
/* If stack is full, an error message is printed.       */
void push(int n)
{
  if (top < MAXSTACK - 1)
    {
    top++;
    stack[top] = n;
    }
  else
    printf("error -- stack full.\n");
}
```

```
/* pops the top value from stack. Prints an error    */
/* message  and returns a negative value for top      */
/* if stack is empty                                  */
int pop(void)
{
  int temp = top;

  if (top >= 0)
    {
    top--;
    return (stack[temp]);
    }
  else
    {
    printf("error -- stack empty.\n");
    return (0);   /* stack empty: return 0, clear stack */
    }
}
```

Example 9.15 Operations on STACK_ITEM data, an improved version

```
/**********************************************************/
/*    FILENAME : stack.c                                  */
/*    FILE CONTAINS FUNCTIONS FOR OPERATIONS ON A STACK */
/*    STACK IS IMPLEMENTED USING AN ARRAY OF FIXED SIZE */
/*    ELEMENTS OF THE ARRAY ARE OF THE TYPE GIVEN BY A   */
/*    typedef STATEMENT AS BEING TYPE STACK_ITEM         */
/*    STACK_ITEM IS int IN THIS FILE                     */
/*    FUNCTIONS IN FILE:                                 */
/*        push()                                         */
/*        pop()                                          */
/*                                                       */
/*    FILE WRITTEN: JULY  14, 1975                       */
/*    PROGRAMMER: A. B. SEE                              */
/*    MODIFIED BY: HU ISHE                               */
/*    MODIFICATION DATE: FEBRUARY 29, 1993               */
/**********************************************************/



#define MAXSTACK 20      /* max. number of items in stack */
int top = -1;

typedef int STACK_ITEM;
STACK_ITEM stack[MAXSTACK];    /* array of integers      */
```

```
/* pushes an argument onto the stack if not full.  If  */
/* stack was already full, an error message is printed.*/
void push (STACK_ITEM n)
{
  if (top < MAXSTACK-1 )
    {
    top++;
    stack[top] = n;
    }
  else
    printf("error -- stack full.\n");
}



/* pops the top of the stack; prints an error message  */
/* if one tries to "pop" from an empty stack.          */
/* Stack is empty if top is negative                   */
STACK_ITEM pop(void)
{
  int temp = top;

  if (top >= 0)
    {
    top--;
    return (stack[temp]);
    }
  else
    {
    printf("error -- stack empty.\n");
    return (0);            /* stack is empty -- return 0 */
    }
}
```

The only change that is necessary to be able to use precisely this same code for another type of data is that the nature of the data as described in the typedef statement must be changed by a new typedef statement. However, we really need to change the documentation each time we change the definition of the data type of the stack element by using the typedef to agree with the code. There is a good rule of thumb to follow when trying to read and understand a program: if the documentation and the code don't agree, then they are both wrong.

There is a better, more modular way of writing this code. We will still use the typedef construction. However, we will remove all mention of the data type from the file of stack operations and place them in a separate header file "stack.h" in which the data type is given. Example 9.16 shows the header file, and example 9.17 shows a better version of the stack operations file.

Example 9.16 Header file stack.h for stack operations using typedef

```
/************************************************/
/*    FILENAME : stack.h                        */
/*    CONTAINS CONSTANTS FOR STACK OPERATIONS   */
/*    STACK USES AN ARRAY OF FIXED SIZE         */
/*     ELEMENTS OF ARRAY ARE OF TYPE GIVEN BY   */
/*    typedef STATEMENT  TYPE STACK_ITEM        */
/*    STACK_ITEM IS int IN THIS FILE            */
/*    stack is an array of elements of type STACK_ITEM */
/*                                              */
/*    FILE WRITTEN: JULY  14, 1975              */
/*    PROGRAMMER: A. B. SEE                     */
/*    MODIFIED BY: HU ISHE                      */
/*    MODIFICATION DATE: FEBRUARY 30, 1993      */
/************************************************/

#define MAXSTACK 20              /* max. size of stack */
int top = -1;
typedef int STACK_ITEM;
STACK_ITEM stack[MAXSTACK];      /* array of int  */
```

Example 9.17 Operations on STACK_ITEM data

```
/************************************************/
/*    FILE NAME : stack.c                       */
/*    FILE CONTAINS FUNCTIONS FOR STACK OPERATIONS */
/*    STACK IS IMPLEMENTED USING AN ARRAY OF FIXED SIZE */
/*    ELEMENTS OF THE ARRAY ARE OF THE TYPE GIVEN BY A */
/*    typedef STATEMENT AS BEING OF TYPE STACK_ITEM */
/*    STACK_ITEM is a synonym for int           */
/*    Stack is an array of elements of type STACK_ITEM */
/*    CONSTANTS ARE IN THE FILE stack.h         */
/*    FUNCTIONS IN FILE:                        */
/*        push()                                */
/*        pop()                                 */
/*    FILE WRITTEN: JULY  14, 1975              */
/*    PROGRAMMER: A. B. SEE                     */
/*    MODIFIED BY: HU ISHE                      */
/*    MODIFICATION DATE: FEBRUARY 31, 1993      */
/************************************************/

#include "stack.h"


/* pushes an argument onto the stack if not full.  If  */
```

```
/* stack was already full, then print error message.    */
void push (STACK_ITEM n)
{
  if (top < MAXSTACK - 1)
    {
    top++;
    stack[top] = n;
    }
  else
    printf("error -- stack full.\n");
}



/* pops the top value off stack. Prints an error message  */
/* if one tries to "pop" from an empty stack.             */
/* A negative value for top means that the stack is empty */
STACK_ITEM pop(void)
{int temp = top;

if (top >= 0)
  {
  top--;
  return (stack[temp]);
  }
else
  {
  printf("error -- stack empty.\n");
  return (0); /* stack empty: return 0 to clear stack */
  }
}
```

The only change that is necessary to be able to use precisely this same code for other projects with stack operations is to change the header file. Of course the use of the type STACK_ITEM must be enforced by the programming team. I once saw code written by a programmer who was fired from a project because he did not follow the company's required pattern for the names of data types. Each of the individual program modules written by this programmer was correct but together they were useless since they had to be rewritten in order to fit the rest of the system. Clearly the use of the typedef statement supports the idea of using code in different contexts.

The major problem with using the typedef declaration for pure object-oriented programming is that many C compilers do not normally check for type agreement even without typedef and therefore are not likely to check if the program uses typedef. In addition, only one renaming of any typedef definition is active in a program at any one time. The unfortunate conclusion is that C does not really support the use of object-oriented programming.

Even with this limitation, we can provide some of the facilities for an abstract data type in C. By the term "abstract data type" we mean that the essential features of the concept can be hidden completely from the person using this type.

One problem with the previous code for stack operations is the direct visibility of the top of the stack to the rest of the program. We can remedy this lack of hiding by redefining the data type stack as a structured type. One way to do this is shown in examples 9.18 and 9.19. Note the differences among this and the previous two sets of examples.

Example 9.18 Header file stack.h for stack operations using typedef

```
/**********************************************************/
/*    FILENAME : stack.h                                */
/*    CONTAINS CONSTANTS FOR STACK OPERATIONS           */
/*    STACK USES AN ARRAY OF FIXED SIZE                 */
/*     ELEMENTS OF ARRAY ARE OF TYPE GIVEN BY           */
/*    typedef STATEMENT  TYPE STACK_ITEM                */
/*    STACK_ITEM IS int IN THIS FILE                    */
/*    stack is an structured data type                  */
/*                                                      */
/*    FILE WRITTEN: FEBRUARY 29, 1993                   */
/*    PROGRAMMER:  HU IS SHE                            */
/**********************************************************/

#define MAXSTACK 20                    /* max. stack size*/
typedef int STACK_ITEM;
struct stack
  {
  STACK_ITEM stack[MAXSTACK];          /* array of int  */
  int top;
  };
typedef struct stack STACK;
```

Example 9.19 Operations on STACK_ITEM abstract data type

```
/**********************************************************/
/*    FILENAME : stack.c                                */
/*    FILE CONTAINS FUNCTIONS FOR OPERATIONS ON A STACK  */
/*    STACK IS IMPLEMENTED USING AN ARRAY OF FIXED SIZE  */
/*    ELEMENTS OF THE ARRAY ARE OF THE TYPE GIVEN BY A   */
/*    typedef STATEMENT AS BEING OF TYPE STACK_ITEM      */
/*    STACK_ITEM is a synonym for int                   */
/*    A STACK is an abstract data type                  */
/*    elements on STACK are of type STACK_ITEM          */
/*    CONSTANTS ARE IN THE FILE stack.h                 */
```

```
/*    FUNCTIONS IN FILE:                                  */
/*        initialize()                                    */
/*        push()                                          */
/*        pop()                                           */
/*    FILE WRITTEN: JULY  14, 1975                        */
/*    PROGRAMMER: A. B. SEE                               */
/*    MODIFIED BY: HU ISHE                                */
/*    MODIFICATION DATE: FEBRUARY 32, 1993                */
/**********************************************************/

#include "stack.h"


/* New function needed because of new declaration     */
/* initializes the stack top to -1                    */
void initialize(STACK s)
{
  s.top = -1;
}


/* pushes an argument onto the stack if not full.  If */
/* stack was already full, then print error message   */
void push (STACK s, STACK_ITEM n)
{
  if (s.top < MAXSTACK - 1)
    {
    s.top++;
    s.stack[top] = n;
    }
  else
    printf("error -- stack full.\n");
}


/* pops the top value off stack. Prints an error message  */
/* if one tries to "pop" from an empty stack.             */
/* A negative value for top means that the stack is empty */
STACK_ITEM pop(STACK s)
{
  int temp = top;

  if (s.top >= 0)
```

```
    {
    s.top--;
    return (s.stack[temp]);
    }
  else
    {
    printf("error -- stack empty.\n");
    return (0); /* stack empty: return 0 to clear stack */
    }
}
```

Any program wishing to use the stack operations on the abstract data type may simply include the two files of examples 9.18 and 9.19 and change the typedef statement to agree with the appropriate type. The size of the arrays could be changed as needed. In fact, a change to the STACK data structure that allows a linked list representation of a stack using pointers instead of a representation that uses arrays should only affect the two stack operations files and not the rest of the code. This is a fairly high level of abstraction - the highest that is available in C.

Note that a high level of abstraction such as the abstract data types allows any function using an instance of the abstract data type to be completely independent of the details of this type. In the exercises you will be asked to confirm this statement by writing a program that operates on a stack using the code for array implementation of stacks given in this section and to modify the stack operations without changing the rest of your system. An appropriate data structure for a linked-list implementation of a stack would be

```
typedef int STACK_ITEM;
struct stack
  {
    STACK_ITEM info;           /* array of int  */
    struct STACK *top;
    };
```

typedef struct stack STACK;

With the functions push( ), pop( ), and initialize( ) recoded to meet this interface, any other portions of the program can be used without modification to use this implementation. Of course the program will have to be recompiled since the include file has been changed.

9.5 Unions

A union is a data structure somewhat related to the data structures that can be created using the C struct facility. Data in programs may take various forms. The struct facility is appropriate for programs that use data that is always going to be interpreted in the same way. The storage of a struct is determined at one time and all the component fields are fixed in their interpretation by the C compiler. This is the way that records are usually treated in Pascal and in most other modern languages.

Unions are a way to consider data of different forms that may have some common use. They are similar in nature to variant records in Pascal, which are used much less frequently than fixed-format records. Here is an example of the need for the union concept that uses some simple ideas from geometry.

Suppose that we wish to have a method of computing the area of geometric figures such as various triangles, quadrilaterals, and pentagons. One approach might be to use a program containing code something like

```
if (type == right_triangle)
    area = base * height ;
if (type == non_right_triangle)
    {
    s = (a + b + c)/2;
    area = sqrt((double) (s*(s-a)*(s-b)*(s-c)) );
    }
if (type == square)
    area = s * s ;
if (type == rectangle)
    area = l * w ;
if (type == parallelogram)
    area = a * b * sin (theta);
if (type == rhombus)
    area = c * d /2 ;
. . . . . . . . . .
```

This type of code is acceptable if it is used only once in a program. As an alternative, we could use a switch statement and replace the types of the geometric objects by numerical values such as 1 for right_triangle, 2 for non_right_triangle, etc. However, suppose that the area of the figure will be computed several times and that we do not know at compile time what the actual geometric object might be. This could happen if the user of the program was able to select the geometric object. We might try to write a function that performs the area calculation.

What parameters need to be passed to this function? We need to be able to pass any parameter that is necessary for any instance of the geometric object. Thus we would need a function declaration of the form

```
double area(
    char type[],    /* name of the object type */
    float base,     /* for right triangles */
    float height,   /* for right triangles */
    float a,        /* for non right triangles */
    float b,        /* for non right triangles */
    float c,        /* for non right triangles */
```

```
float s,          /* for squares */
float l,          /* for rectangles */
float w,          /* for rectangles */
float p_a,        /* for parallelograms */
float p_b,        /* for parallelograms */
float theta,      /* for parallelograms */
float r_c,        /* for rhombuses */
float r_d         /* for rhombuses */
)
```

This function would violate most of the rules of good software engineering. It has a huge number of parameters that are never used in any single function call. Since many C compilers don't perform any checking of the number and type of parameters, using this function is almost certain to lead to errors in that we don't know or care about the values of parameters passed. In addition, this code is ugly and inelegant. Use of more mnemonic names would have caused the function declaration to cover several lines – even more ugly and inelegant code. Note that using a switch statement would only change the line

```
char type[];        /* name of the object type */
```

of the function declaration to

```
int type;  /* number identifying type of the object */
```

and we would then have to determine what the numerical value of type actually meant in terms of the geometric object's type.

We need a method of keeping all of the relevant data needed to compute the area of any of the geometric objects together in a single data structure. The solution uses the C concept known as a union. In example 9.20, we show one way of doing this. Of course, we would want this information to be in a header file.

Example 9.20 A header file for the use of unions in problems involving plane geometry

```
/* header file geometry.h       */
struct geometric_type
  {
  char *polygon_type;
  union choice_type
  {struct rt_triangle_type
    {
    float base;
    float height;
    } right;
  struct non_rt_triangle_type
    {
    float a;
```

We now know how to create unions for use in programs. The next example shows how to use them. Note that the compiler has absolutely no understanding about how the data stored in the union can be used. It is the responsibility of the programmer to check that the type of data in the union is the type of data that the programmer wants. Example 9.21 uses the declarations in example 9.20 and the additional declaration

```
float area
```

to show how a union might be used in practice. Note the complex manner in which we refer to the various fields of the union. This complexity is caused by the structure of the data in which each of the fields of the union (except for s) is a structured type and thus has fields itself. In addition, the union is itself embedded in a struct and thus there must be four dots used to describe the most complex variable chain. The example groups the assignments as if the types of the object were known (rt_triangle, non_rt_triangle, etc.); this is completely unnecessary since the union can hold only one version of its possible choices at a time.

Example 9.21

```
#include <stdio.h>
#include <stdlib.h>
#include "geometry.h"

main(void)
{
  float area;
  /* rest of the code in example 9.20, after the variable
  declarations */

  if (object.type == "rt_triangle")
    {
    object.choice.right.base = 3.0;
    object.choice.right.height = 4.0;
    }
  if (object.type == "non_rt_triangle")
    {
    object.choice.general_triangle.a = 4.0;
    object.choice.general_triangle.b = 5.0;
    object.choice.general_triangle.c = 6.0;
    }
  if (object.type =="square")
    object.choice.s = 10.0;
  if (object.type == "rectangle")
    {
    object.choice.rectangle.l = 10.0;
    object.choice.rectangle.w = 5.0;
    }
```

```
if (object.type == "parallelogram")
   {
   object.choice.parallelogram.p_a = 10.0;
   object.choice.parallelogram.p_b = 20.0;
   object.choice.parallelogram.theta = 1.0;
   }
if (object.type == "rhombus")
   {
   object.choice.rhombus.r_c = 20.0;
   object.choice.rhombus.r_d = 30.0;
   }

printf("%s\n",object.type);   /* Note - not initialized */

printf("%2.1f\n",object.choice.right.base );
printf("%2.1f\n",object.choice.right.height );
printf("%2.1f\n",object.choice.general_triangle.a );
printf("%2.1f\n",object.choice.general_triangle.b );
printf("%2.1f\n",object.choice.general_triangle.c );
printf("%2.1f\n",object.choice.s );
printf("%2.1f\n",object.choice.rectangle.l );
printf("%2.1f\n",object.choice.rectangle.w );
printf("%2.1f\n",object.choice.parallelogram.p_a );
printf("%2.1f\n",object.choice.parallelogram.p_b );
printf("%2.1f\n",object.choice.parallelogram.theta );
printf("%2.1f\n",object.choice.rhombus.r_c );
printf("%2.1f\n",object.choice.rhombus.r_d );

object.type = "rt_triangle";
area = (object.choice.right.base) *
                (object.choice.right.height);
printf("Area = %3.1f\n",area);

object.type = "rhombus_type";
area = (object.choice.rhombus.r_c) *
                (object.choice.rhombus.r_d)/2;
printf("Area = %3.1f\n",area);
}
```

The output shows clearly that we made an error in not initializing the value of object.type. The compiler thus allows us to print out all of the possible formats in the union. We were fortunate to have the program avoid a crash.

```
(null)
10.0
20.0
```

```
10.0
20.0
1.0
10.0
10.0
20.0
10.0
20.0
1.0
10.0
20.0
Area = 200.0
Area = 100.0
```

Note that we could have initialized the value of object_type to something like "rt_triangle" by using the function strcpy( ) as in

```
strcpy(object_type, "rt_triangle");
```

This initialization of the value of object_type would have generated a run-time error on most systems when we attempted to access the portions of the union that have become invalid because of the initialization.

Here is another example of the use of unions. Earlier in this chapter we considered a tree that was used for computing the value of an expression. The nodes of the diagram of the tree in Figure 9.3 were of two different types: ints and operators. The easiest way to encode the actions of such a tree in C is to use the union construction, with a union taking on one of the two types int or character, where the character represents one of the allowable binary operations. Note the use of both structures and unions in a fairly complex data type presented in the code of example 9.22, which describes a portion of the tree (the lower-left corner) of Figure 9.3.

Example 9.22

```
#include <stdio.h>
#include <stdlib.h>

struct compute_tree
  {
  struct compute_tree *left;
  union info_type  /* note the different components */
    {
    int value ;
    char operation ;
    } info ;   /* name for this part of structured type */
  struct compute_tree *right;
  };
```

```
void tree_traversal(struct compute_tree *t );

main(void)
{
   struct compute_tree *tree, *temp ;

   tree = (struct compute_tree *)
           malloc(sizeof(struct compute_tree));
   tree->left = NULL;
   tree->right = NULL;
   tree->info.operation = '+' ;/* note syntax, precedence */

   temp = (struct compute_tree *)
           malloc (sizeof(struct compute_tree));
   temp->left = NULL;
   temp->right = NULL;
   temp->info.value = 2 ;   /* note syntax and precedence */
   tree->left = temp;

   temp = (struct compute_tree *)
           malloc (sizeof(struct compute_tree));
   temp->left = NULL;
   temp->right = NULL;
   temp->info.value = 3 ;   /* note syntax and precedence */
   tree->right = temp;

   /* tree is now initialized - call for tree traversal */
   tree_traversal(tree);
} /* end main */



void tree_traversal(struct compute_tree *t)
{
   struct compute_tree *tree_pointer;

   tree_pointer = t;
   if (tree_pointer != NULL)
     {
     tree_traversal(tree_pointer->left) ;

     /* note format of next statement */
     if (tree_pointer->info.operation == '+' )
```

```
      {
      printf("node contents: %c\n",
                  tree_pointer->info.operation);
      printf("The value of the sum is %d\n",
                  tree_pointer->left->info.value +
                  tree_pointer->right->info.value );
      }
    else
      printf("node contents: %d\n",
                  tree_pointer->info.value );

    tree_traversal(tree_pointer->right );
    } /* end if */
}       /* end tree_traversal */
```

You will see unions again in the exercises. Relatively few C programs use the union facility; you will need it primarily for systems programming work.

9.6 Advanced Bit Operations: Fields

C allows a very complex data object to be implemented as if it were a structure. This structure is the field. The purpose of a field is to specify at a fairly low level how objects are to be stored. We generally want to access particular bits of a data object and expect them to be in a particular place. We can specify a set of bits that appear within an int variable by indicating the number of bits to be grouped at a time. The most common need for access to bits is in software that must interface directly with the operating system or in the operating system itself.

To be specific, suppose that a particular computer has 16 bits used for the storage of integers and that these integers are represented at the bit level as follows:

The bits are numbered from 0 to 15, with bit 0 the lowest.

Bit 15 is the sign bit.

Bits 14 through 0 represent the number in base 2.

Then we can declare the data structure

```
    struct
      {
      unsigned sign_bit :1;
      unsigned numb_bit :15;
      } bit_integer;
```

to represent the number.

The purpose of this representation is to allow us to access the individual bits of a number and so to be able to take action depending on particular bits. One way that this concept is used is to access what in operating systems terminology is called an "interrupt vector." (The purpose of an interrupt vector is to provide a fast connection between an action that interrupts, such as pressing of keys that stop a running program or the disk controller signaling the CPU that it has finished the desired reading of data from the disk, and a set of actions that must be taken by the lowest level of the operating system, such as returning control of the read/write heads of the disk to the CPU.) In one simple situation, the various bits of two 8-bit byte computer words are combined and used as a single word. The leftmost of the two bytes is ignored, and the actions of the operating system are dependent on the various bits.

Example 9.23 Code using structs and fields

```
struct interrupt_vector
  {
  unsigned left_byte :8;
  unsigned bit_7 :1;
  unsigned bit_6 :1;
  unsigned bit_5 :1;
  unsigned bit_4 :1;
  unsigned bit_3 :1;
  unsigned bit_2 :1;
  unsigned bit_1 :1;
  unsigned bit_0 :1;
  } interrupt_vector;


    . . .
if (interrupt_vector.bit_0  == 0)
/* bit is 0, take appropriate action no. 0 */

if (interrupt_vector.bit_1  == 1)
/* bit is 1, take appropriate action no. 1 */
    . . .
```

There are a few things to keep in mind about bits and fields:

- The bits in a field must be contiguous.
- They should be declared as unsigned.
- They must be a portion of a variable of type int.
- They cannot overlap int boundaries.
- Most code that uses bits and fields is not portable.
- Other features of fields are the same as for structs.

There are other ways of getting access to individual bits on a computer other than using fields of structs. We will meet them in the next chapter.

9.7 Software Engineering Project: Changed Requirements

Since we now know about structured data types in C, we can change the project requirements to allow the storage of structured data types in our simulated disk and memory. The major weakness of our simulation is that we cannot have both character and int data in the array elements of the disk. This has meant an encoding of the names of the files. The new requirements are to allow inclusion of the name of the file and allow the data in the file to be incorporated in the disk.

We discuss the results of the new requirements in the next section.

9.8 Software Engineering Project: The Next Prototype

The new requirements really mean a new organization of data. This data organization must be flexible enough to allow us to change the type of data on the disk to allow for both character and int data.

The major change is in the definition of the type of element that appears on the disk. There are two likely possibilities.

We could choose to have data stored in a structure such as

```
struct data_type {
        int contents;
        char name_char;
        } data_element;
```

Only one of the portions of the struct is in use at any one time either as a place for a character of the name of the file or the contents of a location. If we do this, we can reserve extra space for later expansion of functionality such as you are asked to do in the exercises.

Alternatively, we could choose to have the data elements on the disk to be in the form of a union

```
union union_data_type {
        int contents;
        char name_char;
        } union_data_element;
```

This has the advantage of not wasting space in memory at the expense of being slower code because of the type checking at run time.

Which method do we choose? The selection is up to you. Your decision should be based on the following factors:

- How much work will I have to do? Can I use most of my existing code?
- What needs to be changed? What can I modify easily?
- How will the system perform? Is the system so small that performance does not matter?
- Which method am I most comfortable with? Which is easier to test thoroughly?

Note that some functions such as initialization will have to be rewritten in either case. Note also that if we had used typedef for the data type used in memory and the disk, then we would only have had to change a header file and recompile unchanged functions.

Summary of Chapter 9

In this chapter, we were introduced to the fundamental C language construction for combining data that can be of the same or different types: the struct. Combining data into a struct means that memory can be allocated for its storage and for access to the component parts. Structs can be used to store any combination of data.

Like all other variables in C, any variable that is a struct must be declared as having a type. The syntax of the declaration of a struct type is

```
struct struct_type {
      part1_type part1;
      part2_type part2;
      part3_type part3;
      };
```

A variable of this type can be declared as

```
struct struct_type s;
```

or in conjunction with the type declaration as in

```
struct struct_type {
      part1_type part1;
      part2_type part2;
      part3_type part3;
      } s;
```

The most common use of structs is in combination with pointers which are used for access to a struct variable. The common form is that a pointer to a struct is used as an indirect access to the parts of the struct. If ptr is a pointer to a struct with three parts named part1, part2, and part3, then the parts can be accessed by constructions such as

```
(*ptr).part1 = x;
```

or

```
y = (*ptr).part2 + (*ptr).part3;
```

An alternative notation for access to the parts of the struct is

```
ptr->part1 = x;
```

and

```
y = ptr->part2 + ptr->part2;
```

The most important C library function to be used with structs is malloc( ), which allocates memory of the correct size for the storage of a struct. Since the storage allocator function malloc( ) returns only "pointers to void," the cast operation is used to coerce the return type to the desired form.

The call to malloc( ) reserves space in memory for the variable and indicates the appropriate use by the cast operation. Initialization of the space is the responsibility of the programmer. A related function, calloc( ), can be used to allocate memory for an array of structs; this function will perform initialization of the space to 0. Recall that we met this function in Chapter 8.

The portions of a struct can be of any fixed form, including pointer types. The use of pointers to variables of the same type allows the incorporation of recursive data structures such as trees.

A typedef statement can be used together with structured data types to provide the C language version of abstract data types.

Variable-sized portions of data can be incorporated into a common structure by using the C construction called a union. A union permits different portions to have different types at run time depending on the nature of their usage.

Exercises

1. This exercise uses the linked-list structure of section 9.2. In that section, we created a list of nodes by first creating the first node. All the remaining nodes were created by going to the first node in the list (the list head) and then walking down the list until we got to the end. Once we found the end of the list, we created a new node and added it to the list. A far more useful approach in many situations is to keep the list in some order. This means that there is an ordering of the information fields of the nodes and that insertion of a node at any place on the list is possible.

(a) Write C functions insert( ), insert_after( ), delete( ), and delete_after( ) that allow us to manage a list by inserting or deleting nodes at any place on the list.

(b) Use the functions in part a of this question to read a list of integers and to place them in a linked list so that traversing the list from the head to the end at any time, we always have the information fields of the nodes in decreasing order.

2. The function insert( ) in example 9.6 has a problem if the list has not yet been created. Rewrite this function to work if the list does not yet exist. This will involve checking the parameter list_head to see if it is NULL.

3. Write C functions to implement a circular queue. If you are not familiar with this concept, consult a text on data structures.

4. Consider the data structure called a deque. This structure is somewhat similar to a queue but allows data to be inserted or deleted both at the front and the rear of the deque. Write insert and delete routines that implement the insertion or deletion of data. The deque is to be implemented as a linked list of nodes, and the information to be stored in the nodes is to be of type int.

5. Write C functions that operate on a stack that is to be implemented using a linked list. Thus the stack that you are manipulating does not have a predetermined maximum size.

6. Write a C program to transform an expression from infix to postfix form. Use stack operations that you have written earlier. However, the elements on the stack should be floating point numbers. The program should use trees in the manner that was indicated at the end of section 9.2.

7. Write a C program that evaluates an expression that is given in postfix form. The program should use trees in the manner that was indicated at the end of section 9.2.

8. Write a C program to add two positive, arbitrary-precision integers. Each of the integers is to be represented as a linked list of nodes where each node contains three binary digits. Thus the number 101110001 is represented as three nodes with contents 101, 110, and 001, respectively. The sum of the two numbers is to be presented as a binary integer in standard form.

9. Repeat exercise 8 using subtraction of binary numbers instead of addition.

10. Repeat exercise 8 for decimal integers, with three decimal digits stored in each node.

11. The purpose of this exercise is to develop a software tool that will provide a low-level analysis of a source code file. The input to your program will be a file containing a syntactically correct program written in FORTRAN. The output of your program will be a listing of the frequency of various tokens. For example, if the input is a source code file whose contents are

```
      INTEGER I , J
      REAL A , LOTS
C This is a dumb program
      I = 1
      J = I + 1
      IF (I.EQ.J) A = 0.0
      IF (I.EQ.J) A = 0.0
      CALL SIN(LOTS)
      WRITE(6,100)I
 100     FORMAT(1X,I4)
      STOP
      END
```

the output will be something like:

```
TOTAL APPEARANCES OF RESERVED WORDS: 9
RESERVED SYMBOLS:
      ,          4
      =          4
      +          1
      -          0
```

```
        /              0
        *              0
        **             0
        (              5
        )              5
COMMENTS: 1
TOTAL OF OTHER TOKENS:    27
```

The reserved words in this text are INTEGER REAL IF IF CALL WRITE FORMAT STOP END

The "other tokens" are I J A LOTS I 1 J I 1 I .EQ. J A 0.0 SIN LOTS 6 100 I 100 1X I4

The reserved symbols are easy to test. To check to see if a token is a reserved word, you will have to search a list of reserved words. Use a procedure or function for this operation. I suggest that you use a binary search on the sorted list of reserved words in FORTRAN.

You will probably need a function called compress( ) that eliminates blanks and combines continuation lines.

12. Do the analysis of exercise 11 for input files written in the C language. Use the list of reserved words given in Appendix 1.

13. Do the analysis of exercise 11 for input files written in the Ada language. The list of Ada reserved words can be found in example 9.13.

14. Write a program that fills up and manipulates a stack. Use the abstract data type used for stacks developed in examples 9.18 and 9.19. After the program works, change the code of the stack manipulation portion to use a linked-list representation of stacks with dynamic storage allocation using malloc( ). This is a good illustration of the power of abstract data types.

15. Write a program that manipulates a stack. The purpose of this program is to be able to store the contents of a tree such as we saw in Figure 9.3; note that this tree had two different types of information stored in its nodes. The contents of the stack that you are to implement are allowed to be either ints or chars. Use the abstract data type used for stacks developed in examples 9.18 and 9.19. Hint: use unions.

16. Rewrite the code for queues using the typedef and structured data type construction in order to develop an abstract data type for queues.

17. Rewrite the code for trees using the typedef and structured data type construction in order to develop an abstract data type for trees.

Software Engineering Exercises

18. In the text, we developed specifications for structured data on the disk. Use the suggestions in the text to design and implement a system using a structured data type on the disk and incorporating all of the initializations and functionality that we have discussed.

19. In the text, we developed specifications for structured data on the disk. This means that we can incorporate information about the organization of the contents of the files in addition to the knowledge that we already have about the way that the files are stored (sequential, indexed sequential, or random access). We can think of a file as having a file header that describes the organization of the contents of the file as well as the actual contents of the file.

For example, we can agree that the file is to be interpreted as a file whose contents are to be interpreted as integers. This means that each place in the arrays used to simulate the disk or memory corresponds to a single piece of data. If we have a file whose contents are to be interpreted as floating point numbers, then we might have a header to be able to describe the type of data as being comprised of two successive locations, one for the integer part and one for the decimal part.

Implement these features for files of integers, characters, floating point, and double-precision numbers.

CHAPTER 10

Advanced Input and Output

In this chapter, we consider the input and output facilities that are available in the C programming language. As we indicated earlier, input and output are not part of the formal definition of the C language. All I/O functions are performed by library functions. The standard I/O library is automatically linked to C programs by the C compiler when the statement

```
#include <stdio.h>
```

is incorporated in the program. This is different from the manner in which other library functions are generally treated. In order to use other library functions, we often have to include a header file in the program and also link the library explicitly. The I/O library is automatically linked to C programs and is accessed via the header file. The advantage to using this preprocessor directive in your programs is to make them run slightly faster on many systems, since on these systems the use of the include file allows the replacement of functions by macros, which are expanded in-line and therefore reduce the overhead of function calls.

This chapter contains three sections. Section 10.1 provides a general discussion of those I/O features for file access that are provided by nearly all C compilers. It makes no special use of the UNIX operating system and may be read at any point in the text. Section 10.2 provides a set of I/O utility functions that are available for formatting data both for reading and writing. The code and functions described in the first two sections are available under both UNIX and non-UNIX systems and may be used easily in either. Section 10.3 provides a discussion of those I/O features that are specific to C programs running under the UNIX operating system. Section 10.3 also includes an introduction to defensive programming with UNIX system calls.

```
             START OF FILE ------->| a |
                                   | b |
                                   | c |
                                   | d |
                                   | e |
             OFFSET = 5   --------> | f |
                                   | g |
                                   | h |
                                   | i |
                                   | j |
                                   | k |
                                   | l |
                                   | m |
                                   ---- <---- position of pointer
```

Figure 10.2 The action of fopen("name","a");

The values "a+", "r+", and "w+" are somewhat similar in function but are not universally available on all C compilers. These values mean that the programmer must be sure to protect the state of the data that is in the file at all times. Use of the '+' option requires the use of certain function calls to move the file pointer after a switch from input to output. These function calls are discussed in Appendix 2.

There is a limited number of file pointers that can be used in any given program; you should expect portability problems with your programs if the number of file pointers is more than eight, which is the number suggested as a minimum in the ANSI standard. Many systems allow a lot more; the system that was used to test the programs in this text allows a maximum of 30 files to be opened by fopen( ) at any time.

Every C program has at least three files opened automatically when it begins execution: stdin, stdout, and stderr. These files respectively represent input from the terminal,

```
                                   _____ <---- position of pointer
             START OF FILE ------->| a |
                                   | b |
                                   | c |
                                   | d |
                                   | e |
             OFFSET = 5   -------->| f |
                                   | g |
                                   | h |
                                   | i |
                                   | j |
                                   | k |
                                   | l |
                                   | m |
                                   ----
```

Figure 10.3 The action of fopen("name","r");

```
                                    ——— <---- position of pointer
            START OF FILE  ------->| a |
                                   | b |
                                   | c |
                                   | d |
                                   | e |
            OFFSET = 5     -------->| f |
                                   | g |
                                   | h |
                                   | i |
                                   | j |
                                   | k |
                                   | l |
                                   | m |
                                    -----
```

Figure 10.4 The action of fopen("name","w");

output to the terminal screen, and error messages, which are usually sent to stdout also. (In this context, the word "terminal" means the computer itself if you are using a stand-alone computer system without terminals.) Thus you should not assume that you may have any more than 8 (5 – 3) files open unless you know the default limits for your system. These designations of the standard three files are compatible with the UNIX standards for file access, as we will see in the next section.

This attachment of special meaning of input and output devices to standard numbers in C is similar to the way that unit numbers such as 3 for the tape drive unit, 5 for terminal input, and 6 for terminal output are typically reserved in FORTRAN.

Example 10.3 uses the function fopen( ) to open files. Note the use of the mode. Also note that we opened a total of 8 files (the 5 here plus the 3 from the standard files. The last statement in the program is a UNIX system call named system( ) which allows us to access general utilities available using the UNIX shell. The arguments to that system call, "ls -l f*", simply cause the contents of the directory to be listed in the long form in which detailed information about the files is included. The f* is an example of a wild card in which any sequence of zero or more characters is allowed. Thus file1, file2, file3, .., file7, fred, f, all match, but File3 does not.

Example 10.3

```c
#include <stdio.h>

main(void)
{
  FILE *fp[7];
  int i;

  fp[1] = fopen("file1","a");
  fp[2] = fopen("file2","r");
```

```
fp[3] = fopen("file3","w");
fp[4] = fopen("file4","a");
fp[5] = fopen("file5","a");
fp[6] = fopen("file6","r");
fp[7] = fopen("file7","w");
system("ls -l f*");
for (i = 0; i < 7; i++)
  fclose(fp[i]);
}
```

Only that portion of the output of this program that concerns the files we opened is presented below. The important features of the output appear in the first, fifth, and ninth columns. The information in the first column concerns permissions. The rw means that the person who opened the files had permission to read and write each of the files. The dashes indicate that no other people in my group or in the rest of the world, have any permission to read the files at all. This was independent of the mode included in the call to the function fopen( ). The 0 in the fifth column indicates that the size of each file is 0 bytes, as expected, since we have put nothing in the files. The ninth column has the name of the file.

```
-rw-------    1 rjl      scs      0 Apr 27 19:29 file1
-rw-------    1 rjl      scs      0 Apr 27 19:29 file3
-rw-------    1 rjl      scs      0 Apr 27 19:29 file4
-rw-------    1 rjl      scs      0 Apr 27 19:29 file5
-rw-------    1 rjl      scs      0 Apr 27 19:29 file7
```

Notice that not all of the files were created. The files named file2 and file6 were not created because the mode given was "r". Since neither of these files existed previously, these files were not opened for reading.

Incidentally, when the same code was run on another UNIX system, there were slightly different permissions because the default parameters were set differently. On the other system, the output was

```
-rw-r--r--    1 rjl               0 Apr 27 19:29 file1
-rw-r--r--    1 rjl               0 Apr 27 19:30 file3
-rw-r--r--    1 rjl               0 Apr 27 19:29 file4
-rw-r--r--    1 rjl               0 Apr 27 19:29 file5
-rw-r--r--    1 rjl               0 Apr 27 19:30 file7
```

and as before the two files that were to have been opened with mode "r" did not exist previously and therefore they were not opened. On both systems opening an existing file with the "r" mode worked..

Note that we could have chosen the name of a file to be opened by a command line argument instead of by hard-coding it into the program. In example 10.4, we repeat the code that was presented in example 5.23 in order to show a program in which we read data in the form of character data from an input file.

Example 10.4 Program to read data from a file

```c
/* Program uses files given as command-line arguments */
#include <stdio.h>

main(int argc, char *argv[])
{
   FILE  *fp;
   int c;

   if (argc == 1)  /* no filename on the command line */
     {
     printf("Error in read - not enough arguments\n");
     exit(0);
     }
   else   /* a filename was present on the command line */
     {
     fp = fopen(argv[1],"r");
     while ((c = getc(fp) ) != EOF)
       printf("%c",c);
     fclose(fp);
     }  /* end else */
}
```

Note that in example 10.4 we have opened the file with read permissions only. Note also that we have used a function called getc( ) instead of getchar( ). In the file stdio.h, getchar( ) is defined as the higher-order software in the sense that it is defined in terms of getc( );

```c
#define getchar()        getc(stdin)
```

Clearly, getc( ) works for arbitrary files while getchar( )works only for stdin.

In example 10.5 we present a portion of a program that uses a variable called msg to determine which action it will take. It will read from either a file named "generic.doc" or from a file whose name was entered by a user. Note the use of both scanf( ) and getc( ) for input and putchar( ) for output.

Example 10.5

```c
#include <stdio.h>

main(void)
{
   FILE *fp;
   int c,k;
   int i = 0, j = 0;
   int msg = 1;
   char message[80],  usrfile[15];
```

```
/* Omitted code to change value of msg would go here. */
if (msg == 1)
  {
  if ((fp = fopen("generic.doc","r")) != NULL)
    while ((c=getc(fp)) != EOF)
      {
      message[i++] = c;
      for (k = 0; k < i; k++)
        putchar(message[k]);
      }
  }  /* end msg == 1 */
else if (msg == 3)
  {
  printf("Input filename?: ");
  scanf("%s",usrfile);
  printf("File read is %s\n",usrfile);
  if ((fp = fopen(usrfile,"r")) != NULL)
    while ((c=getc(fp)) != EOF)
      message[i++] = c;
  for (k = 0; k < i; k++)
      putchar(message[k]) ;
  }  /* end else if msg ==3 */
}
```

At this point we know how to read text data from files. Writing text data to a file is equally easy. Instead of the function putchar( ), we will use putc( ). As before, putchar( ) is actually a special case of putc() restricted to stdout as may be seen from

```
#define putchar(x)        putc((x),stdout)
```

In example 10.6 we show how to copy from one file to another. The arguments are passed as command-line arguments. A count of command-line arguments is given in order to be sure that there is a file for input and a file for output. The program works correctly if the file to be copied from already exists; it crashes if the input file does not exist.

Example 10.6 General-purpose copy program — aborts if the input file does not exist

```
/*-------------------------------------------------------------*/
/*  ----   FIRST ATTEMPT TO WRITE COPY PROGRAM -              */
/*    Copy files whose names are given as command             */
/*    line arguments .........general version                 */
/*    Works if the input file exists - problem if             */
/*    the input file does not already exist                   */
/*-------------------------------------------------------------*/
```

```
#include <stdio.h>

main(int argc, char *argv[])
{
  int c;
  FILE *fp[3];

  /* one file pointer not used - index wasted for clarity */

  if ( argc == 3 )
    {
    fp[1] = fopen(argv[1],"r");
    fp[2] = fopen(argv[2],"w");
    while ((c=getc(fp[1])) != EOF)
      putc(c,fp[2]);
    fclose(fp[1]);
    fclose(fp[2]);
    }
  else
    printf("Error - incorrect number of arguments\n");
}
```

The problem with this program is that a count of the number of arguments is not sufficient to check for the existence of the file. The next version of the copy program solves this problem by providing a check for the existence of the input file at the appropriate time – when the input file is opened for reading. The defensive programming technique used here is typically used for programs with calls to the file system (or to the operating system). In this technique, we test the value returned by the function call. If the value returned by the function call is not one that is possible with normal execution, then we stop normal execution and take some error action. The function fopen( ) is expected to return a value of type "pointer to a FILE" and thus NULL is the appropriate flag to be tested for an unsuccessful attempt to open the file specified in argument 2 for reading. No such defensive programming technique need be used in the second call to fopen( ) if we know either that the output file does not already exist or that if it did exist, then it would have the correct access permissions. It is probably best to make sure by programming the access to all files defensively. Example 10.7 shows us how to do this in a correct copy program.

Example 10.7 Correct copy program — a general version that works on any system

```
/*-----------------------------------------------*/
/* ----  CORRECT COPY PROGRAM                    */
/* Copy files whose names are given as command-  */
/* line arguments .........general version       */
/*-----------------------------------------------*/
```

A somewhat different type of function is fgets( ) which reads its input one line at a time. The syntax of fgets( ) is

```
fgets(char *input_line,int MAX_LINE,FILE *file_pointer);
```

The function fgets( ) reads in a line at a time from the file pointer's file, with at most MAX_LINE characters per line (including the newline character) being read into the string pointed to by the pointer input_line. The string is terminated by a '\0'. If the end of file is reached, then fgets( ) returns the value NULL.

Incidentally, we have constantly referred to such operators as getc( ), getchar( ), putc( ), putchar( ), isalpha( ), etc., as being functions. In nearly every C language implementation, they are implemented as macros instead of as functions. This means that the code for these operations is expanded in the place where the C preprocessor and the compiler find them. As a result, such operations are much faster than if they were subject to the overhead of function calls. Thus I/O in C is quite fast. In operations such as fgets( ) that are implemented as C functions rather than as macros, register variables are frequently used instead of normal memory access locations.

In addition to having functions such as ftoa( ) for changing the type of tokens, isupper( ) for testing the value of a token of a particular type, getc( ) for reading from arbitrary files, and fgets( ) for reading entire lines, there are C functions for reading data into and out from strings. One way of doing this is to use the C I/O function sprintf( ) and its relative sscanf( ). The syntax of these two functions is

```
sprintf(char *string, char *control, any_type
            arg1, arg2 ..) ;
```

and

```
sscanf(char *string, char *control, any_type
            arg1, arg2 ..) ;
```

The function sprintf( ) is similar to printf( ) in that the arguments arg1, arg2, etc., are formatted according to the control specification given. However, the output is written to the string specified as the first argument instead of to stdout. The function sscanf( ), which is similar to scanf( ), is the opposite of sprintf( ) in that it takes a string argument and a control specification in order to put the tokens in the string that are separated according to the instructions in the control specification into the variables specified in arg1, arg2, etc. Thus the statement

```
sprintf(name, "temp_file%d",i);
```

changes the contents of the character string called name from "temp_file" to "temp_filenn," where nn is the decimal value of i. It is also useful for changing the format of an integer to a character string, as in

```
sprintf(val, "%d", 77);
```

which changes the int 77 to its ASCII equivalent as a character string and stores this string in the variable "val."

Conversely, the statement

```
sscanf(name, "temp_file%d",i);
```

changes the contents of the variable i by reading everything in the character string called name from the end of the nine-character substring "temp_file" to the end of the string and then interpreting this remainder as a variable of type int. Also,

```
sscanf(val, "%d", x);
```

changes the value of the ASCII string val to an int called x.

As an example of how the function sprintf( ) might be used, suppose that we wish to create some files with the names temp_file1 . . . temp_file10 and that we wish to refer to these files by their names. The program in example 10.8 creates 10 files and opens them for writing using the defensive file manipulation strategy that we saw earlier.

Example 10.8

```
/*-----------------------------------------------------------*/
/* Program to open 10 files using names generated            */
/* using sprintf() to place a meaningful number in each      */
/* filename.                                                  */
/*-----------------------------------------------------------*/

#include <stdio.h>

main(void)
{
  FILE *fp[];
  char name[11]; /* large enough for file names */
  int i;

  for (i=0; i <= 10; i++)
    {
    sprintf(name, "temp_file%d",i);
    if ( (fp[i] = fopen(name,"w") ) == NULL)
      {
      fputs("Error in open\n",stderr);
      exit(1);
      }
    }
}
```

The incorporation of numbers into filenames is an essential feature of many computer systems since it allows temporary files to be easily identified by many processes. During the time that this chapter was written, I remained logged on to a workstation computer for a considerable period of time. Many temporary files were created during this period. The files in the directories /tmp and /usr/tmp (I was the only user on this UNIX-based system) were

```
/tmp:
total 195
-rw-------   1 rjl          57344 May 30 16:47 Ex12407
-rw-------   1 rjl           5120 May 30 16:42 Ex12746
-rw-------   1 rjl              1 May 11 14:20 MTda00843
-rw-------   1 rjl          10240 May 30 16:44 Rx12407
-rw-------   1 rjl           4096 May 30 16:42 Rx12746
-rw-------   1 rjl           2089 May 11 09:55 Text111.0
-rw-------   1 rjl           2051 May 11 13:03 Text657.0
-rw-------   1 rjl              0 May 11 13:05 Text753.0
-rw-------   1 rjl         105240 May 30 16:48 Text839.0
-rw-------   1 rjl              0 May 10 15:06 tty.txt.a00111
-rw-------   1 rjl              0 May 11 10:17 tty.txt.a00657
-rw-------   1 rjl              0 May 11 13:05 tty.txt.a00753
-rw-------   1 rjl              0 May 11 14:20 tty.txt.a00839
-rw-rw-rw-   1 rjl            328 May 30 16:04 winselection
```

and

```
/usr/tmp:
total 6
-rw-------   1 root          4619 Mar  1 11:51 ESa01626
drwxr-xr-x 10 root           512 Mar  1 11:48 transcript/
```

Of these files, only two did not have an integer portion as part of their name. It is clear from the listing of two of these files in Figures 10.5 and 10.6 that temporary files are used by the editor, storage allocator, and other processes. The first temporary file, shown in Figure 10.5, is used by the editor to keep a copy of the most recent changes to a file. As you can see, I was entering a portion of a program into the text of this chapter and testing it. The second temporary file, shown in Figure 10.6, indicates an error in allocating storage for a complex computation that I attempted during the time that this book was being written. Both files have been formatted slightly to make them somewhat easier to read.

In summary, C offers several advanced I/O features. It allows different means of accessing files and of reading or writing the data from either standard input and output or from files. The data can be read using one of several formatting functions such as:

```
scanf()
fscanf()
sscanf()
```

that read their input from stdin, other input files, or specified strings; all of the data formatting is done according to a control specification that is given as an argument to the appropriate function.

```
|)t2.c$|)0D~4HD$48dr#include <stdio.h> main(){FILE
*fopen(), *fp;char name[12]; int i,j;for (i=0; i <=
10; i++) {sprintf(name,"temp_file%d",i); printf(
"%s\n",name);fp= fopen(name,"w"); printf("%d\n"
,i);printfThe file number is %d\n",j);sscanf (,name
,"temp_file%d",j);printf("The file number is%d\n",j);
}system("ls -l");system("rm temp_file*");}for (i=0; i
<= 0; i++)for (i=0; i <= 5; i++)  char name[12],
file_name;char name[12], *file_name; sscanf(name,
temp_file%d",j);strcpy(file_name,name);sscanf(name,"te
mp _file%d",j);sscanf(name,"temp_file%d",j);strcpy
(file_name,name);name[10='\0;name[10]='\0';name[9]='\0
'
```

Figure   10.5 The UNIX temporary file Ex12746

```
        10      34      286 appendix1
XYY#        39     626     2149 appendix2
!||#        49     120     1152 appendix3
\#       11      54      398 appendix4
BB#        28      75      891 appendix5
Ree#         1      12       75 appendix6
H))        98    1049     6467 chap0
HH       437    2878    17718 chap1
8gg      1060    7220    43158 chap10
o       364    2122    12120 chap11
'''        66     222     1646 chap12
_GG       540    3176    19008 chap2
ff       796    5243    31706 chap3
N      1366    8383    48864 chap4
$$      1552    9103    55006 chap5
<CC       135    1335     7862 chap6
sbb       737    5083    32610 chap7
*      1359    8260    48422 chap8
a       616    4088    22790 chap9
??      9378   59532   355117 total
0^^faculty1-->3%>>
nn.WX~Vx}~U|}T8{|SXz{RxyzQxyP8wxOXvwNxuvMtuL8stKXrs
    JxqrIpqH8opGXnoFSpid 743: killed due to swap
problems in xalloc: no swap space    !-2
    cd b*/C
    xAA
```

Figure   10.6 The UNIX temporary file Text657.0

Formatted output is performed in C by using the three related output functions

```
sprintf()
fprintf()
sprintf()
```

that write their output to stdout, other output files, or specified strings; all of the formatting is also specified in a control argument.

If the input is known to consist of character data only, then the functions

```
isalpha()
isdigit()
islower()
isspace()
isupper()
atof()
atoi()
itoa()
```

can be used for formatting the data into appropriate forms and for testing the character for being upper case, lower case, numeric, etc. These functions are available to programs by means of the preprocessor directive to include the file ctype.h, which is described in Appendix 4.

Character strings are operated on by using the functions

```
strcpy()
```

and

```
strcmp()
```

10.3 File Input and Output in C: UNIX Operating System Version

This section considers the I/O facilities available under UNIX C compilers. It assumes that the reader has some familiarity with UNIX, at least at the level of knowing how to find files in the hierarchical UNIX file system, understanding the use of permissions, and knowing the difference between ordinary users and the "root" or "super-user."

The UNIX operating system uses a somewhat different philosophy for file access. Instead of a file pointer that controls a data structure called a FILE, UNIX has the notion of a "file descriptor" that is associated with a program during the period in which the program executes. When a program uses a file, the file descriptor corresponding to that file is in use; if the program ceases to use the file and cleans up properly, then the file descriptor is available for use and may be associated with another file. Thus a file descriptor can be thought of as an index into an array of files.

In general, a maximum of 20 file descriptors may be associated with any program at a time; the number may be smaller because a system administrator wishes to restrict the amount of resources that a user has available. Three of these file descriptors are automatically opened for a running C program: standard input (stdin), standard output (stdout), and standard error (stderr). These three files associated with these file descriptors are the same as those that are available in non-UNIX systems.

Instead of opening and closing files using the fopen( ) and fclose( ) functions that returned pointers to a variable of type FILE, UNIX implementations of C use three primary functions named creat( ), open( )), and close( ). All three of these functions are called system functions because they deal directly with the operating system. The life history of a file will always have a call to creat( ) before the first call to open( ); after the file has been created, open( ) and close( ) can be called many times. The function creat( ) is the most unusual of the three functions and so we discuss it first. Note the unusual spelling of creat( ).

The function creat( ) returns an integer value that is 0 if the function call was successful or the value -1 in the event of an error. Successful execution of creat( ) also associates a file descriptor with the given file. The syntax of creat( ) is

```
int creat(char *file_name, int permissions)
```

The character string file_name is interpreted as follows. If a slash character ('/') is present in the string, then directories indicated by the path are searched. If no slash is present, then only the current directory is used.

The permissions are interpreted as an octal number representing the bits for the read, write, and execute permissions for the owner, group, and world. As we will learn in Chapter 11, octal constants always begin with the letter O.

The function creat( ) behaves differently depending on the existence of the file that is to be created and also on whether the owner of the program that calls creat( ) is the superuser or not. In this text, we consider the behavior for ordinary users; for more information on the use of creat( ) by super-users, consult a UNIX systems programming manual. We also assume that the user has the correct read and write permissions on the directory in which the file is to be created.

If the file does not exist, then creat( ) creates the file by forming an i-node, that is, by making a link between the file and the UNIX file system so that the file can be accessed from within the current directory. The read and write permissions on the file are those specified in the second argument. The file has an initial length of 0, and the file is opened for writing even if the given permissions don't match. Other file system actions are taken; to obtain more information on the details of such file system actions, see a reference on the UNIX operating system. If the file to be created did not already exist, then the creat( ) system call is presumed to be successful and the function creat( ) returns 0. As a side effect of the function, which is in fact an essential reason for calling the function in the first place, an integer value is given to the file as a file descriptor. This means that the next file to be created will have another file descriptor that is larger than the previous one. This pattern will continue unless file descriptors are released or we run out of available file descriptors.

If the file already exists, then creat( ) returns a value of -1 indicating an error state. In this case, creat( ) ignores the permissions argument and changes the length of the file to 0, thereby eliminating all data currently in the file. This action requires only that the user has execute permission on the directory to which the file is linked. Needless to say, the use of creat( ) can cause many problems if used in the wrong manner.

Example 10.9 shows a simple use of creat( ) for alternatively correctly creating and removing a file named "creation."

Example 10.9

```
/*-------------------------------------------------------*/
/* Create files using the UNIX operating                 */
/* system function creat()                                */
/*-------------------------------------------------------*/

#include <stdio.h>

main(void)
{
   if (creat("creation",0644) == -1)
     {
     printf("Error in create\n");
     unlink("creation");
     }
   else
     printf("No error in creation\n");
}
```

The output from six successive executions of the program is given below. The alternation of output corresponds to the existence or nonexistence of the file named "creation" at the time that the program is being executed. The UNIX function call unlink( ) removes the file given as its argument.

```
No error in creation
Error in create
No error in creation
Error in create
No error in creation
Error in create
```

Note that what we have really done in example 10.9 is to use an event, namely the prior existence or nonexistence of a file, to signal information back to a program. Note also that this event is external to the program and thus can be used by many different programs at the same time. This provides a means for implementing semaphores for communicating between processes.

A *semaphore* is a flag that signals a process that it cannot use a resource until another process, which currently is using the resource, releases it. Semaphores are one of nine methods for interprocess communication available in UNIX. Each of the methods is quite complex and requires considerable familiarity with the details of the operating system to be able to implement it. For this reason, many processes use the simpler method of testing the value returned by creat( ) as a semaphore.

The idea is quite simple. All processes attempting to use a resource agree in advance upon the name of a particular file whose existence or nonexistence is to serve as a semaphore. Any process wishing to use the critical resource then checks the existence of the file by applying creat( ) to it with the file's name as the first argument. If creat( ) returns a positive integer, then there was no problem and the process may proceed. If creat( ) returns –1, then the file already existed, and the process must wait until the file no longer exists, thereby indicating that the resource is available. A file used for this purpose is often called a "lock file".

This method was used on an Ada compiler designed for a small UNIX-based computer. The memory was somewhat limited on this machine and hence only one user could use the compiler at a time. A file named something like "ada.lk" was the file whose existence was the key to access to the compiler. The read/write permissions were allowed for everyone by using the octal permissions O666. If a user wished to use the Ada compiler, then the lock file's existence was checked using the function creat( ). If the value returned by

```
creat("ada.lk", 0666)
```

was 0, then the user could continue compilation. If the value returned was -1, then the user simply waited. Obviously this slows down the work of the waiting user; however, a slowing or delay in computation is better than having an error in the compilation caused by having no room in the compiler's internal data structures.

See the exercises for more information on the use of semaphores using the creat( ) function.

The next example shows the proper use of creat( ) for the creation of multiple files. The files all have names formed by using the sprintf( ) function in order to include numbers in strings.

Example 10.10

```
#include <stdio.h>

main(void)
{
  char name[10];
  int i, fp[10];

  for (i=0; i <= 9; i++)
    {
    sprintf(name, "temp_file%d",i);
    printf("%s\n",name);
    if (fp[i]= creat(name, 0644) == -1)
      {
      printf("error\n");
      exit(1);
      }
    }
  system("ls -l temp*");
  exit(0);
}
```

The output of example 10.10 is

```
temp_file0
temp_file1
temp_file2
temp_file3
temp_file4
temp_file5
temp_file6
temp_file7
temp_file8
temp_file9
-rw-r--r--  1 rjl              0 May 26 15:34 temp_file0
-rw-r--r--  1 rjl              0 May 26 15:34 temp_file1
-rw-r--r--  1 rjl              0 May 26 15:34 temp_file2
-rw-r--r--  1 rjl              0 May 26 15:34 temp_file3
-rw-r--r--  1 rjl              0 May 26 15:34 temp_file4
-rw-r--r--  1 rjl              0 May 26 15:34 temp_file5
-rw-r--r--  1 rjl              0 May 26 15:34 temp_file6
-rw-r--r--  1 rjl              0 May 26 15:34 temp_file7
-rw-r--r--  1 rjl              0 May 26 15:34 temp_file8
-rw-r--r--  1 rjl              0 May 26 15:34 temp_file9
```

Now that we know how to create a file using the C functions that are available under UNIX, it is time to use UNIX file operations for something useful. Perhaps the simplest real example of the UNIX file operations is obtained by rewriting the file copying program of example 10.7 using creat( ), open( ), and close( ) instead of fopen( ) and fclose( ). As could have been predicted from their names, the two pairs of functions open() and fopen( ) and close( ) and fclose( ) have similar purposes. The prototypes for these two functions are

```
int close(int fd) ;
```

and

```
int open(char *name, int mode);
```

The first argument to open( ) is a character string of the file, and the second argument is the mode: one of "0," "1," or "2." The value returned is a file descriptor. The value −1 is returned if there is an error such as the permissions being wrong, the file already existing, etc.; otherwise it returns a file descriptor. The argument to close( ) is a file descriptor. It returns −1 to indicate an error if the file was already closed.

Once the files are opened, the functions getc( ) and putc( ) that we have used many times can be used with the UNIX C functions. However, it is customary to use two new functions for the actual reading and writing of data from files – read( ) and write( ). The prototypes for these two functions have the syntax

```
read(int file_descriptor,char buffer[buffer_size],
        int number_of_bytes);
```

and

```
write(int file_descriptor, char buffer[buffer_size],
      int number_of_bytes);
```

and are designed to read and write at the low level of byte access rather than at the higher level of data structure such as characters, integers, or floating point numbers. The first argument to both read( ) and write( ) is an integer that indicates the file descriptor for the proper file. The second argument is a buffer that indicates where the data is to be read to or from. The third argument is the number of bytes to be transferred during the read or write. Note that the number of bytes that we wish to read from a file is declared in the third argument of the function and thus this number is determined before the execution of the function read( ). If the number of bytes indicated in the third argument to read( ) is less than the number of bytes remaining in the file, then the number of bytes read is the number remaining in the file and the value returned by read( ) is 0, indicating the end of the file. Each of the functions read( ) and write( ) returns the value of –1 if an error occurs.

Compare the program given in example 10.11 to that given in example 10.7. Note that the general structure is the same but that the functions fopen( ), fclose( ), putc( ), and getc( ) have been replaced by UNIX equivalents.

Example 10.11 Correct copy program — UNIX operating system-specific version

```
/*-------------------------------------------------*/
/* Program to copy files, names are command-       */
/* line arguments .........UNIX version            */
/*-------------------------------------------------*/

#include <stdio.h>

#define BUFSIZE 512

main(int argc,char *argv[] )
{
   int n;     /* number of bytes read */
   char buffer[BUFSIZE];
   int fd[];
   /* one file descriptor not used -  for clarity */

   if ( argc == 3 )
     {
     if ( (fd[1] = open(argv[1], 0) ) == -1)
       {
       fputs("Error in open\n",stderr);
       exit(1);
       }
```

```
       if ( (fd[2] = creat(argv[2], 0644) ) == -1)
         {
         fputs("Error in creat\n",stderr);
         exit(1);
         }
     while ( (n = read(fd[1],buffer,BUFSIZE) ) > 0 )
       if (write (fd[2],buffer,n) !=n )
          {
          fputs("Error in write\n",stderr);
          exit(1);
          }
     close(fd[1]);
     close(fd[2]);
     }
   else
     printf("Error - incorrect number of arguments\n");
}
```

The program in example 10.11 uses the functions open( ) and creat( ) in an obvious way. The interesting part of the program appears in the while-loop to read from the input file. The loop condition

```
     while ( (n = read(fd[1],buffer,BUFSIZE) ) > 0 )
```

means that there are more bytes to be read from the input. The comparison

```
       if (write (fd[2],buffer,n) !=n )
```

means that the number of bytes read from the input is the same as the number of bytes written to the output. Note also that the program closes the open files at the end of its execution, using explicit calls of the function close( ). A complex program with a large amount of error checking might have many such calls to close( ) depending on the program execution path. To avoid this complexity, many C programmers simply call exit( ) with a parameter of 0. This function call closes all open file descriptors, and the parameter of 0 indicates successful execution.

The value of BUFSIZE indicates the size of a buffer for storing data; a buffer is necessary for fast program execution since the I/O devices may have very different effective data-transfer rates at different times, depending on other use of the computer by different users or operating system requirements. The use of buffers is especially important in operations such as animation that are both CPU- and I/O-intensive. For most uses, BUFSIZE is either 1 (for unbuffered I/O) or a multiple of the size of a standard disk block (usually 512). The exercises describe an experiment to determine the effect of changing the value of BUFSIZE on program speed.

10.4 Software Engineering Project: Changed Requirements

The next set of changes to our memory–disk simulation system is quite simple. We allow the system to be driven by obtaining the commands from an input file or by reading them from the terminal when a user enters them interactively. This means that we have to consider two possible environments – a user-friendly one, in which the user is prompted for input with an opportunity for a user to correct incorrect or missing data, and an environment in which a user has no interaction because all of the commands come from a file. This second situation is commonly called a batch system.

Specifically, the software should be able to take either of two execution paths. If the system receives the command for interactive input and response, then the software should respond as before. However, if the command is for the software to act as a batch system, then all of the user interface commands and prompts should be removed from the software.

10.5 Software Engineering Project: The Next Prototype

The first step in the design of this system is to determine how and when to get the information about whether the system is to be interactive or batch. We want to get this information as early as possible in the execution of the program. It should be clear by now that the only appropriate way of entering this choice is before the program begins execution; that is, by using command-line arguments to convey the choice. To be consistent, obtaining the choice of interactive or batch mode by command-line argument suggests that we should also obtain the name of the input file in batch mode from the command line. A batch-oriented system might also send its output into a file; this might be inappropriate for an interactive system in which the user must see the prompts in order to enter data.

Let's consider the beginning of the user interface first. Suppose that the name of the executable file is "program1." Some likely candidates for a command line might be

```
program1
```

or

```
program1 - i
```

or

```
program1 i
```

for an interactive system, and

```
program1   input
```

or

```
program1   -b input
```

or

```
program1   input output
```

or

```
program1   -b input output
```

or

        program1   b input

or

        program1   b input output

for a batch-oriented system. Other possibilities include the use of "batch" instead of "b" or "interactive" instead of "i"; the number of possibilities is large.

We will follow the principle that the simplest interface is best and use the command line

        program1

to mean that the program is interactive; we use the command line

        program1 input

to mean that the program is batch and reads commands from a file named "input"; and we use the command line

        program1 input output

to mean that the output should be written to a file named "output." This means that our program should be able to handle the case of one, two, or three command-line arguments. If the number of arguments is one, then the program is meant to be interactive. If there is more than one argument, then the program is a "batch" program and the second command-line argument is the name of the input file. If a third command-line argument is given, then it represents the name of the file to which output is to be written. If there are any additional command-line arguments, they are ignored.

This involves a major restructuring of the program that we have written in the previous chapters. To make the changes, we want to remove messages to the user, all menus, and prompts to the user. The easiest way to do this is to set a flag that indicates that these interface components are to be omitted at the time that they would be used in an interactive system. This can be done most easily by encapsulating them into functions that manipulate the screen as necessary.

Note that this solution will slow down the performance of the code. This will not cause any problem for the interactive code, because of the general slowness of user response compared to computing times. The batch code will be slowed also but will be slightly sped up by the omission of the screen output.

Summary of Chapter 10

This chapter considered the problem of reading, writing, and using files from within C programs. C includes many functions for manipulating files.

An important notion in C is that of a file pointer. In order to use file pointers to access a file, a program has to have a pointer declared as pointing to a variable of the predefined type FILE. Files are opened with the function fopen( ) and closed with the function fclose( ). Files can be opened with permissions to read, write (at the beginning), or to append (to the end of the file). Once a file pointer points to a file and the file is opened, we can read the contents as characters by using the function getc( ).

The function getchar( ) is a special case of getc( ) and is used when the input data comes from standard input (stdin). In a similar manner, scanf( ) is a special case of fscanf( ) in that scanf( ) reads its input from stdin and fscanf( ) reads its input from the given file.

The UNIX operating system allows an additional type of file access, based on the notion of a file descriptor. A file descriptor is a number used to denote which entry in the file table of a UNIX process is intended. File descriptors 0, 1, and 2 are reserved for stdin, stdout (the user's terminal), and stderr (usually errors are also displayed on the user's terminal), respectively. A file is created by using the creat() UNIX system call. Files can be opened using the UNIX system calls open() and close().

UNIX file access also allows a lower-level means of reading bytes of data using the read( ) and write( ) system calls. The UNIX file access commands are more powerful than the general C file access commands, since they allow the programmer to have some control over the access permissions on the files being accessed. UNIX systems allow both the general file access commands and the special UNIX system calls.

Exercises

1. Write two C functions atof( ) and ftoa( ) that change ASCII characters to floating point data and the reverse, respectively.

2. Write two C functions fgets2( ) and fputs2( ) that read and write data one line at a time. Assume that the data is in character format.

3. Most semaphore operations depend upon the writing of two functions called P( ) and V(( ) that act on semaphores by "acquiring" or "releasing" them; that is, by making sure that no other process can use the resource because it does not have the semaphore (acquiring the semaphore) or that any process that wishes to use the resource can have it (releasing the semaphore). The notation P( ) and V( ) is used because the words "acquire" and "release" begin with P and V, respectively, in Dutch, which was the native language of the primary mover of the use of semaphores in computer systems (Edsgar Dijkstra). Write the two functions P( ) and V( ) to manipulate a semaphore file named /tmp/lockfile using the function creat( ).

4. Design and implement an experiment to determine the effect of changing the value of BUFSIZE on reading text data. Compare your results with those of a C program using the non-UNIX concepts presented in the first section of this chapter. The precise determination of actual running time is difficult on a multiuser UNIX system because of system overhead and the effect of other users. Therefore you should repeat your experiments three times in order to get an average time.

5. Repeat the experiment in exercise 4 using three different types of data: integer, floating point, or bit data. Compare your results to the results you obtained in exercise 4.

as a constant within a C program, and the hexadecimal constant described here would be denoted in a C program by

    X1B

for clarity.

The next program shows how the printf( ) statement gives the correct values for the number 27 in base 10, base 8, and base 16, respectively. The control specifications %d, %o, and %x are used to change the format of the number as needed.

Example 11.1

```
#include <stdio.h>
main(void)
{
  printf("%d %o %x \n",27,27,27);
}
```

The output of example 11.1 is

    27 33 1b

(The output for hexadecimal numbers (base 16) uses the form "1b"; the input of 1B would be treated the same as 1b for a scanf( ) function.)

In the rest of this chapter, we will see why bit operations are necessary. We will learn the basic operations that can be performed on bits and how these operations are carried out in C.

There is one fact that is somewhat surprising. There have been essentially no changes in the C language facilities for bit operations in ANSI C from the older versions. Perhaps the initial design of C was outstanding in this regard. Perhaps this is because any changes to these lower level features would have caused great difficulty in lower-level programming. Generally speaking, the lower the language level, the harder it is to make the program modular and to follow good software engineering practice.

11.1 Why Bit Operations Are Sometimes Necessary

Bit operations are necessary when a program must control specific devices and the high-level construction of integers or other higher-level variables is not sufficiently fine-grained for us to be able to have the proper control of our program's data.

As a first example, we consider a program to move a simple rectangular object across a computer screen. The simplest type of display available is a monochrome monitor in which each position on the monitor is represented as a value of a location in a special area of memory called the display memory. On many such computer systems and in particular on most personal computers, the computer and the software are designed to be easily upgraded to color systems later by merely replacing the monochrome monitor by a color monitor. This means that the video memory has to be able to handle both color and monochrome data, even if the only available monitor is monochrome. We will assume that this is the case in our discussion.

Our model of the video memory looks like a rectangular array of locations called pixels (for picture elements). Each pixel represents a point on the screen ,and there is a one-to-one relationship between pixels on the screen and bytes in this video memory. Since we are considering only a monochrome system, the choices for each pixel value are ON and OFF, and this corresponds to the values 0 and 1 in the corresponding memory locations. We therefore want to be able to tell if the contents of a memory location are 0 or 1. We think of the video memory as an array

```
int arr[HEIGHT][WIDTH];
```

where HEIGHT and WIDTH are the integer values of the maximum number of rows and columns, respectively.

Initially, the screen is blank, and this is done by setting each element in the array to 0. If an array value is set to 1, then the corresponding pixel is on. Thus the picture shown in Figure 11.1 is obtained from the code in example 11.1.

Example 11.2

```
#include <stdio.h>

#include "video_memory.h"
/* Not the name of a real file.  It is given here        */
/* as an illustrative example only.  The values of       */
/* HEIGHT and WIDTH would be in this file.               */

main(void)
{
  int i, j;
  int video_memory[HEIGHT][WIDTH];

  j = WIDTH/2 ;
  for ( i = 1; i < HEIGHT; i++)
    video_memory[i][j] = 1;

  /* The next function is not a real function name.    */
  /* It is here to illustrate the video system function */

  display_video_memory();
}
```

In example 11.2, the array elements are set to 1 in the desired places. This code will run relatively fast.

Suppose now that we wish to create the object shown in Figure 11.2 and move it horizontally across the video screen from right to left.

The object in Figure 11.2 is a two-dimensional rectangle of height 4 and width 8. It is represented as an array of 32 dots, and we assume that it is initially in a position just to the right of the region to be displayed on the monitor screen. You should think of the

Figure 11.1 A single vertical line of dots is drawn

object as being just to the right of a window and therefore invisible. Imagine that it will move past the window to become partially visible, then completely visible, then partially visible again, and finally invisible again. The problem is how to represent the values of the array that represents the video memory and how to compute these values fast.

In most computer graphics systems, an object is considered to have a set of world coordinates that describe its position. These world coordinates are transformed to actual screen coordinates (the video memory in our example) by means of a special graphics function. To follow the same design here, we assume that there is a function named world_to_screen(args) that takes as a parameter a two-dimensional array named args and produces as its result a two-dimensional array that we call the video memory. The two-dimensional array args has values between predetermined minimum and maximum values for x and y.

To make matters simple, assume that the object to be moved from right to left has the world coordinates changed as the object moves and that the picture is updated by the following algorithm:

```
for (time = min_time; time < max_time; time ++)
  for (x = world_x_min; x < world_x_max; x++)
    {
    get_new_world_coordinates(args);
    world_to_screen(args);
    };
```

```
........
........
........
........
```

Figure 11.2 A pixel representation of a rectangle

We now have the object changed to a set of screen coordinates and are faced with the problem of rapidly updating the screen. In this example, we probably just want to cover any existing object by the moving object. We need to be able to change rapidly the values in the two-dimensional array video_memory[ ][ ]. These values can be either 0 (if the object cannot be seen) or 1 (if it can). What we need is a way to have only the values 0 and 1 result from these operations.

The first attempt is to multiply the values in the various array positions. If the corresponding values are both 0, then the product is 0, and this means that the object should not be displayed, which is what we want. If the corresponding values are both 1, then the product is 1 and the pixel should be lit, which is also what we want. You should note that it is not possible to tell where the new object begins and ends, because the boundary is blended into the background. If the value of a particular element of video_array[ ][ ] is 0 and the corresponding value of the object is 1, then the pixel should be lit since we wish to show the object. This doesn't work since the product is 0. A similar problem occurs if the video_array[ ][ ] value is 1 and the corresponding value of the object is 0. It is easy to see that using addition of the array values also doesn't work since 1 + 1 = 2. We could always use a combination of arithmetic operations based on the expression

```
a * (1 - b) + b * (1 - a) + a * b
```

which works correctly for all possible values of a and b chosen from the set {0, 1}. This method is too slow since it requires three multiplications, two subtractions, and two additions to compute a single value of the video_array[ ][ ] used for the video display. Using comparisons and if-else statements is also too slow for this simple computation.

What we really need is a way to use the individual pieces of information from the array elements. That is, we need to use the information as single bits and perform an "OR" operation that returns the value 1 if at least one of the two values used is 1 and returns 0 if both have the value 0. This is a bit operation. If we wished to show the outline of the moving object against the background of the same type, we would want to use the exclusive OR, which returns 0 if the two values are either both 0 or both 1 and returns 1 otherwise.

We would use similar constructions if we wanted to change the color on a color display system. Such systems ordinarily store the colors as a collection of values that are determined by a collection of bits in a fixed size. Each pixel is associated with one of these colors. The number of bits for the choice of colors is determined by the hardware and is usually one of 4, 8, 12, 16, 24, or 32. A color graphics display is commonly described by a triple of integers:

horizontal number of pixels * vertical number of pixels * pixel depth

and so a high quality workstation display might be described as being 1,024 by 1,024 by 16. Using convoluted arithmetic expressions for the simple idea of comparing pixel colors is not at all satisfactory from the viewpoints of performance or understandability of the code.

Another example of a bit operation comes from the UNIX wait command. This command is used to convey information from a running program called a "child process" to another running program, called the "parent process", that the child process has terminated its execution. The child process conveys its information by means of a status code that is stored in an integer variable called status. Status is accessed by means of a pointer to its contents, and so the syntax for the wait( ) function is

```
wait(&status)
int status;
```

Wait returns an integer value representing the number that was assigned to the child process by the operating system. We are much more interested in the contents of status in this section.

The size of the storage location for the integer status is usually different on different machines. To keep this code portable, the only portion of status used is the rightmost two bytes. These two bytes are interpreted as follows:

- If the child exits with no "fatal errors," then the rightmost byte of status is 0 and the next byte is the child process's argument to the function exit( ).
- If the child exits because of a "fatal signal," then the rightmost byte is nonzero. The 7 rightmost bits of this rightmost byte give the number of the signal (there are 19 standard UNIX signals), and the leftmost bit of the rightmost byte is 1 if a core dump is to be done and 0 if no core dump is to be done.

We could always check for the leftmost bit of the rightmost byte on byte-addressable machines by comparing at a higher level such as

```
if ( (status >127 ) && (status < 255)
     core_dump_bit =1;
```

Compare this to the actual code

```
if ((status & 128) == 1)
     core_dump_bit = 1;
```

which can be written more cleanly as

```
core_dump_bit = status & 128;
```

using the bit operation '&' that will be discussed in the next section.

The code using these bit operations is easier to understand than the original since it does not use as many comparisons with constants. It is also shorter. It has the additional advantage of executing faster, which is a critical concern when writing operating system code.

By the way, we can denote octal constants by starting them with an O as in O666 and hexadecimal constants by starting them with an X or x as in X31 or x31.

11.2 Elementary Bit Operations

In the previous section, we saw how bit operations can be applied in programs. In this section, we discuss the operations that can be performed on bits.

The first operation that we discuss is the "bitwise OR" operation that takes as input two values and returns a value that is obtained by performing the "OR" operation on the individual bits in the encoding of the two input values. The "OR" operation on bits produces a single bit output that is 0 if both input bits are 0, 1 otherwise. The "OR" operation in C is denoted by a single 'I' symbol and has the syntax

```
output = input1 | input2
```

In most C compilers, this operation is not defined for inputs that are of type float or double. An example of the use of the 'I' for an "OR" operation is given in example 11.3.

Example 11.3

```
#include <stdio.h>

main(void)
{
   int i = 16, j = 20, k = 10;
   char a = 'a', x = 'x';

   printf("%d\n",i |j );
   printf("%o\n",i |j );
   printf("%d\n",i |k );
   printf("%o\n",i |k );
   printf("%d\n",a );
   printf("%o\n",a );
   printf("%d\n",x );
   printf("%o\n",x );
   printf("%d\n",a|x );
   printf("%o\n",a|x );
}
```

It has the following output:

```
20
24
26
32
97
141
120
170
121
171
```

The output is obtained in the following way. The numbers i and j are converted to binary giving the bit patterns 10000 for i, 10100 for j, and 01010 for k. (Most of the leading 0's have been omitted.) The "OR" operation produces the pattern 10100 (decimal 20 and octal 24) for i|j and 11010 (decimal 26 and octal 32) for i|k. The bit pattern of the character 'a' is 1100001 (decimal 97 and octal 141) and the bit pattern of the character 'x' is 1111000 (decimal 120 and octal 170). The "OR" of 'a' and 'x' produces the pattern 1111001 (decimal 121 and octal 171) for a | x.

The next operation that we discuss is the "bitwise AND" operation that takes as input two values and returns a value that is obtained by performing the "AND" operation on the individual bits in the encoding of the two input values. The "AND" operation on bits produces a single bit output that is 1 if both input bits are 1, 0 otherwise. The "AND" operation in C is denoted by a single '&' symbol and has the syntax

```
output = input1 & input2
```

In most C compilers, this operation is not defined for inputs that are of type float or double; it is generally defined for the char and int (including unsigned, short, and long) types. An example of the use of the '&' for an "AND" operation is given in example 11.4.

Example 11.4

```
#include <stdio.h>

main(void)
{
   int i = 16, j = 20, k = 10;
   char a = 'a', x = 'x';

   printf("%d\n",i&j );
   printf("%o\n",i&j );
   printf("%d\n",i&k );
   printf("%o\n",i&k );
   printf("%d\n",a&x );
   printf("%o\n",a&x );
}
```

The output of example 11.4 is

```
16
20
0
0
96
140
```

As before, the numbers i and j are converted to binary, giving the bit patterns 10000 for i, 10100 for j, and 01010 for k. The "AND" of i and j produces the pattern 10000 (decimal 16 and octal 20) for i&j and 00000 (decimal and octal 0) for i&k. The bit pattern of the character 'a' is 1100001 and the bit pattern of the character 'x' is 1111000; hence the "AND" is 1100000 (decimal 96 and octal 140).

Warning: Be careful not to confuse the "bitwise AND" and "bitwise OR" operations '&' and '|' with the "logical AND" and "logical OR" operations (denoted by && and ||) that we have been using in most of this book. They produce quite different results. For example, replacing | by || and & by && in examples 11.3 and 11.4 radically changes the output to

```
1
1
1
1
97
141
120
170
1
1
```

and

```
1
1
1
1
1
1
```

respectively. This is one of the most difficult errors to detect in practice, since the apparent logic of the program is correct but the output makes no sense.

The bitwise "OR" operation '|' is often called the "inclusive OR" since it has output 1 if one or both of the input argument bits have the value 1; the output for each bit is 0 if both bits are 0. There is another bit operation called the "exclusive OR" that gives the result 1 for the output bit if one, but not both of the input argument bits has the value 1; the resulting output bit will be 0 if the input argument bits are either both 0 or both 1. The exclusive OR operator is denoted by ^.

The use of the exclusive OR operator is shown in example 11.5.

Example 11.5

```c
#include <stdio.h>
main(void)
{
    int i = 16, j = 20, k = 10;
    char a = 'a', x = 'x';

    printf("%d\n",i^j );
    printf("%o\n",i^j );
    printf("%d\n",i^k );
```

```
        printf("%o\n",i^k );
        printf("%d\n",a );
        printf("%o\n",a );
        printf("%d\n",x );
        printf("%o\n",x );
        printf("%d\n",a^x );
        printf("%o\n",a^x );
}
```

Example 11.5 produces the output

```
4
4
26
32
97
141
120
170
25
31
```

You should use the bit patterns for the variables i, j, k, a, and x given earlier to convince yourself that the output is correct.

C has a negation operator "NOT" that changes every bit pattern to its "one's complement." This terminology means that every 0 bit is changed to a 1 and that every 1 bit is changed to a 0. The syntax for the "NOT" operator is

~ bit_pattern

and an example of its use is shown in example 11.6.

Example II.6

#include <stdio.h>

```
main(void)
{
    int i = 16, j = 20;
    char a = 'a', x = 'x';

    printf("%o\n",i );
    printf("%o\n",~i );
    printf("%o\n",j );
    printf("%o\n",~j );
    printf("%o\n",a );
    printf("%c\n",~a );
```

```
    printf("%o\n",x );
    printf("%o\n",~x );
    printf("%c\n",~x );
}
```

On one computer, example 11.6 has the output

```
    20
    37777777757
    24
    37777777753
    141

    170
    37777777607
```

All of the results of the conversions are displayed in octal form. (The last one is also displayed in character form.) The results are surprising until the method of conversion is clear. For example, the number 16 (decimal) has the octal representation 20 and corresponds to 001 000, where we have used spaces between groups of three bits for clarity. Adding the leading 0's to the binary representation of this number gives the number

```
    00 000 000 000 000 000 000 000 000 001 000
```

Changing all of the bits in this number gives the result

```
    11 111 111 111 111 111 111 111 111 110 111
```

which has the octal equivalent (with spaces for clarity) of

```
    3  7  7  7  7  7  7  7  7  5  7
```

and this is how the value of 37777777757 for the expression ~20 is computed.

There are two other strange results in the output. The blank line after the 141 is caused by the fact that the character 'x', whose ASCII value is 141 (octal), is changed by the "NOT" operator to the octal number 37777777535, which does not have a reasonable ASCII equivalent in the sense of being a printable character. When this example program was run on one computer, a beep was heard. The beep was caused by the last printf( ) statement of the program in example 11.6 and is also a result of the ASCII value of the character ~x not being visible (although it is audible).

There are two other bitwise operators in C: the left and right shifts. The left shift operator, denoted by two less-than signs (<<), shifts the binary representation of its argument some number of bits to the left. The number of bits to be shifted is determined by the second argument, and this second argument is an integer. Thus after a left shift of 1 bit, 110001 is changed to 1100010. The right shift operator, denoted by >>, performs a similar action while shifting bits to the right. The syntax of the left shift operator is

```
    bit_pattern << number_of_bits_to_be_shifted_left
```

and the right shift operator has the similar syntax

```
        bit_pattern >> number_of_bits_to_be_shifted_right
```

Example 11.7 shows the operation of the left shift operator <<.

Example 11.7

```
#include <stdio.h>

main(void)
{
  int i = 16, j = 20;
  char a = 'a', x = 'x';

  printf("%o\n",i << 1 );
  printf("%o\n",i << 2 );
  printf("%o\n",j << 3 );
  printf("%o\n",a << 1 );
  printf("%o\n",a << 2 );
  printf("%c\n",a << 2 );
  printf("%o\n",x << 1 );
  printf("%o\n",x << 2 );
  printf("%c\n",x << 2 );
}
```

The output is

```
        40
        100
        240
        302
        604

        360
        740
```

Notice again that the output contains a blank line caused by the fact that the shifting left of 'a' by two bits results in an unprintable character. Use the bit patterns for i, j, a, and x given earlier in this section to check the results of running the program of example 11.7.

A summary of bit operations is given in Table 11.1.

Bit operations are often used to test the value of a single bit that has a relation to the state of some device or subsystem. For example, we may wish to test the value of the right-most bit in the variable stored in a location called "interrupt vector." This bit can be accessed by a mask such as the binary number 00000001 in a code fragment like

```
#define MASK 0001
...
if ( (interrupt_vector | MASK) == 0000)
        /* then bit is 0, take an appropriate action */
```

Table 11.1 Summary of bit operations

OPERATION	NOTATION
OR	|
AND	&
EXCLUSIVE OR	^
NOT	~
LEFT SHIFT	<<
RIGHT SHIFT	>>

Compare this code with the code presented in Chapter 9 that used fields to accomplish some of the same results.

The shift operation can be used to pack many pieces of data into the same place. Masks can be used to retrieve this data. This type of data compression and data retrieval operation is very important in image processing systems that generate thousands of images per day, with each of these images needing at least one megabyte for storage.

For example, on a 32-bit word computer that is word-addressable, we can place 4 8-bit ints as follows. Let a, b, c, and d denote the four ints and let var denote the address of the word where the ints are to be stored. We store the first 8-bit int, a, in the first 8 bits of its address by assigning a to var:

```
var = a;
```

The next assignment is to the next 8 bits:

```
var = (var << 8) | b;
```

The remaining assignments are, in order,

```
var = (var << 8) | c;
```

and

```
var = (var << 8) | d;
```

The values are retrieved by using masks and shifting right if necessary. For example, to retrieve the value of b, we take the AND with the mask whose value is octal 000000111000,

```
b = (var & 0000000111000);
```

to set the proper bits in b and then shift right to get the bits in first position:

```
b = (b >> 8);
```

There is one final note about bit operations. They are frequently used in programs that are machine-specific in the sense that they act on the lowest level of information available to the computer. As such, they generally are not portable between different computer systems. The results obtained from running the programs of this chapter will probably be different, especially if you use computers with different storage sizes for int, char, float, or double.

11.3 Software Engineering Project: Changed Requirements

The next change to our prototype involves the use of bit operations for finding free memory space. We have used the first-fit algorithm for the determination of the next available memory block when an insertion is needed. It was easy to implement this by searching through all of memory to find the first free block.

The new requirement is to implement the free list of unused memory as an single bit vector instead of as an array (or a list as we could have implemented it in Chapter 8). A bit vector is a memory unit that is used to simulate the contents of a boolean array. The bits are either 0 or 1, and this means that the memory location corresponding to the position of the bit is either empty or full.

11.4 Software Engineering Project: The Next Prototype

Our new requirement is to implement the free list for access to memory blocks in our project as a bit vector using the ideas of this chapter. The only function that we have to change is the one that manages the free list. The way that this function should work is simple – each bit represents a specific memory block. We can access a bit directly by using a mask to obscure all the other, unwanted bits.

One way of using the masks is as follows. To test the rightmost bit, we simply take the bitwise AND of the bit vector with the octal number 0001. A value of 0001 means that the value of the rightmost bit is 1 and a value of 0000 means that the rightmost bit is 0. All other bits can be selected by using a similar procedure with other masks. This method clearly involves the creation of as many masks as there are bits to be tested, that is, as many masks as there are possible entries on the free list.

Another method is simply to determine the first bit that has a value of 0. We can use a function to select the bit by shifting the input until the bitwise exclusive OR of the number and the octal number 0000 has the value xxx1, where we don't care about the first three octal digits. The exclusive OR operator will return a value of the form xxx1 if the rightmost bit is a 0, which is the situation that we want. This is the preferred method since it doesn't require the creation of a large number of masks and keeps the program simple.

The header for the new function find_free_block( ) should be of the form

```
find_free_block(list_vector)
double list_vector;
{
/* body of find_free_block goes here */
}
```

with the free list passed as a parameter named list_vector. The reason for this is that the shifts would only change a copy of the input parameter while we are testing and the free list would not have to be reset to the correct order. The value that is identified as needing to be changed because of a memory insertion or deletion is determined by this function. The actual change to the free list should be made elsewhere in the program.

In the exercises you will be asked to analyze the performance of the new system based on this design and to implement the design.

Summary of Chapter 11

C permits operations on individual bits. Bit operations can be used to control the behavior of several different aspects of the contents of memory locations. Typical applications of bit operations include setting or releasing a bit that represents a pixel in a graphics display, reading the contents of a memory location that represents the status of some system function and interpreting the values of particular bits in this memory location, and speeding up access to lists that can be represented as bits in a computer memory location.

Some of the operations that can be performed on bits and the notations used for these operations are

OR	|
AND	&
EXCLUSIVE OR	^
NOT	~
LEFT SHIFT	<<
RIGHT SHIFT	>>

These can generally be used on int and char expressions.

The bitwise AND and OR operations | and & are different from the logical AND and OR operations || and &&; this can cause serious problems if the two operations are confused.

Exercises

1. Write a C function that has a single variable of type int. This function will produce as output the value of the input exclusively "ORed" with the value of MASK where MASK = 037777 in octal. Note the size of MASK might be larger than the size of the int variable that was input. Repeat this for the "AND," "OR," and "NOT" operators.

2. Write a C program that finds the largest value that can be stored in a variable of type int on your system. Do this by reading the system manual and writing your program to check the sign bit. Compare the speed of this program with that of a program that increments an integer value that was originally 0, until the value becomes negative. This should give you some idea of the speed of bit operations as compared to integer arithmetic.

3. Write a C program to compare the speed of multiplication by powers of 2 using shift operations and using standard arithmetic.

4. Read a manual for a medium- or high-performance computer graphics system. A system based on a personal computer may not have the functionality of the more elaborate (and more expensive) graphics systems. Count the number of times that bit operations are used, especially in functions that control the use of input or output devices or that manipulate color look-up tables.

5. What is the output obtained from the following function? How portable is the code of this example?

```
mystery(n)
short n;
{
short i;
for (i = 15; i >= 0; i--)
    {
    if (( n & (1 <<i) ) == 0)
        printf("0");
    else
        printf("1");
    }
i = getchar();
}
```

6. Many operating systems keep track of unused memory by using a "free list." Frequently this free list is implemented as a bit vector rather than as an actual list. Simulate this by the following procedure.

(a) Memory is to be simulated as an array of 128 integers. Initially, each memory location should be set to 0 to indicate that the location is free. This simulates memory locations being empty until they are loaded with data.
(b) The free list is a set of 128 consecutive bits.
(c) Use a random number generator (either one that is already on the system or one that you create yourself) to generate 100 integers in the range 0 to 127.
(d) When a random integer is obtained, the corresponding bit in the free list vector is checked to see if the corresponding memory position is available. For example, if a 32 is obtained, then bit 32 is checked to see if memory position 32 is available. If it is, then bit 32 is set to 1 and memory[32] is set to the value 999. If memory position 32 is not available, then the value of memory[32] will be set to –1 to indicate that a request was made for that location and that the location was not available because of prior use. In an actual operating system, the free list would have been searched for a free memory location.

Software Engineering Exercises

7. In this chapter, we discussed the use of a bit vector to describe the free list for access to our simulated memory. Implement this system.

8. Analyze the relative speed of the two methods discussed for implementation of the free list using bit operations.

9. In this chapter, we discussed the use of a bit vector to describe the free list for access to our simulated memory. The disk also needs to have the available blocks kept on some type of a free list. In the previous prototypes, we have implemented the free list as an array. Implement the free list for the disk simulation in our project as a bit vector using the ideas of this chapter.

Towards C++

You have probably heard a lot of discussion about the C++ language and object-oriented programming. Some people claim that using the technique of object-oriented programming with languages such as C++ will automatically solve most of the major problems in software engineering. This was the intention of Bjarne Stroustrup, who is commonly considered to be the creator of the C++ language. Object-oriented languages are actually much older than C++; one of the earliest object-oriented languages was Simula, which was developed in 1967.

Proponents of the object-oriented approach believe that the combination of object-oriented design and object-oriented programming provides a more natural framework for the software development process and for the reuse of previously developed software. Unfortunately, most experienced computer professionals have a healthy skepticism about the ability of any new programming paradigm to provide easier solutions to software engineering problems. It is difficult for the person new to this subject to distinguish between what is clearly true, what is clearly untrue, and what requires special analysis of its utility in a given situation.

You may also have heard the statement that C++ is a superset of C. C++ is technically a superset of C in the sense that a program in C will generally be compiled without major changes by a C++ compiler, except for differences in access to the standard libraries. However, anyone faced with the problem of using C++ for a software system of any size has found that there are several subtle differences in the semantics of C and C++, at least in the way that the semantics of the languages are implemented by various compiler writers. There is no official standard for C++ that is as universally accepted as the ANSI standard for C.

12.1 C and C++ Solutions to a Simple Problem

It is impossible to provide a complete introduction to C++ in this book because of the need to develop fully the object-oriented paradigm for software development. Instead, we present a description of a small problem and two solutions: one using the standard facilities of the C language and the other using the object-oriented facilities of C++.

The problem we consider is that of writing a program to perform high-precision binary arithmetic; only the addition portion is shown in our sample solutions. The input to the program consists of three things: a binary integer, an arithmetic operator, and a binary integer. After the input is read in, the operation is to be performed and the result is to be printed.

There are additional specifications intended to simplify the problem: all the data is to be read in using character format, and we can assume that the input is error-free, that the binary integers (which were read in as arrays consisting of one of the two characters '0' and '1') required no more than 80 characters for storage, and that the three inputs are entered on different lines.

The solution using C is presented in example 12.1.

Example 12.1

```
/* C program to compute the sum of two binary integers */
/* Integers are entered as character strings, with the */
/* characters being either 0 or 1.                      */
/* All data entry is from the terminal and no error     */
/* checking of the input is done.                       */

#include <stdio.h>
#define MAXLINE 80


/*------------------------------------------------*/
/*      FUNCTION PROTOTYPES                        */
/*------------------------------------------------*/
void convert(char x[MAXLINE], char y[MAXLINE]) ;
void sum(char x[MAXLINE], char y[MAXLINE], int max_len) ;


/*------------------------------------------------*/
/*      GLOBAL DECLARATIONS                        */
/*------------------------------------------------*/
int len1, len2;   /* lengths of the input strings */
int max_len;
int first = 1, second = 2, larger;
char num1[MAXLINE] , num2[MAXLINE] ;
```

```
void main(void)
{
  puts("Please enter the first binary number.");
  scanf("%s",num1);
  puts("Please enter the second binary number.");
  scanf("%s",num2);
  len1 = strlen(num1);
  len2 = strlen(num2);
  if (len1 > len2)
    {
    max_len = len1;
    larger = first;
    }
  else
    {
    max_len = len2;
    larger = second;
    }
  convert(num1, num2);
  sum(num1,num2, max_len);
}


/*-----------------------------------------------------*/
/*  Converts the two character strings to the same     */
/*  length by padding the shorter string with 0's.     */
/*-----------------------------------------------------*/
void convert(char x[MAXLINE], char y[MAXLINE])
{
int i;
extern int max_len;

  if (larger == first)
    {
    for (i = len2 - 1;i >= 0 ;i--)
      y[i + max_len -len2] = y[i];
    for (i = 0; i < max_len - len2; i++)
      y[i] = '0';
    }
  else
    {
    for (i = len1 - 1;i >= 0 ;i--)
      x[i + max_len -len1] = x[i];
```

```
      for (i = 0; i < max_len - len1; i++)
        x[i] = '0';
      }
}


/*-------------------------------------------------*/
/*    Performs the addition                        */
/*-------------------------------------------------*/
void sum(char x[MAXLINE], char y[MAXLINE], int max_len)
{
  static int temp[MAXLINE +1];        /* initialized to 0 */
  int xtemp[MAXLINE], ytemp[MAXLINE];
  int i ;
  int carry = 0;

  printf("\n");
  /* temp has indices 1 off to allow for carry to the   */
  /* leftmost place.  The arrays x and y  have data in */
  /* positions 0 ..max_len - 1                          */
  for (i = 0; i < MAXLINE; i++)
    {
    /* convert from int to char */
    xtemp[i] = x[i] - '0';
    ytemp[i] = y[i] - '0';
    }
  i = max_len;

  do
    {
    temp[i+1] = xtemp[i] + ytemp[i] + carry ;
    if ( temp[i+1] > 1)
      {
      carry = 1;
      temp[i+1] = (temp[i+1] % 2) ;
      }
    else
      carry = 0 ;
    }
  while (i--);

  temp[0] = carry;
  if (carry == 0)
    for (i = 1; i <= max_len; i++) /* ignore first zero */
      printf("%d",temp[i]);
```

```
    else
        for (i = 0; i <= max_len; i++)
            printf("%d",temp[i]);
}
```

This program is fairly straightforward. It prompts the user for input and reads the input character by character. No error checking of the input is done. The first and third input lines of characters are placed into two arrays called first and second, and the operation specified in the second input line (addition) is performed using a binary version of the standard algorithm for addition. Before the call to the function sum( ) that performs the arithmetic computation, the two arrays are coerced to the same length by the function convert( ), which pads the shorter array with the character '0'. The result of the arithmetic computation is then printed.

The I/O in this example is performed by the standard C functions getchar( ) and printf( ), using appropriate control specifications for these functions. Other standard I/O functions also could have been used, at least for the printing of messages to the user of the program.

Our solution was somewhat constrained by the facilities available in the C language. Notice that we used a function called add( ) to perform the addition instead of calling a function whose name is the single character '+'. Also notice that we used a global array since C does not allow functions to return entire arrays. (Of course, C does allow functions to return pointers.)

From the perspective of object-oriented software design, the major flaw in this solution is that a person modifying this C program would be able to perform computations that are not appropriate, and which have unexpected results. The reasoning is that someone might try to do something inappropriate such as computing the cosine of this binary number, which would lead to unexpected results. Only the discipline of the programmer prevents this; the language does not. Even the use of typedef does not prevent access to the internals of function representations using common or external variables.

The C++ solution to this problem is somewhat similar to the C solution in the sense that it uses the same algorithm for performing the arithmetic computation. However, the basic data element is not an array any longer. Instead, we define a class of object called "Binary." In the definition of this class, we incorporate all the transformations that are allowable on objects of this class. Allowable operations on this data object will be read, print, and add. This means that no other operations are possible, unless we explicitly allow them. The enforcement of these restrictions is done by the compiler, thus removing some responsibility from the programmer.

The C++ solution to the same problem is presented in example 12.2. We will use a slightly different style of indentation to reinforce the program being written in C++ and not in C.

Example 12.2

```
// C++ program to compute the sum of two binary integers.
// Integers are entered as character strings, with the
```

```
// characters being either 0 or 1.
// No error checking of the input is performed.

#include <stdio.h>

#define MAXLINE 80

class Binary {
      char num[MAXLINE] ;
      int len;
public:
      int length(Binary word)  { return (strlen(num) ; } ;
      int max_len;
      void print();
      void read();
      void convert(Binary x, Binary y);
      sum(Binary x, Binary y, int max_len);
};


void Binary :: print()
      {int i;

      for (i = 0; i < max_len; i++)
            cout << num[i] ;
      };


void Binary :: read()
      {
      scanf("%s", num;
      len = strlen(num);
      };

/////////CONVERT/////////////////////////////////
void Binary :: convert(Binary x, Binary y)
{
int i
extern int max_len;
extern int larger, first, second ;
extern int len1, len2;

if (larger == first)
      {
      for (i = len2 - 1;i >= 0 ;i--)
            y.num[i + max_len -len2] = y.num[i];
```

```
              for (i = 0; i < max_len - len2; i++)
                    y.num[i] = '0';
              }
       else
              {
              for (i = len1 - 1;i >= 0 ;i--)
                    x.num[i + max_len -len1] = x.num[i];
              for (i = 0; i < max_len - len1; i++)
                    x.num[i] = '0';
              }
       }


/////////SUM///////////////////////////////
Binary :: sum(Binary x, Binary y, int max_len)
{
static int temp[MAXLINE +1];           // initialized to 0
Binary  xtemp, ytemp;
int i ;
int carry = 0;

cout <<"\n";
// starts at index 1 to allow carry into leftmost place.
// arrays x and y have data in positions 0 ..max_len - 1

for (i = 0; i < MAXLINE; i++)
       {
       /* convert from int to char */
       xtemp.num[i] = x.num[i] - '0';
       ytemp.num[i] = y.num[i] - '0';
       }
i = max_len;

do
       {
       temp[i+1] = xtemp.num[i] + ytemp.num[i] + carry ;
       if ( temp[i+1] > 1)
              {
              carry = 1;
              temp[i+1] = (temp[i+1] % 2) ;
              }
       else
              carry = 0 ;
       }
while (i--);
```

The advantages that are claimed for the use of an object-oriented language such as C++ over a procedural language such as C are primarily in the areas of program understanding, consistency of data, and, most importantly, the ease of development of libraries of pre-compiled and tested objects and their allowable transformations. Clearly, none of the features should be expected to show up to any great effect in a small program such as the one presented here.

A dream of software engineers is to develop a collection of interchangeable software modules with known specifications of their performance, cost, reliability, and interface, with the access to this collection similar to the way that an electrical engineer chooses components for a circuit or a mechanical engineer chooses a spring for some mechanism. The hardware engineers can look at something like a catalog for this information. This is somewhat more promising for C++ than for C because of the ability of C++ to restrict allowable transformations on data objects.

On the other hand, there is a considerable concern about the additional requirements for testing of object-oriented software written in languages such as C++ over that of software written in languages such as C. Real-time performance of software that resolves overloading of operators at run time (such as in C++) is also a concern in many applications.

A fundamental feature of C++ that has not been illustrated in the example presented in this chapter is the ability of developing new classes of objects that inherit some of their properties from parent classes. An example of the utility of this concept can be seen by studying the geometric examples presented in Chapter 9 when we discussed unions in C. There were several geometric objects that could have been implemented in C++ as classes, with appropriate subclasses that would inherit some properties. For example, a square may be considered to be a subclass of a rectangle and as such would inherit some, but not all, of the properties of a rectangle. There are obviously many questions that need to be answered before an efficient and flexible object-oriented design can be created and implemented. See the exercises for more information about inheritance.

It seems clear that both C and C++ will be popular and important programming languages for many years. For further reading, consult the article by Hashemi and Leach [Hashemi 1992], which provides additional information about some of the issues encountered when migrating from C to C++.

Summary of Chapter 12

C++ is an object-oriented language that allows the use of the C language facilities for program control to be incorporated into new systems that use a new paradigm for the organization of data and allowable operations. The fundamental concepts of C++ are classes of objects and the restrictions of allowable transformations on these objects. New classes of objects can be created from old classes of objects by means of inheritance.

Exercises

1. There are several ways to arrange a hierarchy of objects. For example, we could view a square as a special case of a rectangle, or both of these as being subclasses of an object of class quadrilateral. Write complete class descriptions for each of these approaches to developing a class called "square."

2. Choose any programming example presented in Part II of this book and recode it in object-oriented form in C++.

Software Engineering Exercise

3. Consider the large software engineering project that we have described during the course of our study of the C language. (Recall that we changed our requirements for this software system several times as we learned more about the C language.) Describe how the system's design would be different if we had used an object-oriented paradigm for the system.

(a) Determine the fundamental data objects in our system. Are the fundamental objects the disk, the memory, disk or memory blocks, single data elements for either disk or memory, or something else? As part of your analysis, include the possibility of reusing libraries of transformations on these data objects and the possibility of having new classes of objects inherit properties from existing classes of objects.

(b) Determine the allowable operations on each of the classes that you have determined in part a of this problem.

(c) Encode this new system in C++. (This is a feasible project in a few weeks of full-time work for a student who is learning C++ as the project continues. Of course, such a project for a student who is learning C++ as the project goes on can't result in production quality code. Nevertheless, it is a valuable exercise.)

(d) Take your solution to an expert in both C++ and object-oriented programming for feedback on some of the improvements that could have been made to your design or your code. The feedback could also have been used profitably at the design stage.

Appendix I

Reserved Words in C

auto	break	case	char	const
continue	default	do	double	else
enum	extern	float	for	goto
if	int	long	register	return
short	signed	sizeof	static	struct
switch	typedef	union	unsigned	void
volatile	while			

Appendix 2

The C Standard Library and Other Libraries

int abs(int)   math library
NOTE: This function is in stdlib.h in ANSI C.
     absolute value function
USAGE: int_result = abs(int_argument)

double acos(double)   math library
     inverse cosine function
USAGE: double_result = acos(double_argument)

double asin(double)   math library
     inverse sine function
USAGE: double_result = asin(double_argument)

double atan(double)   math library
     inverse tangent function
USAGE: double_result = atan(double_argument)

float atof(char *)   std library
     changes ASCII string to float
USAGE: float_result = atof(char_string)

int atoi(char *)   std library
     changes ASCII string to int
USAGE: int_result = atof(char_string)

`(void *) calloc(int, int)`   std library

NOTE: Many UNIX implementations have two versions of this function. One is in the standard library and the other is in the malloc library. To use the malloc library, include the file malloc.h and compile with the -lmalloc option.

calloc( ) returns a pointer to a region containing precisely enough memory to hold an array. The first argument to calloc( ) represents the number of elements in the array and the second argument represents the size of an element in the array. The pointer is to char in Kernighan and Ritchie C and the pointer is to void in ANSI C. The two int parameters should always be positive.

USAGE: pointer = (pointer_type *) calloc(number_of_elements, element_size)

`double ceil(double)`   math library

ceiling function – returns a double-precision number that is on the next integer boundary greater than or equal to the argument.

USAGE: double _result = ceil(double_argument)

`double cos(double)`   math library

cosine function

USAGE: double_result = cos(double_argument)

`double cosh(double)`   math library

hyperbolic cosine function

USAGE: double_result = cosh(double_argument)

`int exit(int)`   std library

exit function – terminates execution of the program and provides the status of the program, which is stored in the argument, to the environment. An argument of 0 indicates successful execution; any other argument is used to indicate an error.

USAGE: exit(int_status)

`double exp(double)`   math library

exponential function

USAGE: double_result = exp(double_argument)

`double fabs(double)`   math library

floating point absolute value function

USAGE: double_result = fabs(double_argument)

`int fclose(FILE *)`   stdio.h

close file function – closes the input file given in the argument,
return value of –1 for error

USAGE: fclose(file_stream)

`int feof(FILE *)` stdio.h
feof function – returns 0 unless the END_OF_FILE character has been read from the input stream pointed to by the file pointer; in this case it returns a nonzero value. This is used to detect reading after the END_OF_FILE.
USAGE: if (file_error = feof(file_stream))
                exit(file_error);

`(char *) fflush(int)` stdio library
flush buffer function – empties output buffers if we wish to force their output. Useful in C++ programs when using printf and cout in the same program.
USAGE: fflush(file_stream);

`int fgetc(int)` stdio library
fgetc function – gets character from an input stream Identical to getc( ) in use. Somewhat slower than getc( ) because getc( ) is usually implemented as a macro.
USAGE: ch = fgetc(file_ptr);

`(char *)fgets(int, int,int)` stdio library
fgets function – gets the number of characters specified in the second argument from the input stream specified in the third argument and places them in order in the array of consecutive memory locations starting from position 0 in the array specified by the address of the first argument. A new line in the input is read into the array; this is different from the treatment of gets( ).
USAGE: str_ptr = fgets(starting_address, number_of_char, file_ptr)

`double floor(double)` math library
floor function – returns a double-precision number that is on the next integer boundary smaller than the argument.
USAGE: double_result = floor(double_argument)

`double fmod(double)` math library
floating point mod function – returns the remainder after division of the first argument by the second, or returns 0 if division by 0
USAGE: double_result = fmod(double_arg1, double_arg2)

`(FILE *)fopen(char *, char *)` stdio library
open file function – opens the file stream given in the first argument. The second argument is one of: "r", "w", "a", "r+", "w+", or "a+".
USAGE: file_ptr = fopen(file_name, mode)

`int fprintf(int, char *, var_args)`   stdio library

fprintf function – prints to the file stream specified in the first argument as output. The output is formatted according to the control specifications in the second argument. The variables that get their values printed are in the remaining arguments. The usage

fprintf(stdout, control_char_string, other_args)

is equivalent to the usage

printf(control_char_string, other_args)

See also the functions printf( ) and scanf( ).
USAGE: fprintf(file_ptr, control_char_string, other args);
NOTE: The order of control specifications and arguments to be printed can be changed and any number can be mixed in any order.

`int fputc(char, FILE *)`   stdio.h

fputc function – writes its first argument to the output stream specified by the second argument, which is a pointer to a FILE. The return value is the int equivalent of the first argument. See also the function putc( ), which has the equivalent action.
USAGE: int_val = fputc(ch, file_ptr);

`int fputs(char *, FILE *)`   stdio.h

fputs function – takes the first argument, which is a character string, and places it on the output stream specified in the second argument. The first argument must be terminated by a null byte; this null byte is not written to the output stream. See also puts( ).
USAGE: int_val = fputs(char_ptr, file_ptr);

`void free(void *)`   std library

free function – releases a memory region previously allocated by a call to malloc( ) or calloc( ).
USAGE: free(void_ptr);

`int fscanf(FILE *, char*, var_args)`   stdio library

fscanf function – reads from the input stream specified in the first argument according to the control specifications in the second argument. The variables that get assigned values are in the remaining arguments.
USAGE: fscanf(file_ptr, control_char_string, other args);

`int fseek(FILE*, long int. int)`   stdio.h

fseek function – allows random access to a file pointed to by the first argument. The second argument is used as the file offset from the current position, which is specified in the third argument.
USAGE: fseek(file_ptr, file_offset, current_position);

`int getc(char*)`   stdio library

get character from an input stream
USAGE: ch = getc(file_ptr);

`int getchar(void)`   stdio library

     get character from standard input. This is the equivalent of getc(stdin);

USAGE: ch = getchar( );

`int gets(char *)`   stdio library

     gets function – reads an input string from standard input and places it in consecutive locations beginning in the one pointed to by the argument. Input is read until EOF or a newline character is read. The newline character is NOT placed into the array pointed to by the second argument. This treatment of the newline character is different from that of fgets( ).

USAGE: gets(char_ptr);

`int isalnum(char)`   std library

     isalnum function – returns a nonzero value if the character is in one of the ranges A – Z , a – z, or 0 – 9; returns 0 otherwise – needs the include file ctype.h.

USAGE: if (isalnum(char_arg)) ...

`int isalpha(char)`   std library

     isalpha function – returns a nonzero value if the character is in the range A – Z or a – z; returns 0 otherwise – needs the include file ctype.h.

USAGE: if (isalpha(char_arg))...

`int isdigit(char)`   std library

     isdigit function – returns a nonzero value if the character is in the range 0 – 9; returns 0 otherwise – needs the include file ctype.h.

USAGE: if (isdigit(char_arg))...

`int islower(char)`   std library

     islower function – returns a non-zero value if the character is in the range a – z; returns 0 otherwise – needs the include file ctype.h.

USAGE: if (islower(char_arg))...

`int isspace(char)`   std library

     isspace function: – returns a non-zero value if the argument is one of: blank, space, carriage return, form feed, vertical tab, newline; returns 0 otherwise – needs the include file ctype.h.

USAGE: if (isspace(char_arg))...

`int isupper(char)`   std library

     isupper function – returns a non-zero value if the character is in the range A – Z; returns 0 otherwise – needs the include file ctype.h.

USAGE: if (islower(char_arg))...

`char* itoa(int)`   non-standard

     itoa function – changes int to ASCII string - not always found in C libraries – see sprintf( ).

USAGE: string_val = itoa(int);

`double log(double)`   math library
    natural logarithm function
USAGE: double_result = log(double_argument)

`double log10(double)`   math library
    logarithm to base 10 function
USAGE: double_result = log10(double_argument)

`(void *) malloc(unsigned int)`   std library
NOTE: Many UNIX implementations have two versions of this function. One is in the standard library and the other is in the malloc library. To use the malloc library, include the file malloc.h and compile with the -lmalloc option.

    malloc( ) returns a pointer to a region of size number of bytes; pointer is to char in Kernighan and Ritchie C and pointer is to void in ANSI C. The int parameter should always be positive.
USAGE: pointer = malloc(size)

`(char *)memcpy(char *, char*, unsigned int)`   string.h
    function memcpy – behaves much like the function strcpy( ) – copies from the memory location pointed to by the second argument to the location pointed to by the first argument.; the number of characters copied is given by the third argument. The value returned is a pointer indicating the location of the second argument.
USAGE: source_ptr = memcpy(dest_ptr, source_ptr, num_bytes);

`double pow(double,double)`   math library
    power function – raises the first argument to the second argument
USAGE: double_result = pow(double_arg1, double_arg2)

`int printf(char *, var_args)`   stdio library
    printf function – prints to standard output according to the control specifications in the first argument. The variables that get their values printed are in the remaining arguments. See also the function scanf().
USAGE: printf(control_char_string, other args);

`int putc(char, FILE *)`   stdio.h
    putc function – places the character argument on the output file pointed to by the file pointer specified in the second argument, which is a pointer to a FILE. The return value is the int equivalent of the first argument. See also fputc(), which has equivalent action.
USAGE: int_val = putc(ch, file_ptr);

`int putchar(char)`   stdio.h
    putchar function – writes its argument to the output stream stdout. The return value is the int equivalent of the argument.
USAGE: int_val = putchar(ch);

`int puts(char *)`   stdio.h

puts function – takes its argument, which is a character string, and places it on the output stream stdout. The first argument must be terminated by a null byte; this null byte is not written to the output stream.

There is one difference between puts( ) and fputs( ). The function puts( ) always places a newline character at the end of the character stream, while fputs( ) does not. See also fputs( ).

USAGE: int_val = puts(char_ptr);

`int scanf(char *, var_args)`   stdio library

scanf function – reads from standard input according to the control specifications in the first argument. The variables that get assigned values are in the remaining arguments.

USAGE: scanf(control_char_string, other args);

`double sin(double)`   math library

sine function

USAGE: double_result = sin(double_argument)

`double sinh(double)`   math library

hyperbolic sine function

USAGE: double_result = sinh(double_argument)

`int sprintf(char *, char *, var_args)`   stdio library

sprintf function – prints its output to the string specified in the first argument according to the control specifications in the second argument. The variables that get their values printed are in the remaining arguments. See also the functions printf( ) and scanf( ).

USAGE: sprintf(result_string, control_char_string, other args);

`double sqrt(double)`   math library

square root function – error if argument is negative

USAGE: double_result = sqrt(double_argument).

`int sscanf(char *, char *, var_args)`   stdio library

sscanf function – reads from character string specified in the first argument according to the control specifications in the second argument. The variables that get assigned values are in the remaining arguments.

USAGE: fscanf(file_ptr, control_char_string, other args);

`(char *) strcat(char *, char *)`   string.h

strcat function concatenates the contents of the string pointed to by the second argument onto the end of the string pointed to by the first argument. The value of the first argument is returned. (The end-of-string character of the string pointed to by the first argument is overwritten by the characters from the string pointed to by the second argument.)

USAGE: string_ptr = strcat(string_ptr1, string_ptr2);

`int strcmp(char *, char *)`   string.h

      strcmp function compares the contents of the string pointed to by the second argument with the string pointed to by the first argument. The function returns a negative value if the first string is lexicographically less than the second, a positive value if the first is greater than the second, and 0 if the strings are identical. Since lexicographical order is what is used in dictionaries, this function is useful for sorting alphabetic data.
USAGE: int_value = strcmp(string_ptr1, string_ptr2);

`(char *) strcpy(char *, char *)`   string.h

      strcpy function copies the contents of the string pointed to by the second argument into the string pointed to by the first argument at the beginning of that string. The value of the first argument is returned. (The end of string character from the string pointed to by the second argument is used to terminate the string.)
USAGE: string_ptr = strcpy(string_ptr1, string_ptr2);

`int strlen(char *)`   string.h

      strlen function gives the length of the string pointed to by the second argument as an int; all characters up to, but not including, the end-of-string marker, are counted. The value of this int is nonnegative since the length of an empty string is 0.
USAGE: string_length = strlen(string_ptr);

`double tan(double)`   math library

      tangent function
USAGE: double_result = tan(double_argument)

`int ungetc(char, char *)`   stdio library

      ungetc function – places the character back on the specified input stream to be read by the next call to a "get" function such as getc( ), getchar( ), fgetc( ), fgetchar( ), etc.
USAGE: int_val = ungetc(ch, file_name);

Some UNIX I/O C Functions

      All of these functions can be found in the standard UNIX library and do not require any include files. They are considered to be system calls in UNIX since they involve access to lower-level operating system routines. Some are available on other systems.

`int close(int)`

      close function – the argument is a file descriptor. It is an error if the file is already closed.
USAGE: close(fd);

```
int creat(char *, int)
```
creat function – The first argument is a character string of the file and the second argument is the permissions in octal. The value returned is a file descriptor. If the user is not the super-user and the file already exists, then creat returns -1.

USAGE: if ((fd = creat(filename, octal_permissions)) == -1)
                    error( );

```
int open(char *, int)
```
open function – the first argument is a character string of the file and the second argument is the mode: one of "0," "1," or "2." The value returned is a file descriptor. The value of -1 is returned if there is an error such as the permissions being wrong, the file already existing, etc.

USAGE: fd = open(filename, mode);

```
int read(int, char *, int)
```
read function – the first argument indicates a file descriptor to read from; the second is a buffer location for buffered reads; and the third argument is the number of bytes that the reader requests. The return value is 0 if we read end of file, -1 if an error, and a nonnegative number if the read is successful. The number of bytes that are read may be less than the number requested if there are few bytes remaining; this is not an error.

USAGE: #define BUFFER_SIZE some_int
            char buffer[BUFFER_SIZE];
            num_read = read(file_descriptor, buffer, bytes);

```
int unlink(char *)
```
unlink function – removes a link to a file whose name is the second argument.

USAGE: unlink(filename);

```
int write(int,  char *,  int)
```
write function – the first argument indicates a file descriptor to write to; the second is a buffer location for buffered reads; and the third argument is the number of bytes that the writer requests. The return value is 0 if we read end of file, -1 if an error, and a nonnegative number if the write is successful. The number of bytes that are written must be the number requested; if not, an error occurs.

USAGE: #define BUFFER_SIZE some_int
            char buffer[BUFFER_SIZE];
            num_written = write(file_descriptor, buffer, bytes);

Syntax Summary

The syntax summary is given in yacc format. In this format, the first character string (in this case "program") is where the pattern-matching begins. The leftmost character string in each block is a nonterminal, which is to be expanded into one of the options provided after the colon. Different options are separated by single vertical bars and appear on different lines. Matching continues until each nonterminal in the sequence of replacements is replaced by a terminal. Terminals are actual characters or strings in a C program. We have used italics for nonterminals and have separated each block of possible matching by a semicolon on a line by itself, followed by a blank line. Also, a pair of braces in italics means that the terminals and nonterminals inside can occur either zero or an arbitrary number of times. Braces, commas, semicolons, and other punctuation marks in normal fonts are to be treated as required characters. (In some versions of yacc, these punctuation marks must be enclosed in single quotes.)

program :
> *external_definition*
> |*external_definition program*
> ;

external_definition: :
> *function_definition*
> |*data_definition*
> ;

function_definition: :
> *type_specifier function_declarator function_body*
> ;

function_declarator :
      declarator { parameter_list}
      ;

parameter_list: :
      identifier
      identifier , parameter_list
      ;

function_body:
      type_declaration_list function_statement
      ;

function_statement:
      { declaration_listopt statement_list }
      ;

data_definition :
      externopt type_specifieropt init-declarator_list ;
      | *staticopt type_specifieropt init-declarator_list* ;
      ;

compound_statement:
      {declaration_listopt statement_listopt }
      ;

declaration_list :
      declaration
      declaration declaration_list;
      ;

statement_list :
      statement
      | *statement statement_list;*
      ;

statement: :

    compound_statement

    | *expression* ;

    | if (*expression*) *statement*

    | if (*expression*) *statement* else *statement*

    | while (*exprsssion*)*statement*

    | do *statement* while *expression*

    | for (*expression_1* ; *expression_2* ; *expression_3*) *statement*

    | switch (*expression*) *statement*

    | case *constant_expression* : *statement*

    | default : *statement*

    | break ;

    | continue ;

    | return ;

    | return *expression* ;

    | goto *identifier* ;

    |*identifier* : *statement* ;

    ;

declaration:

    declaration_specifiers init_declarator_listopt ;

    ;

declaration_specifiers:

    type_specifier declaration_specifiersopt

    | *sc_specifier declaration_specifiersopt*

    ;

sc_specifier:

    auto

    | static

    | extern

    | register

    | typedef

    ;

type_specifier:
        char
        | short
        | int
        | long
        | unsigned
        | float
        | double
        | *struct_or_union_specifier*
        | *typedef_name*

init_declaration_list:
        init_declarator
        |*init_declarator , init_declarator_list*

init_declarator :
        declarator initializer

declarator :
        identifier
        |*{declarator}*
        | * declarator*
        |*declarator ( )*
        | *declarator [constant_expressionopt]*

struct_or_union_specifier :
        | struct { *struct_declarations_list* }
        | struct *identifier* {*struct_delcarations_list* }
        | struct *identifier*
        | union {*struct_delcarations_list* }
        | union *identifier* {*struct_delcarations_list* }
        | union *identifier*

struct_declarations_list :
        struct_declaration
        | *struct_declaration struct_declarations_list :*
        ;

struct_declaration :
       type_specifier struct_declarator_list
       ;

struct_declarator_list :
       struct_declarator
       | *struct_declarator* , *struct_declarator_list*
       ;

struct_declarator :
       declarator
       | *declarator* : *constant_expression*
       | : *constant_expression*
       ;

initializer :
       = *expression*
       | = {*initializer_list* }
       | = {*initializer_list* , }
       ;

initializer_list: :
       expression
       | *initializer_list* , *initializer_list*
       | {*initializer_list* }

type_name :
       type_specifier abstract_declarator
       ;

abstract_declarator :
       | (*abstract_declarator*)
       | *abstract_declarator*
       | *abstract_declarator* ( )
       | *abstract_declarator* [*constant_expression*]

typedef_name :
    identifier
    ;

expression :
    primary
    | * *expression*
    | & *expression*
    | - *expression*
    | ! *expression*
    | ~ *expression*
    | ++ *lvalue*
    | -- *lvalue*
    | *lvalue* ++
    | *lvalue* --
    | sizeof *expression*
    | (*type_name*) *expression*
    | *expression binaryoperator expression*
    | *expression* ? *expression* : *expression*
    | *lvalue assignoperator expression*
    | *expression* , *expression*
    ;

primary :
    identifier
    | *constant*
    | *string*
    | (*expression*)
    | *primary* (*expression_listopt*)
    | *primary* [*expression*]
    | lvalue . *identifier*
    | *primary* -> *identifier*
    ;

lvalue :

> *identifier*
> | *primary* [*expression*]
> | *lvalue . identifier*
> | *primary -> identifier*
> | * *expression*
> | [*lvalue*]
>
> ;

An identifier in C is a sequence of letters, digits, and underscores. The first character of an identifier must be either a letter or an underscore.

Operators are given below. Their precedence and associativity are given by the precedence table.

The binary operators are

```
*   /   %   +   -   >>   <<   <  >   <=   >=   ==   !=
&   ^   |   &&   ||   ?:
```

The assignment operators are

```
=   +=   -=   *=   /=   %=   >>=   <<=   &=   ^=   !=
```

Appendix **5**

Precedence of Operations

OPERATOR	COMMENTS ON USE
( )	grouping
[ ]	array elements
->	members of a structure
.	members of a structure
!	negation, right-associative
~	not, for bits, right-associative
++	increment, right-associative
- -	decrement, right-associative
-	unary minus, right-associative
(cast)	change type using cast, right-associative
*	contents operator, right-associative
&	address operator, right-associative
sizeof	size of data types, right-associative
*	multiplication
/	division
%	modulus
+	addition
-	subtraction

OPERATOR	COMMENTS ON USE
$<<$	left shift
$>>$	right shift
$<$	less than
$<=$	less than or equal to
$>$	greater than
$>=$	greater than or equal to
$==$	equal to (comparison)
$!=$	not equal
$\&$	bitwise AND
$\wedge$	bitwise exclusive OR
$\|$	bitwise OR
$\&\&$	logical AND
$\|\|$	logical OR
$?:$	if-else, right-associative
$=$	assignment, right-associative
$+=$	assignment & addition, right-associative
$-=$	assignment & subtraction, right-associative
$*=$	assignment & multiplication, right-associative
$/=$	assignment & division, right-associative
,	comma operator

Differences between ANSI Standard C and Kernighan and Ritchie C

There are many differences between Kernighan and Ritchie C and ANSI standard C. The most important ones are summarized here. They are function prototypes, the use and contents of libraries, malloc and pointers to void, and type conversion and parameter evaluation.

Function Prototypes

Kernighan and Ritchie C does not provide the C compiler with very much information about the types of parameters to functions. This causes special difficulties if the program consists of several C source code files that are separately compiled. ANSI C addresses this problem by using the syntax of function prototypes.

In K & R C, a function named f( ) that returns a float value and uses an int parameter would have a function definition

```
float f(x)
int x;
{ .. body of f ..}
```

In ANSI C, it would look like

```
float f(int x)
{ .. body of f ..}
```

If there were two or more parameters, they would be separated by commas as in

```
float g(double x, float y, int z)
{ .. body of g ..}
```

The general syntax for ANSI C functions is

```
return_type function_name(parameter_list)
```

where parameter_list consists of either the word void or is one or more of the expressions of the form

```
parameter_type1 parameter1
```

separated by commas. More formally, the BNF is

```
function_prototype ::=
            return_type function_name
                 '(' parameter_list ')'
parameter_list ::=
            non_void_parameter_list |
            void
non_void_parameter_list ::=
            parameter_type parameter |
            parameter_type parameter ','
            non_void_parameter_list
```

Every use of a function in ANSI C must be preceded by a function declaration such as

```
float g(double x, float y, int z)
```

before the function is used. In practice, this means that functions are generally declared at the beginning of files. If not, a considerable amount of documentation must be provided.

Libraries

In ANSI standard C, in order to use malloc( ), you must include the header file stdlib.h in your programs (or at least the single function – assuming that you don't wish to rewrite malloc( ) yourself). Implementations of C using Kernighan and Ritchie C do not require the use of, or even the existence of, the file stdlib.h in order to use malloc( ). Some implementations allow the use of a special library that is called the malloc library. Thus a segment of K & R C code to use the standard version of malloc, but not the malloc library, for a character pointer might look like

```
/* sample code for K & R C storage allocation    */
/* without the malloc library                     */
        .
        .
        .
char_ptr = malloc(sizeof (char));
```

while a segment of Kernighan and Ritchie C code to use malloc, which uses the malloc library and therefore must be compiled with the -lmalloc option, for a character pointer might look like

```
/* sample code for K & R C storage allocation    */
/* using the special malloc library              */
#include <malloc.h>
          .
          .
          .
char_ptr = malloc(sizeof (char));
```

For comparison, a segment of ANSI standard C code to use malloc for a character pointer might look like

```
/* sample code for ANSI C storage allocation */
#include <stdlib.h>
          .
          .
          .
char_ptr = (char *) malloc(sizeof (char));
```

malloc and Pointers to void

In ANSI standard C, malloc( ) is defined as always returning a pointer to void; that is, the return value is a pointer to a nonexistent variable. ANSI C always requires the use of a cast operation in order to use the space allocated by the function malloc( ). This means that every use of malloc() in ANSI C must be associated with a cast operation to be able to use the type of the region pointed to by the return value of malloc( ). This differs from Kernighan & Ritchie C, in which we can omit a type case for pointers to char.

Type Conversion and Parameter Evaluation

In Kernighan and Ritchie C, all arithmetic involving a float or double quantity is done in double precision. If the arithmetic is followed by an assignment, then the type of the result is coerced into the type of the "lvalue" on the left-hand side of the assignment statement. If there is no assignment, then no coercion will be done. This means that a function call such as

```
x = 2;
f( 1.5 * x)
```

where x is of type int and f expects an int parameter, will lead to garbage since the temporary variable used for the storage of the product 1.5 * x is interpreted as a double-precision number after the arithmetic but the function expects an int parameter.

This cannot happen in ANSI C since the parameter is changed to the correct form because of the information conveyed by the function prototype.

Initialization

Another important difference is in the initialization of variables. Kernighan & Ritchie C allows only global or static, but not automatic, arrays to be initialized, whereas ANSI C allows any array to be initialized, regardless of its storage class.

Appendix 7

List of Trademarks

AIX	International Business Machines Corporation
Apple	Apple Computer, Inc.
AUX	Apple Computer, Inc.
HP	Hewlett-Packard Company
HP-UX	Hewlett-Packard Company
IBM	International Business Machines Corporation
Microsoft	Microsoft Corporation
Motif	Hewlett-Packard Company
OSF	Open Software Foundation
SCO UNIX	The Santa Cruz Operation
SUN	SUN Microsystems, Inc..
Turbo C	Borland International, Inc.
ULTRIX	Digital Equipment Corporation
UNIX	AT&T (UNIX Systems Laboratory)
X-Windows	MIT
XENIX	Microsoft Corporation

References

Ada, *Reference Manual for the Ada Programming Language*, ANSI-MIL-STD-1815A, 1983.

Boehm, B., *Software Engineering Economics*, Prentice Hall, Englewood Cliffs, NJ, 1981.

Dunsmore, H. E., and Gannon, J. D., "Analysis of the Effect of Programming Factors on Programming Effort," *J. Systems & Software*, **1** (2), 1980, pp. 141–153.

Gehani, N., and Roome, W. D., "Concurrent C," *Software – Practice & Experience*, **16** (9), 1986, pp. 821–844.

Hashemi, R., and Leach, R. J., "Issues in Porting Software from C to C++," *Software — Practice & Experience*, **22** (7), 1992, pp. 599–602.

Horowitz, E., and Sanhi, S., *Fundamentals of Computer Algorithms*, Computer Science Press, Rockville, MD, 1976.

Kernighan, B., and Ritchie, D., *The C Programming Language*, Prentice Hall, Englewood Cliffs, NJ, 1978.

Kernighan, B., and Ritchie, D., *The C Programming Language, Second Edition*, Prentice Hall, Englewood Cliffs, NJ, 1989.

Meyer, A., "An Efficient Implementation of LU Decomposition in C," *Computers in Mechanical Engineering*, 1988.

Pfleeger, S. L., *Software Engineering*, Macmillan, New York, 1987.

Plaugher, P. J., *The Standard C Library*, Prentice Hall, Englewood Cliffs, NJ, 1992.

Pressman, R., *Software Engineering: A Practitioner's Approach*, McGraw Hill, New York, 1992.

Ritchie, D. M., and Thompson, K., The UNIX TIme-Sharing System, *Bell Systems Technical Journal*, **57** (6), 1978, pp. 1905–929.

Rochkind, M., *Advanced UNIX Programming*, Prentice Hall, Englewood Cliffs, NJ, 1985.

Stroustrup, B., *The C++ Programming Language*, Prentice Hall, Englewood Cliffs, NJ, 1992.

Wirth, N., *Algorithms + Data Structures = Programs,* Prentice Hall, Englewood Cliffs, NJ, 1976.

Index